D0762082

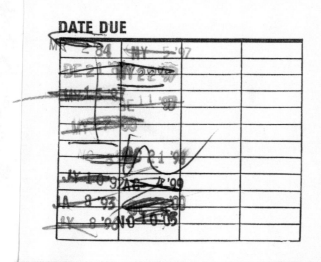

Are You Now or Have You Ever Been in the FBI Files?

Are You Now or Have You Ever Been in the

FBI FILES

How to Secure and Interpret Your FBI Files

by Ann Mari Buitrago and Leon Andrew Immerman

With Forewords by
Jessica Mitford and Hon. John Conyers

Introduction by
William Preston, Jr.

Grove Press, Inc., New York

First Evergreen Edition 1981

First Printing 1981

ISBN: 0-394-17647-2

Grove Press ISBN: 0-8021-4295-8

Library of Congress Catalog Card Number: 79-6155

Library of Congress Cataloging in Publication Data

Buitrago, Ann Mari.
    Are you now or have you ever been in the FBI files?

    Bibliography: p. 221
    1. United States. Federal Bureau of Investigation — Public records. 2. Privacy, Right of — United States. I. Immerman, Leon Andrew, joint author. II. Title.
HV8141.B8   363.2'4   79-6155
ISBN 0-394-17647-2

Manufactured in the United States of America

Distributed by Random House, Inc., New York

GROVE PRESS, INC., 196 West Houston Street, New York, N.Y. 10014

To Bonnie Brower, whose inspired legal work in using the Freedom of Information Act advanced the effort to uncover the truth in the Rosenberg/Sobell case, and insures that others who attempt to dislodge secret government files will meet with less resistance.

TABLE OF CONTENTS

FOREWORD

I am honored to be asked to contribute a foreword to this immensely useful and informative book; but what can I add? I am not an expert in the subject matter, just a fairly innocent bystander. At that, I have noted a certain laxity on the part of agencies that took it upon themselves to investigate us subversives. For example, my husband, Robert Treuhaft, finally succeeded (after the usual years of effort) in prying loose some pages, alleged to be his complete dossier, from both the FBI and CIA. In "Description of Subject," the FBI said: "5'8", stout, balding." CIA said: "5'10", black hair, slender build." Well! it is easy to see which agency Bob finds the more reliable.

Confronted with the expertise of John Conyers as my fellow foreword-writer, perhaps the best I can do is to add a purely personal note about a matter that has been bugging me (to coin two phrases at once, so to speak) for a number of years.

To start with a quotation from *Ramparts*, 1966:

"At a San Francisco cocktail party recently I had the odd sensation of hearing a voice from the past that I couldn't quite place. I studied the face — it was totally unfamiliar. Then it suddenly dawned on me: the voice was one I had heard many times while monitoring the taps in the 'clubs.' It belonged to Robert Treuhaft, a prominent civil liberties lawyer and husband of noted author Jessica Mitford."

This article, by reformed FBI agent William W. Turner, was obviously of more than passing interest to us. The "clubs" referred to, Turner explained, were elaborately equipped business premises that functioned as a façade where in the early 1950s FBI agents fed tapes of tapped lines into a bank of recorders.

Over the years we have made many efforts to get hold of these tapes, which for us would have considerable historical value, to hear again the clear treble voice of my daughter, then aged about ten, chattering on interminably with her school chums: "Do you think Sandra still likes me? Well *I* don't like *her*." "Mean old Miss Harris gave me a C on that stupid Streets and Roads of America test. What did *you* get?" Once in a while my own voice might come on: "When you said a teaspoon of soda, did you mean soda water or baking soda?" I was forever soliciting recipes in those days, hoping against forlorn hope to become a passable cook. Bob's distinctive voice, the one recognized by William Turner, would have been heard but seldom, saying only: "Sorry, we can't discuss this on the telephone. Come around to my office."

Calendar leaves float by. It is now 1976, and I am writing *A Fine Old Conflict*, a memoir of subversive days in the Truman-McCarthy era. What could be a better mind-jogger than my FBI dossier, now presumably available for the asking under the Freedom of Information Act? I send a one-line letter to the FBI: "Supply my dossier within ten days as required by law," and receive a poignant answer: the FBI is swamped with requests, say they. Could I let them have a bit more time? No, I answer sternly in another one-liner; surely the agency that prides itself on instant retrieval of information about criminals through its marvelous computer system can comply with the law. And I add a P.S.: I WANT THOSE TAPES FROM 1951 ON.

They write back long form letters, I respond with more one-liners, eventually Congressman Pete Stark comes to my rescue with some back-up demands, and something resembling a dossier arrives in the nick of time for an appropriate ending to my book. But no tapes.

I still want those tapes:

"Sandra kicked me, she actually *kicked* me, in the schoolyard today. I'm not even going to invite her to my birthday party . . . "

"Sorry to bother you again, but did you say a smidgeon of salt or a pigeon with salt for the *pot au feu à la campagne?*"

"As I told you before, we can't discuss any of these matters on the telephone . . . Yes, that's right . . . probably tapped. Please come to my office, and we'll go into an empty parking lot. The walls have ears these days, get it? Very well then, see you next Tuesday."

Jessica Mitford
Oakland, California
December, 1979

FOREWORD

The right of citizens to information about what their government does is essential to the preservation of freedom.

After a lifetime devoted to the Bill of Rights, the late Supreme Court Justice, William O. Douglas, concluded that the founding fathers adopted the Bill of Rights "to get government off the backs of people." Since governments are unlikely to police themselves, the preservation of freedom in the United States ultimately rests with individual citizens using the safeguards of the Constitution, the judicial process, and access to information. This means that individuals must have full information about what their government is doing, including, and especially, the information governmental agencies collect about citizens.

By enacting the Freedom of Information Act (FOIA) and the Privacy Act (PA), Congress sought to provide individuals the right of access to information in government files and the means to challenge any unlawful denial. Since 1966, when FOIA was enacted, citizens have fought an uphill battle with governmental agencies. Nowhere has this battle been more intense than with the files of the Federal Bureau of Investigation.

Long before the Freedom of Information Act, the FBI had become a law unto itself, answerable to no one but its Director, not to the Attorney General, or the President, or Congress itself. The full extent of FBI lawlessness is still not known. Enough is known, however, of its abuses — FBI harassment of political activists, surveillance and intimidation of civil rights and political organizations, falsification of documents, and vendetta campaigns against leading figures for no other reason than that the Bureau did not like their beliefs or their politics. The past conduct of the FBI caused severe injury to the political fabric of the country. Reform of the FBI, and strengthening the means by which citizens can obtain official information is absolutely critical today.

Experience under the Freedom of Information Act shows that government agencies do not like being accountable to the public and resist efforts of citizens who seek information about their activities. Typically, agencies expand as far as possible their ability to deny information under FOIA's statutory exclusions. Or else they force citizens to go to court to win compliance, which is costly and time-consuming. Law enforcement agencies, in particular the FBI, have been among the worst offenders in thwarting public disclosure of their files.

Ordinary citizens are not the only ones who have been obstructed in obtaining information from governmental agencies, especially the FBI. Congress also has had difficulty in obtaining information, even though in carrying out its legislative responsibilities the Constitution and the laws provide it with privileged access to official information.

In 1978, for example, the House Subcommittee on Crime, which I chair, requested FBI information concerning a federal program under the Subcommittee's jurisdiction. We were considering bills to re-authorize the program, and we needed to learn of any instances of alleged fraud or corruption in the use of Federal funds. Several months passed following our request, and we still had not received one iota of information from the Bureau. When the Subcommittee demanded an explanation, we were told: "Congress has appropriated money to process FOIA requests from the public, but has not given us funds to process Congressional requests." It turned out, in this instance, that because a citizen had requested similar information, the FBI finally furnished us the information after they had processed the request made by the private individual. When the documents arrived, they were too late for use in the inquiry and deletions made by the FBI on their own files rendered the information less than useful.

The Congress soon will consider reform of the FBI through the establishment of restrictions that spell out its authorities and limits on those authorities. Reform is essential and, hopefully, public and Congressional outrage at the revelations of past FBI abuses will generate a serious climate for the discussion of FBI reforms. Chief among those reforms must be the effective protection of the right of citizens to access to FBI information.

Are You Now or Have You Ever Been in the FBI Files? is an invaluable aid to all citizens who wish to obtain information from the FBI. Its publication is a major event in safeguarding our freedom.

John Conyers
Congressman, 1st District,
Michigan
Washington, D.C.
January 23, 1980

AUTHORS' PREFACE

We conceive of this book as a tool which will help the public win the struggle to hold its government accountable. Congress provided the basic instrument in 1974 when it amended and strengthened the Freedom of Information Act (FOIA) that had originally been adopted in 1966. In the Introduction to *A Citizen's Guide on How to Use the FOIA* . . . the House Committee on Government Operations set forth the historic importance of the legislation:

> The Freedom of Information Act (FOIA) is based upon the presumption that the government and the information of government belong to the people. Consistent with this view is the notion that the proper function of the state in respect to government information is that of custodian in service to society. Yet such a presumption did not always prevail. . . . With the passage of the FOIA . . . the burden of proof was shifted from the individual to the government: the "need to know" standard was replaced by the "right to know" doctrine and the onus was upon the government to justify secrecy rather than the individual to obtain access.

Long before Congressional committees documented the fact that the intelligence agencies in general and the FBI in particular had been acting — illegally — as a national police for most of this century, James Madison understood the connection between a self-governing people and information:

> [A] people who mean to be their own governors, must arm themselves with the power knowledge gives. A popular government without popular information or the means of acquiring it, is but a prologue to a farce or a tragedy or perhaps both.

In his opinion in *American Friends Service Committee et al.* v. *William H. Webster et al.*, 485 F. Supp. 222 (1980), Judge Harold H. Greene asserts the importance of the FBI's records "as part of the national heritage." He based his decision in part on Congress' determination of:

> . . . the right of the people of this nation to know what their government has been doing. The thrust of the laws Congress has enacted is that governmental records belong to the American

people and should be accessible to them — barring security and privacy considerations — for legitimate historical and other research purposes.

The aim of the book is to help fulfill the purposes of the Freedom of Information Act: to encourage the use of the Act, to help people make more effective requests for FBI records, and to help them understand the information the released documents contain.

The book grew out of our work with the Fund for Open Information and Accountability, Inc. (FOIA, Inc.) and with the legal teams of its two lawsuits: the Rosenberg/Sobell FOIA case (*Meeropol* v. *Bell et al.*, D.C., D.C., Civ. No. 75-1121) and the lawsuit to stop further destruction of FBI files (*American Friends Service Committee et al.* v. *Webster et al.*, cited above). FOIA Inc., the group which supports both lawsuits, maintains and fosters research on the files released in the Rosenberg/ Sobell case, and engages in educational activities to strengthen and protect the FOIA.

The original idea for the book, however, was suggested to us by co-counsel on the *AFSC* v. *Webster* litigation, David Scribner. It was Dave Scribner who first saw and correctly insisted that the information about the FBI and its files that the Rosenberg/Sobell lawyers and researchers were accumulating should be widely disseminated to journalists, lawyers, researchers, students, teachers, activists, and the general public. He exhorted, encouraged, and nagged us into starting and, more importantly, finishing the project.

It is impossible to overstate our indebtedness to all those involved in initiating and persevering in one of the oldest and largest FOIA cases — the request for all the files of nine federal agencies pertaining to Julius and Ethel Rosenberg and Morton Sobell. The Rosenbergs' sons, Robert and Michael Meeropol, first requested all the files in their parents' and Sobell's case in February, 1975, on the first day the newly strengthened FOIA went into effect. Their attorney was Marshall Perlin. Perlin's involvement as an attorney in the Rosenberg/Sobell case dates from 1953. He fought relentlessly for Sobell's release during Sobell's many years of imprisonment. As attorney for the Rosenbergs' sons he saw the opportunity offered by FOIA for reopening an investigation of the Rosenberg/ Sobell case and uncovering the truth about the government's role.

When the FBI refused to release its files, the Meeropol lawyers — Marshall Perlin, Bonnie Brower, and their associates, Samuel Gruber, David Rein, and Max Millman — brought suit in federal court. A 1976 court order led to the release of 33,000 heavily deleted pages of FBI Headquarters files. For two more years the struggle to secure the rest of the documents continued. This involved Perlin and Brower in weeks of costly depositions, months of research, dozens of court ordered meetings with FBI officials, and regular reports to the court. Not until the summer of 1977, after the court issued a stronger and more specific order, were an additional 150,000 pages of field office and Headquarters files released. Even then, research on the files showed that hundreds of files were still being withheld or had been destroyed. In the fall of 1978 Bonnie Brower told the court:

> It is truly obscene that, almost four years since the [Meeropols] filed their FOIA request, they are compelled to confront the FBI in a continuing, protracted battle for that which they were entitled to obtain nearly four years ago. The FBI's elaborate and continuing pattern of resisting, thwarting, and frustrating the letter and spirit of the FOIA and of this Court's Orders has resulted in the expenditure . . . of an incredible amount of time, energy, and moneys which they do not possess.

The litigation continues, focused at present on challenging the nearly 100,000 pages being withheld, primarily on grounds of alleged national security.

The knowledge acquired by Perlin and Brower, and by others working with the documents under their direction, forms the foundation of this book. Perlin and Brower have generously shared with us their vast knowledge and unique understanding of the FBI's investigative and administrative practices and made available to us all their legal papers and notes. At various stages in the preparation of this manuscript they read, commented, and made many suggestions for its improvement. Bonnie Brower was particularly helpful to us in drafting sections of Chapters II and III and in her unflagging interest in tracking down some of the puzzling "bureauese" that appears in the Glossary in Chapter V.

John Simon read and criticized an early draft and encouraged us to continue. We are indebted to Sebastian and Edward DeGrazia for leading us one to the other and thence to an interested and sympathetic publisher.

Our special thanks to Christine Marwick of the Center for National Security Studies for permission to reprint their excellent material in Appendices of Chapter III.

Hal Candee of the Campaign for Political Rights assisted and encouraged our efforts throughout this project, as did Chip Berlet of the Counterintelligence Documentation Center (a National Lawyers' Guild project). We are grateful to both.

Dorothy Steffens, the Executive Director of FOIA, Inc., deserves more than our thanks. She was our fundraiser, our protector, our foreword-writer recruiter, our negotiator, our reality tester, our critical editor, and our supportive colleague. There is no obstacle in the world that Dorothy Steffens cannot find a way around, through, or over. The benefit to our work of her talent, intelligence, and energy is enormous.

Phyllis Lewis is another gift to harassed authors. She read and criticized parts of the manuscript, caught and announced atrocious errors, cheered us on, gave up precious Saturdays to help us meet deadlines, and she was our friend even when we were unbearable. Paul Shneyer asked embarrassing legal questions and then cheerfully helped us find answers. Mark Gildav, Liz Glass, and Martin Schell typed and typed and typed the manuscript and the dreaded glossary with the thought and care we imagined only an author would be willing to give it. We were stunned and saved when Robert Bland as well as Mark Gildav determined that typing and editing a few chapters was a proper way to spend Christmas weekend.

Some of Columbia University's Professor Harold Fruchtbaum's contributions to this book are recognized in the Notes, but they do not represent all that he contributed through his extensive research on the Rosenberg/Sobell files. The Notes, the bibliography, and the text were also greatly improved by the comments, suggestions, and diligent work of Professor Gerald Markowitz of John Jay College.

Finally, we think no other authors ever had a more delightful and hardworking group of co-workers. Their collective contribution to the Rosenberg/Sobell litigation and to this book includes research on the files that produced the information, reading and criticizing parts of the manuscript, typing and retyping drafts, checking Bibliography and Notes, photocopying, proofreading, asking relevant questions, and much, much more. Without them, doing the book would not have been so much fun. Without their work, there would have been no book at all. To reflect the collective spirit that guided our work together, we list them alphabetically and thank them all equally:

Ayshia Amorer, Thomas Annarumma, Archeline Dure, Salina Earls, Jean Flegenheimer, Dora Friedman, Karl Ginsberg, Henry Giaubert, Ayesha Grice Jihada, Bella Kaplow, Andy Karmen, Michael Key, Ken Krauss, Thomas LaTorre, Judy Levine, Dexter Marshall, Susan McCarn, Denise McGee, Bart Meyers, Eve Olitsky, Gwen Pierce, Bess Polin, Sophia Santiago-Toscano, Miriam Schneir, Walter Schneir, Michael Schuster, Ann Marie Stewart, Rex Thomas, Steve Tischler, Joan Walsh, Barbara Yolleck.

A.M.B.
L.A.I.

INTRODUCTION

Political Surveillance and the FBI

Too many Americans, deluded by the immense size and anonymity of modern civilization, have not yet realized that they actually live in a small town whose mayor for over fifty years was J. Edgar Hoover. For decades this modern inquisitor so controlled the mechanics of surveillance that no deviance or dissent, however trivial, escaped his relentless, often witless, observation. In a society that, during Eisenhower's administration, numbered close to one hundred personal characteristics as "unsuitable" for individuals seeking security clearance, even George Washington might not be "normal" enough to establish his Americanism under such guidelines. Although the excesses of this Orwellian system surfaced during the Watergate inquiry, publicity connected with FBI surveillance tended to feature only the big name stories, Martin Luther King's being the best example. As a result, most people today may mistakenly believe themselves outside the vast "dossier dictatorship" created by government surveillance. If so, they are wrong. Ideological pacification knows no limits. Let us not forget that Hoover's free-fire zones spared no one, not even those in closets.

However random this political intimidation may appear in individual cases, it always had as its ultimate objective stilling the voice of mass insurgency. But even those who "challenged existing power relationships or key government policies," or seemed to, or even had some remote tendency to do so, ranked on top of the most-wanted lists. Yet history has rarely honored the struggle of so many people deprived of their rights under the Constitution, who have remained the unknown victims of a long and pervasive system of social control. It is the task of history to explain the surveillance of and the records kept on these people and to expose their contents. Perhaps then the countless victims of these endless investigations may feel as though some partial restoration of their constitutional rights has finally taken place.

Having an FBI file is, of course, a phenomenon of the last several generations of activists.

The "constitutionally underprivileged" victims of the established order faced an entirely different equation of forces in the century before FDR. Official and pseudo-official violence, illegal intimidation, and killing without fear of retribution characterized the excesses of this earlier era. Labor, agrarian, and radical protest also suffered the ravages of techniques that varied from blacklisting and strikebreaking to martial law. Police agents exercised enormous discretionary authority over the population. Dissenters rarely had files (other than those files in private detective agencies) because the small-scale surveillance system did not need them.

Although governmental and private police power seemed sufficient to contain the manifold forces of change up until a few decades ago, a federal responsibility existed from the beginning, and gained increasing authority over time. Federal troops had, of course, always been the last resort in the face of disturbances beyond the control of other agencies and, in other ways, strong control from the center was in evidence well before the New Deal: in the campaign against moral subversion and so-called diseased states of mind; in the Comstock Law (1873), and in the intellectual reign of terror by postal and customs authorities enforcing Victorian standards of prudery; against political and economic heresy; in conspiracy trials, injunctions, alien exclusion, deportation, and denaturalization legislation (especially the anti-radical laws of 1903, 1917, 1918, and 1920), wartime Espionage and Sedition Acts (1917 and 1918); in the dragnet raids, roundups, and disruptions of labor, leftist, and pacifist organizations (the most spectacular being the Palmer-Hoover "Red Raids" of 1919-1920); and in the campaign against certain government-defined vices, especially in the Mann Act (1910) directed at interstate prostitution, the Harrison Act (1914), the federal Magna Carta of the punitive approach to drug control, and of course, in Prohibition, which will forever symbolize the excesses of government invasions of privacy.

While the results of political repression before the New Deal were substantial, even more significant trends were to determine the nature of surveillance in the years that followed Roosevelt's inauguration. The New Deal revolution institutionalized the centralized bureaucratic management of American life. On the surface this seemed to be a giant step forward for free expression, dissent, and political activism, just as it seemed to be for the economy itself. Physical assaults, police beatings, lynchings, and murders waned in the wake of federally enforced rules of fair play. What was really happening, however, was less an extension of liberty in the shape of due process than an expansion of surveillance and order in the name of efficiency and discipline. Having gained important First Amendments rights, dissenting Americans found themselves threatened by the protective custody of a "generalized surveillance," a day whose coming had been so impatiently and eagerly awaited by J. Edgar Hoover himself.

Nor was the list of victims of this generalized surveillance confined to the activist leadership, since the "overt-act" test of criminality had long since been replaced by an obsession with prevention, with the need to stamp out the remotest tendencies in those mistakenly defined as subversive. Formerly unleashed in the discretionary enforcement of vague municipal ordinances, anticipatory criminality rapidly enlarged the arena of interest for the police and intelligence agencies that had to anticipate behavior in order to attempt to forestall it.

Three of those federal agencies — the Immigration and Naturalization Bureau, Bureau of Narcotics, and Federal Bureau of Investigation — had already perfected the style and programs suitable to their security missions. Exercising extraordinary power, immune from effective executive or Congressional oversight, free to indulge in operational lawlessness which guaranteed results, these autonomous administrators had worked out techniques of infiltration, provocation, disruption, and harassment in the pre-Roosevelt years.

Technological innovations in communications not only widened their targets for eavesdropping but also obliterated the recognizable boundaries of legitimate search and seizure. Intelligence gatherers thereby became the silent, unseen, uninvited witnesses to thousands of constitutionally protected conversations, even of those not targeted for attention. Neither the courts nor the laws could stay abreast of the wire-tappers. Sophisticated improvements in microphone and electronic intrusion, legal loopholes, and the very secrecy of the operations promised that these dragnet invasions of privacy would remain unchecked.

This overaccumulation of information about others was paralleled by the growing tendency of government to resist the release of news about itself. Classification and overclassification, secrecy, and precensorship freed many federal activities from effective accountability at the very time of the Malthusian increases in bureaucracy and in its discretionary authority over those whom it controlled.

These systems of "order maintenance," inventions of earlier internal security crises, were, therefore, all in place and some were actively functioning when Roosevelt took office. Whether they would be reinvigorated and expanded depended on the ideological stance of the new administration. Although certain clear advances in due process and substantive justice and equality took place during Roosevelt's Administration, a pragmatic, partisan leadership could not ignore the currents of archconservatism that dominated the decade. Nor would it break with the definition of consensus engendered by years of collaboration with the institutional power brokers of the national economy. Sensitized to subversion by the social strains of Depression unrest and agitation, appalled by clandestine fifth columns and anarchy abroad, egged on by the vociferous investigators of un-Americanism, the New Deal administrators adopted the idol of absolute security and its prophet, Hoover, at FBI headquarters.

In secret Presidential directives ostensibly focusing Hoover's revived authority on espionage and "subversive activities," the administration quickly established the model for all subsequent surveillance. A frame of mind, reminiscent of the witchcraft delusions, craved protection not only against disloyalty and subversion, but even against the potential for such behavior. It became necessary to inspect and label beliefs as if human beings could be certified "pure" like food and drugs. They attempted to uncover the seeds of "subversion" in ideas and attitudes even though "loyalty" itself remained undefined. As a result, the security establishment developed norms for "loyalty" as slippery as any in history. One was the idea of a "party line" (Japanese, Nazi, Communist or whatever group later became suspect). Anyone supporting policies favored by the "enemy" became subject to novel charges of "guilt by coincidence" or "guilt by verbal association," also described as "parallelism." Additional categories included "guilt by association" (even with close relations), "guilt by sympathy," and "guilt by infiltration" (membership in organizations that might possibly be targets of subversive infiltration, from churches, unions and youth groups to entire industries). Participation in any so-called "front" was, of course, immediately suspect.

But the clearest example of the limitless scope of these security obsessions was the fact that even evidence of loyalty itself did not prove satisfactory, for it was easily perceived as a mask for other more sinister objectives. Before long the Japanese-Americans (Nisei) found out how this was to operate in practice. In spite of a total absence of sabotage or any other hostile activity, they found themselves rounded up en masse after Pearl Harbor and incarcerated in "relocation centers" for the duration of the War, their loyal unanimity being interpreted as a conspiracy to delay violence until some more propitious opportunity arose.

Once put into motion, this immense surveillance machine gathered a manic momentum that sent it hurtling out of control through succeeding decades to its fateful rendezvous at Watergate. Through Depression and war, cold war and reaction, civil rights struggles, student activism, Vietnam protest, black militancy, and women's liberation, it pursued the chimera of total security with an intensity and thoroughness unparalleled in American history. And always it kept growing, adding new enemies and targets, inventing new techniques, welcoming new intelligence collaborators until it seemed as though one half of the country was watching the other half. The disasters that marked the route should be remembered by a people who has not yet taken out comprehensive liability insurance on the Bill of Rights.

For protective legal coloration, political surveillance had numerous supports during and after the Roosevelt era: the Hatch Act (1939) initiated government loyalty tests; the Smith Act (1940), a peacetime sedition act, put drastic limits on free speech; the Internal Security Act (1950) created the Subversive Activities Control Board to register members of Communist or Communist "front" groups, and established an Emergency Detention plan for interning suspected subversives; the McCarran-Walter Act (1952) authorized the deportation of any alien whose activities were deemed "prejudicial to the public interest" or "subversive to the national security"; the Communist Control Act (1954) virtually outlawed the Communist Party; the Anti-Riot Act (1968) penalized interstate travel or communications with the intent to incite riot. Some three hundred federal, state, and local laws were enacted against subversion; and the state and Congressional investigations of "un-Americanism" exposed many to infamy and severe economic penalties.

Thousands of new suspects expanded the government's data base, one that had never been small to begin with. Hoover's first General Intelligence Division index in the 1920s had 450,000 names; there may be some 20 million today. The "infiltration" theory of the late thirties brought hundreds under investigation in industry, labor, education, journalism, the civil rights movement, the armed forces, and in numerous organizations proposing social, economic, and political change. The COMINFIL program of the Cold War era cast an even wider net by adding organizations suspected of Communist influence and developing new categories such as "Racial Matters" and "Hate Groups" (though in this instance the FBI should have investigated itself by its own definition). COMINFIL covered "the entire spectrum of the social and labor movement in the country" and compiled files on some 200 organizations. It also kept an eye on race riots, civil demonstrations, and "similar developments." The Security Index, the Communist Index, and the Reserve Index (a sort of back-up list of substitutes that could not make the subversives' first team) supplied the candidates for emergency detention.

COMINFIL was joined by COINTELPRO in the 1960s, which produced ever new categories to pursue. Of the twelve major acknowledged programs, five had undisclosed foreign targets, but six sighted in on the Communist Party, the Socialist Workers Party, white hate groups like the Ku Klux Klan, black extremists, New Left groups, and militant Puerto Rican nationalists, and a seventh, Operation Hoodwink, tried to pit the Communist Party and organized crime against each other. Between 1960 and 1974 the FBI conducted over half a million separate domestic intelligence investigations, including those on every SDS and Black Student Union member, and conducted a massive penetration of the women's liberation movement. Field offices had to summarize, on a semi-monthly basis, the programs of all civil rights and black nationalist organizations, report the statements, writings, and activities of the "New Left," and cover Vietnam demonstrations (VIDEM), and student agitation (STAG). New indexes naturally sprang to life: "Rabble-Rouser," "Key Activist," "Key Black Extremist," and "Agitator" joined the earlier card files of radicals.

Other more prominent names also bulged the collection. Critics of Hoover and the FBI were placed on a separate list, regardless of their patriotism or political importance. Political gossip and information resulting from other notorious invasions of privacy were sent only to Hoover and his Presidential sponsors, a practice which suggests that there may have been indices for purposes other than internment.

As constitutional protections developed, and civil liberty forces resisted the illegal activities of government agents, the latter went increasingly underground to achieve results. Informers, *agents provocateurs*, and advanced systems of surveillance would provide low-cost maximum repression by means of an internal disruption not subject to anyone's oversight. Justified as mere intelligence fact-finders, these internal security agents could and did wage a secret guerrilla war against organizations on the government's hit list. Undercover intimidation, disruption, and harassment could and did inhibit and destroy opponents without ever having to be tested by legal restraints. Vigilante justice, once overt, however illegal, had long characterized the American enthusiasm for speedy justice, but in the modern era, the vigilantes have been working for the government.

Joined by other intelligence authorities, from state and local red squads to the CIA, National Security Agency, and the Army, and with cabinet-level support elsewhere, the FBI saw the full flowering of political repression in the Nixon years. Hoover's COINTELPRO, the CIA's "Operation Chaos," NSA mail and communications intercepts and openings, army intelligence spying on domestic activism, IRS tax-return harassment, passport and visa controls, deportations, burglaries and "black bag job" break-ins, telephone and banking surveillance, grand jury fishing expeditions, conspiracy trials, intimidation of the press, and special White House units of surveillance and disruption characterized these numerous and damaging tactics.

By the time of Carter's inauguration, impressive results had again been achieved. Among the casualties were members of the Communist Party, the Socialist Workers Party, the Progressive Party, the Peace Movement, the New Left, the Women's Movement, and the Black Panthers. Thousands of people had been fired, charged, and named as subversives. Other massive numbers had been intimidated. Science, scholarship, and their foundation support had felt the chilling effect of the drive against dissent. For several decades domestic reform had disappeared as a serious issue and its 1960s resurgence was met by a savage reaction. In the field of foreign and military policy, ideas and programs were tested by their anti-Communist purity alone.

In the aftermath of Watergate, public revulsion against the excesses committed in the name of security seemed to promise much. The lawless members of the Nixon administration and a few subordinate hirelings suffered some punitive redress. The Attorney General announced new investigative guidelines and restraints while a proposed FBI Charter suggested other built-in checks against police lawlessness. Other intelligence agencies claim they have vacated the field of domestic surveillance. The Freedom of Information Act and its supporters have threatened to hold the government permanently accountable to constitutional standards of behavior.

Some cautionary historical reminders may be in order before the First Amendment is taken off the still-endangered list. Coercive mechanisms and bureaucratic habits have always been difficult to dismantle and alter. Official sanctions usually outlive the protest and crisis that inspired them. "It is far easier," Leon Radzinowicz has written, "to make laws than to unmake them." Nor should the public be too sanguine about the impact of guidelines and charters or, for that matter, constitutional controls themselves. In this instance reform has to reverse a long tradition of government lawlessness, deep-seated executive attitudes regarding national security privileges, an entrenched bureaucratic arrogance and independence, and a long-standing confusion between law enforcement and internal security functions. Although current restrictions and proposals would check the worst abuses of the immediate past, they are laced with exceptions and remain fixated on anticipatory criminality and preventive law, thereby continuing the preliminary inquiry and the use of informers and undercover agents. What looks like a "stonewall" guideline to a reformer may be "a triumphal arch" to a determined bureaucratic operator.

The larger trouble may be the existence of two constitutional systems: the limited, defined powers of the checks-and-balances model and the expansive, vaguely worded authorizations of the Presidential one. "Inherent," "implied," and "emergency" powers to maintain public safety and national security will continue to resist the inroads of effective supervision and accountability.

For over half a century the FBI file, the dissenter's dossier, has stood as a symbol of the vast, irresponsible surveillance the state has conducted on its most activist public. The file has become the therapeutic equivalent of the prison cell, isolating the deviant subjects from the general population and subjecting them to endless unknown observation for the purposes of effective and total control. The many victims of this process should utilize the present interlude between repressions to assert their "unintimidated self-respect" against all systems of government spying. The Freedom of Information Act can give them access and a chance, for once, to write or rewrite their own history. And then in some future inaugural address, a President may rightfully say, "Ask not what your country knows about you; ask what you know about your country."

Prof. William Preston, Jr.
John Jay College of
*   Criminal Justice*
New York City
January, 1980

CHAPTER I

THE FBI FILING SYSTEM

Introduction

An understanding of the way the FBI generates and maintains its files is sometimes a prerequisite to making an intelligent FOIA request. A clear picture of the filing systems also leads to greater comprehension of the documents eventually received, since many of the documents can be fully interpreted only if one understands where and how the document was created and to which office, desk, and file it was sent.

This chapter is designed to explain the workings of the Central Records System and its chief finding tool, the General Index, by taking an investigation through its typical document-generating steps. The "main" files and subdivisions are described, as well as the locations of different types of materials. Three Appendices appear at the end of the chapter: Appendix A — a list of the many types of documents typically found in FBI files; Appendix B — a list of the sorts of materials usually found *only* in field office files; Appendix C — an annotated list of 210 classification categories that form the bases of the FBI's filing and numbering system.

Public knowledge of the FBI's filing system is based mainly on the following sources, from which we have drawn: Notices filed annually in the Federal Register, as required by the Privacy Act; General Accounting Office Report, *FBI Taking Actions to Comply Fully with the Privacy Act;* General Services Administration (NARS — National Archives and Records Service), *Disposition of FBI Field Office Investigative Files;* the FBI Records Management Division report on *The Central Records System;* and, of course, FBI documents released under FOIA. This chapter concerns itself with those aspects of the FBI records which are of most interest to the general public. For a list of other FBI record systems, see the GAO Report, *FBI Taking Actions to Comply Fully . . .* pp. 5-6. (Sources are cited fully in the Bibliography.)

The FBI has been automating its filing system recently but it appears that the structure of the Central Records System and the General Index has not been changed.

Central Records System

The FBI uses many record systems to maintain the billions of pages of documents presently in its possession. As in any organization, the record systems reflect the working parts of the organization's structure.

1

The main organizational units of the FBI are as follows:*

FBI HQ: the headquarters office in Washington, D.C. — variously referred to in FBI communications as "FBI HQ," "Bureau," and "SOG" (Seat of Government).

Field Offices: 59 field offices located in 50 states, Puerto Rico and Washington, D.C. Field offices are supervised by FBI HQ and carry out the bulk of the FBI's investigative work, though some investigations are conducted by the generally smaller "Resident Agencies."

Resident Agencies: 477 resident agencies (RA's) located in the 50 states, Puerto Rico, Virgin Islands, and Guam. Each RA reports to its parent field office, not to FBI HQ in Washington, D.C.

Liaison Offices: A separate component of the FBI structure is made up of the 12 foreign offices known as Liaison Offices, or Legats. These offices assist FBI domestic investigations by providing liaison in other countries.

The principal filing system which the FBI claims contains almost all its investigative, personnel, administrative, applicant, and general records is called the Central Records System. There is a central records system at FBI HQ, and one in each field office and foreign liaison office.

The central records filing systems are arranged by the 210 classification numbers the FBI has designated to represent the breakdown of its investigative and administrative responsibilities. Each central system consists of essentially two parts. There are *"Main" files*, which are principally documents filed roughly chronologically and arranged into "volumes" or "sections" of *approximately* 200 pages each; and there is a *General Index*, which is an alphabetical index to the "main" files. In addition, Headquarters (but not the field offices) maintains an *Abstract System*, which has summaries of important documents in "Main" files.

"Main" Files

The "main" files (sometimes known as "main" subject files) contain many of the documents generated in the course of an investigation of individuals, organizations or events — what the FBI calls "subjects of investigation." Investigations are conducted and files are organized under 210 classification numbers. (These numbers have no relation to the national security classifications — "confidential," "secret," and "top secret.")

File classifications are of four types: personnel, administrative, applicant (investigations of persons being considered for government work), and investigative (violations of Federal law; and intelligence and

---

*A map locating the field offices and resident agencies appears as Appendix E of Chapter III. Appendix D of Chapter III contains a list of FBI field offices and liaison offices.

counterintelligence). A look at the classification titles (see Appendix C, Ch. I) indicates that these distinctions are far from ironclad. For example, "66" is listed as an administrative file title, but released FOIA documents show it is frequently used for informer files. "67" files — Personnel Matters — sometimes contain investigations of critics of the FBI. While the Migratory Bird Act classification — "8" — seems straightforward, "180" (Desecration of the Flag) and "42" (Deserter or Harboring a Deserter) might conceivably be used for political investigations.

A reading of the list of 210 classifications underscores a major finding of the Church Committee investigation of the FBI in 1974. The very foundation of the FBI's filing system shows how heavily and early the FBI was acting as the nation's political police. When the filing system was first created, numbers were assigned to political investigations — "3" (Overthrow or Destruction of Government) and "14" (Sedition).

Numbering Documents

With few exceptions, each document that becomes part of a central records system file is identified by a group of three numbers, for example, 100-15375-17.

The first number indicates the type of investigation and is called the *Classification Number*. In our example, "100" marks the document as part of a "domestic security" investigation. The second number in the group is the *Individual Case Number* in a given FBI office (FBI HQ, field office, or legat). These numbers are assigned in sequence as cases are opened. In our example, "15375" indicates that the document is part of the fifteen-thousand-three-hundred-seventy-fifth domestic security investigation in that office. "100-15375" is the *File Number*, though it is sometimes called the *Case Number*.

The third of the group of numbers, the *Serial* or *Document Number*, records the order in which the document was placed in the file — the first document is numbered "1" and all others follow in sequence. Judging from files released by the FBI, documents placed in a file are not always serialized. Unserialized documents are variously marked — "UR" for unrecorded, or "100-15375✓" (with a check mark in place of the missing serial number) — both indicating a document with no serial number. Other irregularities in serialization, such as separate documents labelled "100-15375-17 incoming" and "100-15375-17 outgoing," occasionally occur.

It is likely that anyone investigated by the FBI will have several file numbers. To begin with, each office involved in a particular investigation (including FBI HQ) will assign a different number to that investigation. But, in addition, an individual may have been investigated and separate files created under more than one classification number, e.g., bank robbery (91), income tax evasion (5), and desertion from the armed forces (42).

When an individual is the subject of a "security" investigation, the FBI says that it utilizes the same file for "all his subversive activities." Here is the FBI's own explanation of its procedure at FBI HQ and in the field offices.

[At FBI HQ] . . . if an individual was investigated as a member of the Communist Party in the 1940's, a 100 case file would have been opened. Five years later, after terminating his membership in the Communist Party, if we utilize him as a security informant, we would not open a 134 (Security Informant) file on him. We would place all the mail in connection with his informant activities in his prior 100 file. Fifteen years later, if he became involved in extremist matters, we would not open a 157 (Extremist Matter) file on him, we would place all correspondence on his extremist activities in the same 100 file. If this man then violated the 176 — Antiriot Law Statute, we would open a new 176 case on him because this is a specific criminal violation or if he robbed a bank we would open a separate 91 (Bank Robbery) file. If we conduct an applicant investigation on an individual, it will go in the classification assigned for the particular category of applicant investigations.

[In the field offices, in security matters] . . . separate case files are established for each separate investigative matter. To illustrate, if an individual was investigated as a member of the Communist Party in the 1940s, a 100 case file would have been opened. Five years later, after terminating his membership in the Communist Party, if he was utilized as a security informant, a separate 134 (informant) file would have been opened on him. Accordingly, all mail relative to the Communist Party membership investigation would have been placed in the 134 (security informant) file.[1]

It is also quite common for the FBI to have information about individuals and/or organizations without keeping a separate file in their name. For example, during an investigation about person A, information about person B (a co-worker, a relative, a person present at a surveilled meeting or phone call) will be gathered and placed in person A's file. Documents containing the information on person or organization B are often retrievable through "see references" which will be explained as part of the General Index system below.

How Files Are Created

The "main" files of the Central Records Systems are built up through decisions by the FBI (usually the field offices) to launch preliminary or full-scale investigations on the basis of information received. The information is likely to have been generated in the course of an ongoing investigation and come from an informer, a technical

4

surveillance (wiretap), or from local police.

To illustrate the process of the development and numbering of FBI files and documents, let us assume the New York Field Office decides to investigate all persons whose names appear on the mailing list of an organization which the FBI considers "subversive." (The Attorney General's 1976 Guidelines prohibit the FBI from opening investigatory files on persons who are simply members of an organization under investigation. However, information about such persons can be placed in the organization's file.) Such mailing lists have frequently been stolen by FBI informers or infiltrators.

Let us say that one of the names on a stolen list is "Maria Andrews," and assume for the sake of simplicity that there is not already a file on her in the New York Field Office. To begin the investigation the New York office opens a Subversive Matter — Communist (100) file captioned "Maria Andrews."*

The file is given the next available file number in the New York office's Subversive Matters classification: e.g., 100-120.

The mailing list and a memo outlining steps to be taken to investigate Ms. Andrews are assigned a serial or document number, e.g., 100-120-1. Subsequent information will be placed in this file and numbered sequentially.

If preliminary investigation persuades the New York office Ms. Andrews warrants continued investigation, authority to proceed to a full investigation will be sought from FBI Headquarters. To accomplish this, New York will send a memo requesting such permission and enclose a report on the investigation to date.

If the Headquarters supervisor approves New York's request to continue an investigation, it may issue some instructions on how to proceed. A Headquarters file on "Maria Andrews" corresponding to the New York file is opened and assigned the next available number for the Headquarters Subversive Matters classification, e.g., 100-80. The memo

---

*A common occurrence throughout an investigation arises when more than one "Maria Andrews" is known to the FBI. A fair amount of paper is generated while an office tries to determine if this "Maria Andrews" is identical to the Maria Andrews on whom the FBI already has information. A goodly amount of paper moves around while an office tries to determine the name of an observed or overheard person they wish to investigate. A file on an individual whose name is unknown will be entitled "Unsub." ("Unknown Subject"). Often an alias or an informant's name will appear in the title of an "Unsub." file, e.g., "Unsub., with alias Tom," or "Unsub., Harry Black informant." If Ms. Andrews were married, the file might be captioned in both her name and her husband's name. If they subsequently divorced, the spouse's name might be dropped.

Three other options are open to the field office at this initial stage: the information on Maria Andrews could be assigned to a "dead file," a "general file," or her name entered on the "General Index" as a "see reference." ("General Index," "general file," and "see reference" are explained below. On "Dead file," consult Glossary, Ch. V.)

5

received from New York would be numbered 100-80-1 and the Headquarters reply memo numbered 100-80-2. If Maria Andrews at any time had lived or was active outside the territory of the New York Field Office, e.g., in Milwaukee, other field offices may be requested by the New York office to look into her school or work records, her associates and her living arrangements. To house the letter of instruction and the results of their investigations, these offices will open their own files on Maria Andrews using their next 100 numbers, e.g., in Milwaukee the file might be 100-40 and the request from New York would then be serialized as 100-40-1.

If Ms. Andrews lived, worked, or traveled in other countries or in territories covered by a Resident Agency or legat, it is possible that similar memos may go to those offices which will, in turn, open "Maria Andrews" files.

Each of these sets of numbers (100-120, 100-80, 100-40) represents Maria Andrews' "main" file in the central records system of, respectively, New York, Headquarters, and Milwaukee FBI offices. These files are known as "corresponding" files. No effort is made to have each of these corresponding files bear the same case number or to have the same document in different offices bear the same serial number. Occasionally corresponding files will have different classification numbers, e.g., New York's 105-1234 may be the corresponding file to Headquarters' 65-4231, provided that they have the same "title" or "caption." Documents placed in the files may include interoffice memos, airtels, teletypes, letters, letterhead memos, search slips, correlation summaries, reports, serial chargeout slips, FBI forms, etc. (See Appendix A of this Chapter for a more complete list of various types of documents found in the FBI files. Explanations of many of these terms are in the Glossary, Ch. V.)

As pages accumulate, new "volumes" (called "sections" at FBI HQ of files will be opened. Each volume of a file seems to be bound by a separate metal clip but, apart from subfiles, documents are serialized in one sequence without regard to their divisions into volumes. Two hundred pages per volume is the rough rule, but it is very rough. (When a file is released under the FOIA, the fact that it is divided into volumes is not always readily apparent.)

Any field office involved in an investigation is either an Office of Origin ("OO") or an Auxiliary Office ("AO"). A particular field office is designated the "OO" for a particular investigation by Headquarters at the time it authorizes the investigation. Ordinarily, the "OO" is the field office nearest the subject's place of major activity. However, because field offices observe strict territorial lines (consult Map, Appendix E in Ch. III), it is possible to live geographically closer to one field office but fall within the jurisdiction of, and therefore be investigated by, a different field office. The "OO" has the primary responsibility for the case, but it can request reports from other field offices which are designated "AO"s for this case. Auxiliary offices supply supporting information, which may require undertaking investigations at the direction of the "OO" or Headquarters. Generally "AO"s pass along to the "OO" any information or "leads" they come across, usually asking if they should pursue the lead.

If a subject of an investigation changes residence or place of activity, the field office nearest the new location is usually designated the new "OO" for the investigation. There is an FBI form — FD 128 — to secure this change of responsibility. (In federal government applicant/employee investigations, Headquarters is designated the "OO," e.g., Loyalty of Government Employee (121) and Department of Energy Applicant (116) cases.)

Uniqueness of Each Office's Files

The "OO" in a given case maintains the most complete file and the most valuable documents pertaining to the investigation, including virtually all original materials, e.g., surveillance logs, interviews, notes, tapes, signed statements, confessions, interviews with informers, and the like. (See Appendix B for a list of materials found in field office files, but usually not in Headquarters files.)

In reporting to Headquarters, the "OO" for the most part transmits summary reports of the results of its investigation and only occasionally some primary source material. *Thus, it is the field offices — especially the "OO" for any case — that contain the primary source material of an investigation.*

Awareness of the unique character of "OO" files is crucial to those requesting files and those trying to analyze them. Bear in mind that the FBI does *not always transfer* the entire old "OO" file to the new one if the "OO" of an investigation shifts.

In addition, there are investigations for which the field office files may be the *only* files. Preliminary investigations opened and closed within the 90-day time limit that has governed reporting requirements since the early 1970's were never reported to FBI HQ. These investigations are characterized by the FBI as investigations which resulted in no prosecutions, or where allegations were unfounded, and/or for which no FBI jurisdiction existed. The agency admits that the vast majority of these closed preliminary cases are security investigations. It is likely that since they were not regularly reviewed by Headquarters, "preliminary" investigations have been used by field offices to conduct harassing and illegal operations.

While field office files are unique repositories of primary investigative material, Headquarters files have their own importance. They contain material not found in field office files, e.g., records of dissemination by Headquarters of investigative material to other government officials, agencies of other countries, and friendly news media. Headquarters files may also document the dissemination of material among Headquarters

7

supervisors. Headquarters "control files" (see below) need not have a counterpart in the field offices.

Thus, whether a reader is trying to get all of his or her own FBI files or is trying to get all those files relevant to analyzing a particular subject, it is essential that files be retrieved from both Headquarters and from the field offices.

"Control Files"

The FBI has been most evasive about revealing the scope, nature, and meaning of the term "control file." But recently, in a report submitted in Federal court, the following explanation was provided:

> Control files are separate files established for the purpose of administrating [sic] specific phases of an investigative matter or program. The institution of a control file in an investigative matter or program is left to the discretion of the individual with the administrative responsibility for the particular investigative matter or program. A control file is an administrative tool for managing a particular investigative matter or program. For this reason, control files are not created in each and every investigative matter or program.[2]

In a 1978 report on the Central Records System, the FBI's Records Management Division supplied the following additional information.

> . . . we have control files which are maintained for the purpose of having all information regarding a specific matter immediately available without the necessity of reviewing numerous case files. An example is "Threats Against the President." Individual case files are opened for each threat on which we conduct an investigation; however, a copy is placed in the control file so that all such threats are recorded in one place.
> . . . While there is not a central list of all categories [of control files], a partial listing is maintained of certain categories . . . those more frequently used.[3]

While the FBI may establish control files in connection with such investigative areas as gambling, jewel thieves, organized crime, and the top ten fugitives, released FBI documents show that there is another use for control files. Some control files deal with tactics and strategies, policy decisions, top level instructions, and other matters that pertain to and coordinate a number of individual investigations in a general area of intelligence or political inquiry. It is not certain that the information found in these files — including plans for illegal operations — is always placed in the related individual "main" file.

Among the documents released in connection with the Rosenberg/Sobell case, for example, is one from a New York file, the title of which was deleted by the FBI. The document states:

It is intended that instant case, entitled [deleted] will operate as a control file and will contain only reports and other correspondence relating to the over-all investigation of this matter and its over-all supervision. [Several lines deleted by FBI.]

Since the control file will be entirely separate from all of the individuals involved, the investigation of this matter will be accomplished through investigation of the individual subjects, their contacts with each other and with other persons. The results of the investigation of the individuals and their contacts will be reported in the individual case files.

The control file will be used for reporting in summary form pertinent and significant information obtained in all of the individual investigations. *The reports in this control file will summarize the results of correlations, evaluations and analyses of the information obtained in the individual investigations.*

The Washington Field Office is being designated as Office of Origin in the control file and will be the only office submitting reports in this file . . . [4] (Italics added.)

In addition, documents indicate that some control files are established to coordinate the plans and authorizations for counterintelligence programs (COINTELPROs). For instance, an FBI document published by the Counterintelligence Documentation Center directs that:

Offices receiving copies of this letter are instructed to immediately establish a control file, captioned COUNTERINTELLIGENCE PROGRAM; BLACK NATIONALIST-HATE GROUPS; INTERNAL SECURITY and to assign responsibility for following and coordinating this new counterintelligence program to an experienced and imaginative Special Agent well versed in investigations relating to black nationalist, hate-type organizations . . .

The purpose of this new counterintelligence endeavor is to expose, disrupt, misdirect, discredit, or otherwise neutralize the activities of black nationalist, hate-type organizations and groupings, their leadership, spokesmen, membership, and supporters, and to counter their propensity for violence and civil disorder.[5]

General Files

At Headquarters each of the 210 classifications has a Zero (0) and a Double Zero (00) file placed at the front of the first file drawer preceding the first case in each classification. These are called "General Files." For example, in the American Legion Contact (136) classification there is a 136-0 and a 136-00 file in front of 136-1.

The 0 file contains complaints and miscellaneous nonspecific data relating to the classification which do not warrant opening a separate case file. When three or more pieces of correspondence on the same subject appear in this file, a separate file is established with its own number and the documents from the General File are placed in this separate file and are renumbered. Documents in the 0 and 00 files are numbered serially, for example, 136-0-44 or 136-00-44.

The 00 file houses "all policies and procedures" that pertain to the classification. Each time there is a basic change in policy, procedure, instruction, or guideline in reference to the classification, the document indicating the change is placed in the 00 file. (The Double Zero file is entirely different from the "Office of Origin" files on investigations. "OO" normally stands for "Office of Origin." Only when preceded by a file classification number (e.g., "136-00") does "OO" denote a general file.)

The field offices also maintain 0 and 00 files, but file them somewhat differently from Headquarters.

Subdivisions of "Main" Files

In addition to the volumes of the "main" files that run approximately chronologically as an investigation proceeds, there are specialized subdivisions created in conjunction with these volumes.

Subfiles

Subfiles are sections of "main" files. Documents in subfiles seem always to be serialized separately from the principal sections of the "main" files. Subfile documents would be numbered, e.g., "100-120-SubA-1," or "100-120-Sub 2-1." (Sometimes the word "sub" will be omitted in the number, e.g., "100-120-A-1" or "100-120-2-1.") A single subfile can consist of more than one volume.

Subfiles are either lettered (Sub A, Sub B, etc.) or numbered (Sub 1, Sub 2, etc.). Lettered subfiles are filed physically with the other volumes of the "main" file. Typically, they contain the results of physical surveillances (FISURs), prosecutive summaries, newspaper clippings, requests and authorizations for mail covers, and photo collections. Inventories of oversize items are kept in "1B" subfiles. (See below on "Bulky Exhibits.") However, none of these sorts of material (including logs of FISURs) is invariably placed in subfiles. The decision to open subfiles in a given case is within the discretion of the FBI office conducting the investigation. Another type of information for which subfiles are sometimes used concerns subdivisions of organizations. Subfiles may exist on geographical branches or on particular activities of an organization. For examples of lettered subfiles, See Ch. IV, Document 5.

Numbered subfiles seem to be used for the results of wiretaps, bugs, and FBI burglaries, and they seem to be located away from the file drawers housing the principal sections of "main" files. Numbered subfiles include "JUNE" material. See below for a discussion of "Separate Locations for Some Records."

1A Envelopes

These envelopes contain such items as physical evidence, photos, interviews, confessions, and statements made by subjects of investigations. It seems that 1A envelopes are filed in front of the first regular serial. Items in 1A envelopes are numbered 1-A-1, 1-A-2, etc.

Enclosures Behind Files (EBFs)

EBFs contain material relating to an investigation that fits in a standard file drawer. They may include, often in multiple copies, lab reports, photos, testimony at Congressional hearings, search slips, and correlation summaries.

EBFs are numbered by the case number and the serial number of the document they are placed behind in the "main" file. For example, the cover sheet to an EBF in Maria Andrews' Headquarters file would read: "Enclosure 100-80-220" to indicate that it is associated with serial 220 in her file.

The FBI asserts that EBFs are used only at FBI HQ.

General Index

The FBI currently houses hundreds of millions of documents in its files. In order to retrieve material from these files, the FBI maintains an alphabetical index — which it refers to as the General Index. The central records system of each office, in Headquarters, and in each field and foreign office, has its own General Index to its Central Records System. (See Ch. IV, Document 20.)

The FBI General Index consists of 3 x 5 cards on various subject matters (groups, individuals, events, cases, projects, publications, etc.), but are predominantly on individuals. The General Index of each office is a single alphabetical set of records. The approximately 59 million cards in the Headquarters General Index contain the names of about 20 million people. A card will sometimes contain, in addition to a name, such identifying data as address, birthplace and date, sex, race, and Social Security number. (The General Index is the *only* index searched by the FBI in processing FOIA and PA requests, unless it is specifically requested to search other indices and locations.)

Each General Index contains two sorts of cards interspersed with each other: *"Main"* cards and *"See Reference"* cards. "Main" cards list the main file number or numbers for the individual (or group, event, etc.) named on the card. To return to our example, a search of the New York General Index would reveal that Maria Andrews' New York main file is 100-120. The cards would also inform the searcher of the existence of any other main files the New York office happened to have on Ms. Andrews. However, since each General Index is entirely separate, a search of the New York index would not show the existence of her Headquarters or Milwaukee files.

The FBI claims that its policy is to destroy the "main" index card when the file the card refers to is destroyed. Thus, a search of the

11

indices would probably not show that the FBI had once kept a main file on an individual, if the file has been destroyed. Occasionally, however, there are clerical slipups and a "main" card may be found although the file it refers to has been destroyed. The FBI recently claims it has begun to record titles and file numbers of files destroyed. It is not certain whether this information is kept in the General Index.

The second sort of cards found in the General Index are the *"see"* cards, also known as "see ref" or "see reference" cards. A "see" card indicates that the name on the card is mentioned in one or more documents in another person's or organization's "main" file. The FBI alleges that it attempts to destroy "see ref" cards when the file which the card mentions is destroyed. If an individual is referenced to many other files or appears frequently in one or more files, the FBI may eventually prepare a composite "see ref" card and destroy the numerous individual "see ref" cards.

Imagine that the second document in Maria Andrews' New York file is a report which happens to include some information on her friend George Young. If the information on George is deemed to have sufficient importance apart from its bearing on the Maria Andrews investigation, the FBI will have a copy of the report placed in a main file on Young. However, the FBI may choose instead to place a "see ref" card under Young's name in the New York General Index, indicating that he is mentioned in a document in Andrews' main file. The card will read something like "George Young, 100-120-2, page 5," sending the searcher to page 5 of the second document in Maria Andrews' file for the information on George Young. But if the FBI does not expect the information on Young to be remotely useful, it will not file any "see ref" card to 100-120-2 under Young's name.

The fact that information is filed as a "see reference" rather than placed in a "main" file on the individual does not indicate that the information is trivial. For example, copies of intercepted correspondence received by the FBI from a CIA mail opening project "were not to be filed in the individual's case file (though cross-referencing permitted retrieval) but in a secure area separate from other FBI files."[6] Evidently this illegally opened mail was retrievable only through "see reference" cards.

Thus, in summary, much of the FBI's information on an individual may not be contained in any file specifically on that individual. That is, for example, one may be mentioned many times in the files on an organization to which one belongs, without the FBI's placing this information in one's main file or, indeed, without the FBI's even opening such a main file captioned under one's name. Much of the information not contained in a person's main file can be retrieved through "see reference" cards which show where, in files other than a person's own, information on that person exists. But some of the information which the FBI has on an individual may not be retrievable through the General Index of each office. This will be the case when the information is not contained in the individual's main file and is not retrievable by means of "see reference" cards to other files under the person's name because the FBI did not anticipate wanting to locate it again. Further, if "main" or "see ref" cards once existed on an individual, the destruction of the files to which the cards referred may well mean that the cards themselves have been destroyed. Thus, the absence of any reference to an individual (group, etc.) in FBI indices at present does not preclude the possibility that the FBI at one time had information there.

Abstract System

The abstract system is a device employed in the Central Records System of Headquarters files *only*. It consists of 3 x 5 cards prepared on every important communication sent from or received by Headquarters. The cards contain file number, subject matter, source of communication, type of communication, status of communication or case, and narrative synopsis. They are filed numerically by file and serial number. In HQ, the serialization of file documents was done from abstract cards.

The FBI says that it is no longer serializing from the abstracts but rather that a computer now generates the next sequential number in a file. The substance of the communication is not fed into the computer, but only the date, the sender, the recipient, the status (whether the case is pending, closed or RUC — see Glossary), and the national security classification — if any. Abstracts are still being done pending a decision on whether to continue the system.

The FBI claims that when a file is destroyed the abstract cards are destroyed.

Separate Locations for Some Records

Some of the documents in special, restricted locations were originally part of "main" files which are part of the Central Records System, although many of the specially located documents were kept out of the central records entirely. When documents were removed from main files, a Permanent Serial Chargeout form was inserted in their place. These chargeout slips record the new location, but this location is sometimes deleted when the slip is released under FOIA. (A form called Serial Removal Chargeout appears in some files and may indicate temporary removal of a document.) In their normal course of work, FBI personnel do not "charge out" individual documents from volumes but, rather, the entire volumes themselves, which are kept only as long as needed.

Bulky Exhibits ("Bulkies")

"Bulkies" include material gathered as part of an investigation which is too large to fit in a standard file drawer, e.g., a typewriter, clothes, sometimes books or pamphlets, as well as oversize documents. These items, labeled with the main file number, are kept in a separate room or in vaults.

"Bulkies" are usually lettered "1-B." Items in them are serialized separately from the "main" files, e.g., 100-120-1B-2 designates the second bulky item in Maria Andrews' Bulky Exhibit file in the New York office. Inventories of Bulky Exhibits are recorded on "Green Sheets" which are generally kept with the "main" files in subfiles labeled "1-B." In Ch. IV, Document 19 is an example of a "Green Sheet."

Headquarters Confidential Files

Since the 1920s confidential files of varying types have been kept in the offices of former Director J. Edgar Hoover and, at least since the 1940s, in the offices of other top officials, such as Assistant Directors.

In 1941, Hoover reorganized his confidential files.[7] Some material ("memoranda on undercover and SIS [Special Intelligence Service] employees; name, number and brief autobiography of confidential informants; list of technical surveillances and history of each; list of surveillances maintained on diplomatic representatives at the sanction of the State Department . . . ") was transferred to the National Defense Division to be maintained so as to be "immediately available." Material to be kept in a confidential file by Hoover's secretary, Miss Helen Gandy, was restricted to "items of a more or less personal nature of the Director's and items which I might have occasion to call for from time to time, such as memoranda to the Department on the Dies Committee, etc." At the same time, Hoover created a file for the use of Assistant Directors to be maintained in Assistant-to-the-Director Louis B. Nichols' office. (Hoover's memo reorganizing the confidential files was itself marked "INFORMATIVE MEMORANDUM — NOT TO BE SENT TO FILES SECTION." This memo may have been part of the blue/pink paper procedure described under " 'DO NOT FILE' Files," below.)

The Justice Department reported to the Senate Select (Church) Committee in 1975 that the confidential files in Hoover's office were transferred to Asst. Director Mark Felt's office after Hoover's death and, as of 1975, were stored in the Special File Room of the Files and Communications Division and "indexed into the Bureau's indices." (Access to files kept in this room is extremely limited.) Although Hoover's secretary and top aides claim that none of his confidential files was destroyed, many members of Congress, the press, and scholars continue to have doubts.[8]

Documents from these confidential files released during the mid-1970s congressional inquiries into FBI practices bear two markings: "Official and Confidential" ("OC") and "Personal and Confidential" ("PC," or "PF"). A 1971 (discovered in 1975) inventory of 164 "OC" folders showed Hoover kept files on Elizabeth Bentley, Alger Hiss, three top Bureau officials, and E.R. Butts.[9] Documents released from these files include memos from 1939 to 1952 from Hoover to all Special Agents in Charge (SACs) instructing them in developing lists of persons to detain during a national emergency, the so-called Detention Plan.[10]

Documents marked "Personal and Confidential" that were turned over to the Church Committee contain tidbits of political intelligence which Hoover passed on to various Presidents (from Roosevelt to Nixon) and memos reporting on political favors performed by the FBI — name checks of signers of anti-Viet Nam telegrams, of critics of the Warren Commission, or Roosevelt's defense policies. One document contains an index to the logs of FDR's wiretaps on his aides.[11] A list turned over to the House Government Operations Subcommittee investigating the destruction of Hoover's files shows the transfer of eight files from "PC" to "OC."[12]

In many other cases where records are kept separately from the central records, they are kept in the offices of top Bureau officials. For example, Rosenberg/Sobell files contain documents on Permanent Serial Chargeout moved from the "main" files to "Mr. Lamphere's Office."[13] Another example involved the 17 wiretaps allegedly instituted by Nixon and Kissinger to uncover the source of leaks to the press concerning the secret bombing of Cambodia in 1969. These taps were filed apart from other National Security wiretaps and were not listed on the FBI's ELSUR Index (see below). Until Assistant Director William Sullivan gave them, in 1971, to Assistant Attorney General Robert Mardian to turn over to Nixon (because, Sullivan said, Hoover could not be trusted with them), these wiretap logs were kept first in Hoover's and then in Sullivan's office.[14]

Another instance in which taps were kept out of central records involved Charles Radford, a staff assistant to the Joint Chiefs of Staff. Radford was suspected of leaking classified material (a Nixon-Kissinger conversation) to columnist Jack Anderson in 1972. An FBI memo stated:

Our records [on this Radford tap] have been kept completely isolated from other FBI records and there are no indices whatsoever relating to this project.[15]

It is not clear whether these records were kept in a top official's "OC" file or in a Special File Room.

Field Office Confidential Files

Documents released in connection with the Rosenberg/Sobell case indicate that field offices also maintain Personal and Confidential files.

These files seem to be recorded in the General Index but are evidently maintained in locations separate from the central records. One New York document bears the notation: "Attention P & C Files, 10th Fl." Field Office officials, especially SACs and ASACs, sometimes have personal files in which they keep sensitive FBI records. SAC safes are the repository of "DO NOT FILE" documents, which are explained below.

Special File Rooms

References are found on released documents to rooms with restricted access, e.g., "Special File Room, Division 5" (the Domestic Intelligence Division). William Sullivan reports that in one wiretap case:

> DeLoach [Hoover's liaison with LBJ] recommended to Hoover that the file concerning these taps be maintained in the Special File Room, and that because of the highly sensitive nature of the information contained in the file, it should be afforded strictly limited handling.[16]

The FBI claims that files housed in these special rooms are recorded in the General Index and can be located through a search of that Index, although there is no way to be certain of this. We do know that one control file relevant to the Rosenberg/Sobell case was housed in a special file room but was listed in the General Index. Even clerks assigned to summarizing FBI investigations were not given access to this file, however.

Special FBI Offices

The FBI operation code-named "Brilab" (for "bribery labor") was supposedly an instance of the new (post-1975) style in FBI investigations. A phony Los Angeles company (involved in insurance) was fabricated by the FBI, allegedly to ferret out widespread organized crime and political corruption in the South and Southwest. Investigations of this type (which seem now to be an FBI staple) may have generated their own form of record concealment:

> The Brilab investigation involved extensive court-authorized electronic surveillance as well as undercover operations, according to [Federal law-enforcement] officials, and was handled secretively within the bureau.
> As a result, Brilab agents operated out of special offices whose locations were kept secret from other agents, and all the information gathered for the investigation was kept separate from normal FBI files.[17]

We do not know how much, if any, of the "Brilab" material is destined to be integrated into the Central Records Systems. It seems that at least part of the "Brilab" information was gathered with a view that it would someday be made public in criminal trials. But when documents are originally kept out of the Central Records, it is easier than it would otherwise be to make the more embarrassing documents vanish.

The device of "special offices" is not new in itself. As Jessica Mitford recounts in her Foreword to the present book, during the 1950s FBI agent William Turner listened to the wiretap on Mitford and her husband Robert Treuhaft from one of the FBI's "Clubs." The "Club" in San Francisco, according to Turner,

> . . . was in a building on Sacramento Street that fronted as a marine architect's office. Ships' blueprints on drawing boards cluttered the main floor, but in the basement was the monitoring area with its jumble of wires and banks of amplifiers and recorders. The tapped conversations were fed into the room by means of lines leased from the telephone company under a fictitious business name. The Oakland plant was high up in a downtown office building inside a suite with drawn blinds and double-locked doors; there was nothing but a number on the entrance door.[18]

However, at least by Turner's account, the logs and recordings gathered at the "Clubs" were taken daily to the regular FBI offices. The results of electronic surveillances are discussed below under " 'JUNE' Unit," and "ELSUR (Electronic Surveillance) Logs."

"DO NOT FILE" Files

According to the Church Committee Final Report:

> The FBI developed a special filing system — or, more accurately, a destruction system — for memoranda written about illegal techniques, such as break-ins, and highly questionable operations, such as the microphone surveillance of Joseph Kraft. Under this system — which was referred to as the "DO NOT FILE" procedure — authorizing documents and other memoranda were filed in special safes at headquarters and field offices until the next annual inspection by the Inspection Division, at which time they were to be systematically destroyed.[19]

Though as described, the "DO NOT FILE" procedure is a system of destruction rather than a filing system, the Church Committee in 1975 found a 1966 "DO NOT FILE" memo from Sullivan to DeLoach about "black bag" jobs, so apparently the annual destruction is not invariable.

Another procedure for keeping documents out of central records was the use of pink or blue paper for memoranda submitted to Headquarters. As outlined by Hoover in the early 1940's, these memos, unlike those on white paper, were not given file numbers. According to "General Instructions for Bureau Supervisors" (March 1, 1942):

There are three types of paper used in the bureau at the present time; e.g., white, blue, and pink, for the preparation of memoranda.

1. White — All memoranda prepared by supervisors which are to be made a permanent part of the Bureau files should be prepared on the white memorandum form.

2. Blue — Memoranda prepared solely for the benefit of the Director which will possibly be seen by the Director and other officials and eventually be returned to the Director to be destroyed or retained in the Director's office, should be prepared on the blue memorandum form.

3. Pink — If the memorandum is prepared merely for temporary usage such as ordering supplies, requesting work to be done through the Chief Clerk's Office, then the pink form is to be used.[20]

"JUNE" Unit

"JUNE" (or "JUNE mail") documents contain the fruits of FBI burglaries and electronic surveillances, and also record the preparation and authorization for such activities. In the field offices, "JUNE" subfiles appear to be numbered subfiles kept physically separate from other files in a restricted access "JUNE" unit. It does not seem that all field offices, particularly smaller ones, have "JUNE" units. Some "JUNE" subfiles bear the label on their cover pages:

THIS SUBFILE IS NOT TO BE REMOVED FROM "JUNE" UNIT. INFORMATION CONTAINED HEREIN, IN ITS PRESENT FORM, IS FOR THE SOLE USE OF AGENT HANDLING THIS CASE.

The "JUNE" system was begun in June, 1949, to keep information on electronic surveillances separate. It was a response to the FBI's embarrassment over the Judith Coplon case in which documents released by court order revealed that the FBI was obtaining political information through wiretaps.

Some Headquarters "JUNE" subfiles consist of documents removed (via "Permanent Serial Chargeouts") from "main" files to restricted places. However, Headquarters sometimes also follows the practice of not entering "JUNE" material into central records in the first place.

Apparently, any "JUNE" subfile will bear the same file number as the "main" file with which it is connected.

The presence of "Permanent Serial Chargeouts" in a file may indicate the existence of a "JUNE" subfile. If documents in a file contain information which seems to be derived from an electronic surveillance or a burglary, this is also a sign that a "JUNE" subfile possibly exists. (In Ch. IV, Documents 13 and 18 are taken from "JUNE" subfiles.)

ELSUR (Electronic Surveillance) Logs

ELSUR includes both TESUR (technical surveillance, i.e., wiretaps) and MISUR (microphone surveillance). FBI agents listening to ELSURs take notes (called "logs") on what they hear. Some conversations are tape recorded. It appears that under normal circumstances ELSUR logs are placed in numbered subfiles bearing the same basic file number as the "main" file on the person under surveillance. For example, if the New York "main" file on Maria Andrews is "100-80," an ELSUR log on her might be numbered "100-80-Sub 2-3" or "100-80-2-3." Some, if not all, ELSUR logs are kept in "JUNE" subfiles. It does not appear that any ELSUR logs are filed in the principal sections of "main" files, or that any are referred to in the General Index. The ELSUR Index is discussed below. Reports and other documents in the principal sections of "main" files draw on ELSUR logs, but these documents often attempt to disguise the source of their information. (In Ch. IV, Document 13 is a MISUR log and is taken from a New York "JUNE" subfile labelled "Sub 1.")

Special Indices

The FBI claims that most of its special indices contain information which can be retrieved through a search of the central records systems. These indices, it says, were only established to provide readier access to routinely needed information without a time-consuming search of the large, centrally located General Index. However, when the General Accounting Office made a study in 1977, it found that some of these specialized indices contain information (names, as well as other data) that would not turn up in a central records system search of any other of the eleven published systems of records. Though the FBI refers to all of them as "indices," some are more than mere indices and are in fact closer to being independent record systems.

There is a related difficulty which concerns the special indices at the various field offices. While the names of all unclassified indices are known, as well as the number of field offices housing each one, the FBI has so far declined, with one or two exceptions, to reveal which field offices have which indices.

The 1977 GAO study, *FBI Taking Actions to Comply Fully with the Privacy Act*, lists the special indices and is available from the Government Printing Office. (See Bibliography for full citation.) The Department of Justice-FBI annual Privacy Act notices published in the Federal Register provide more up-to-date information on indices. A compilation of the most politically relevant indices is available from the Fund for Open Information and Accountability, Inc., 36 W. 44th St., New York, N.Y. 10036.

ELSUR Index
The ELSUR Index (Electronic Surveillance) is a record system entirely separate from the Central Records System. It was authorized

by the Department of Justice in 1966 and is maintained at FBI Headquarters and in 58 field offices. The FBI has admitted to the GAO, however, that three field offices established these indices as early as 1941. The Headquarters ELSUR Index is a "master" list, that is, a list which contains all the cards from all field office ELSUR Indices. The 1977 GAO Report describes the system as follows:

[The ELSUR Index System] consists of cards on individuals who have been the subject of a microphone or telephone surveillance by the FBI from 1960 to present. This includes individuals who were (1) the targets of direct surveillance, (2) participants in monitored conversations, and (3) owners, lessors, or licensors of the premises on which the FBI has conducted an electronic surveillance. In addition to the persons' names, the card would contain the date the voice was monitored, a source number to identify the individual on whom the surveillance was installed, and the location of the field office which conducted the monitoring. It also includes persons who were mentioned from 1960 to 1969. The highly publicized 17 White House wiretaps were initially listed separately on the special coverage index until the summer of 1976 when they were merged into the ELSUR Index.[21]

These ELSUR Indices are finder systems to locate instances of electronic surveillance conducted since January 1, 1960. When a field office initiates an electronic surveillance, it prepares two index cards on the target of the tap, files one in the field office ELSUR index and forwards the other copy to Headquarters for inclusion in the "master" ELSUR index. Two additional cards are prepared each time the agents identify anyone overheard on the tap. MISUR and TESUR index cards are *not* segregated within this index, but become part of the total index. Consequently, a single search of the ELSUR index includes a search for all MISUR and TESUR.

FBI Headquarters claims it stopped including "names mentioned" (in overheard conversations) in 1969 in its Headquarters ELSUR Index, but some field offices continue placing such cards in their ELSUR indices.

Other Headquarters Special Indices

In addition to ten indices that remain classified, 71 investigative indices are maintained at FBI Headquarters. Some are note cards containing identifying information; some are computer tapes; others are photo albums.

Fourteen of these 71 indices contain information that cannot be located through a search of any other FBI record system. An example of such an index is one entitled "Murder of FBI Agents on Pine Ridge Indian Reservation."

Another kind of index among those not keyed into another record system is major case indices. A major case index is described by the FBI as follows:

For major cases or investigations, the FBI establishes special indexes to keep track of all the information. The President John F. Kennedy assassination, the Patricia Hearst kidnapping, and the James Hoffa disappearance are examples of such cases. Usually the field supervisor of a major case sets up an index card system to facilitate assigning and keeping track of investigative leads without having to search the general index . . .

Because of the complexity of some major cases, FBI headquarters computerizes certain information to facilitate its administration. The field offices submit to headquarters the names of people on whom information is developed in conjunction with a major case. They also provide license plate numbers, evidence, and any other pertinent information. Headquarters then computerizes the information and usually on a monthly basis provides the field offices with a printout for each case. It shows the names of persons related to the investigation in alphabetical order, a brief summary of the information attributed to this person, and a reference to the location of the information in the headquarters central records or field office files . . .[22]

Politically relevant Major Case Indices maintained at FBI Headquarters include the titles: Burglary of Democratic National Committee Headquarters (Watergate), and Don Segretti Campaign Violations (Watergate spinoff).

Other Field Office Special Indices

In addition to fifteen field office special indices that are classified, FBI field offices maintain 158 different indices in various forms. Not all field offices maintain all indices. Forty-nine of the 158 indices contain information not fully retrievable through the field offices' Central Records Systems and General Indices.

Among the 49 indices, the following are examples likely to contain information important to those requesting or working with political files:

Major Case Index: The Dallas-Kennedy-Ruby-Oswald Case. The Dallas Office told the GAO that this index is totally separate from its General Index. It states that it searches this index for FOIA and PA requests and has sent all the "relevant" information to Headquarters' Central Records System.

Major Case Index: Investigation of the Unauthorized Disclosure of Classified Information Concerning the U.S.-Vietnam Relations (Pentagon Papers).

Informants in Other field Offices Index. As of February, 1977, two field offices have separated Informants Index cards from the General Index but are instructed to search both for FOIA and PA requests. The identity of the two offices was not published.

Foreign Liaison Office (Legat) Special Indices

In addition to three that are classified, the foreign FBI offices maintain ten special indices. All the information included in them is said to be retrievable through the General Index to the office's Central Records System. Not every legat has every one of the thirteen.

The ten indices are: Check circular file, Fugitive alert file, Identification order (fugitive fliers file), Informant index, Key activist program photo album, Revolutionary Communist Party Photo Album, Royal Canadian Mounted Police — wanted circular file, Stop notice index, Top Ten program file, Wanted flyers file.[23]

APPENDIX A: Types of Documents Found in FBI Files
*Starred items are explained in the Glossary, Ch. V. Document numbers refer to Ch. IV.

*ADEX (Administrative Index) memos (recommendation for preparation of and
   changes in a person's card) [Doc. 2]
  Agent assignment cards
*AIRTELS
*Bulky exhibits and inventories [Doc. 19]
  Cables
*Change-to memos
*Channelizing memos
*Correlation Summaries [Doc. 23]
*Daylets
  Destruction authorizations for serials [Doc. 16]
*File covers [Doc. 3]
  Fingerprint cards
  Floor plans, maps, diagrams
  Income tax forms
  Lab reports
  Letterhead memos (*LHM) [Doc. 6]
  Letters of enclosure, transmittal
*Logs of surveillance (FISUR, MISUR, TESUR, ELSUR) [Doc. 13]
  Memos [Doc. 12]
*Nitels
*1A Envelopes [Doc. 14]
  Personnel records
  Photographs
  Placement of surveillance (requests for and authorizations of)
  Private letters (intercepted by the FBI)
  Public record material (newspapers, books, court papers, etc.)
  Radiograms
*Rap sheets (criminal records)
*Reports by agents [Docs. 4 and 5]
  Reports by informers [Docs. 10, 11, and 32]

Requests to or from other government agencies [Doc. 9]
*RI (*Reserve Index) memos (recommendations for preparation of and changes in a
   person's card)
*Routing slips
*SAC letters
*Search slips [Docs. 21 and 22]
*Serial Chargeouts, Permanent Serial Chargeouts [Doc. 17]
*SI (*Security Index) memos (recommendations for preparation of and changes in a
   person's card) [Doc. 1]
Signed statements (confessions)
*Teletypes [Doc. 7]
Third party letters (e.g. from concerned citizens)

APPENDIX B: Material Found in Field Office Files but Usually Not in Headquarters Files

1A envelopes (may contain photos, signed statements, surveillance logs, copies of
   publications)

Informant reports

Summaries of informant activity

Results of interviews with subjects of investigation

Memos concerning whether or not to proceed with an investigation

Data obtained from burglaries

Agent's memos on phone calls made or received

Letters requesting information from phone company, credit bureaus, etc.

Requests from one field office to another (e.g., to follow up leads)

Agent's memos on following leads, interviewing neighbors, checking records

Memos about receipt and destruction of bulky exhibits

Interview logs

Requests for mail covers (HQ authority was necessary during some, not all, periods
   of time)

Search slips for field office

Correlation summaries for field office

In general, details about how information is received and how to proceed with an
   investigation

Source: FBI Records Management Division report, *The Central Records System,* February 1978, and *Federal Register,* Vol. 44, pp. 58981-86 (Oct. 12, 1979). Over time the FBI makes changes in title and/or description of categories. The categories do not appear to be fundamentally altered by these periodic changes. For a more detailed description of many of the classifications consult the FBI's annual "Privacy Act" notices in the *Federal Register.*

* indicates a classification of matters in which an applicant seeks some legal redress, a government position, etc. Many applicant-related classifications (especially 121) involve security-type investigations.

**indicates security-related classifications.

Bracketed material marked "—authors' comment" is information gleaned from working with FBI Rosenberg/Sobell documents and other sources.

"Obsolete": new files are not created in classifications designated "obsolete." However, documents can continue to be added to files whose classifications have now become obsolete.

* 1. Training Schools; National Service Academy Matters; FBI National Academy Applicants.

** 2. Neutrality Matters.

** 3. Overthrow or Destruction of the Government.

4. National Firearms Act; Federal Firearms Act; State Firearms Control Assistance Act; Unlawful Possession or Receipt of Firearms.

5. Income Tax.

6. Interstate Transportation of Strikebreakers.

7. Kidnapping.

8. Migratory Bird Act.

9. Extortion.

10. Red Cross Act.

11. Tax (Other than Income).

12. Narcotics. Complaints are forwarded to the administrator, Drug Enforcement Administration (DEA), or the nearest district office of DEA.

13. Miscellaneous. National Defense Act; Prostitution; Selling Whiskey Within Five Miles of an Army Camp. (Obsolete)

**14. Sedition.

15. Theft from Interstate Shipment.

16. Violation Federal injunction. (Obsolete) FBI records do not provide an explanation of the nature of this classification.

17. Veterans Administration Matters.

18. May Act.

19. Censorship Matters. (Obsolete 1946)

20. Federal Grain Standards Act. (Obsolete 1921)

21. Food and Drugs. Complaints are referred to the Commissioner of the Food and Drug Administration or the field component of that agency.

22. National Motor Vehicle Traffic Act. 1922-27. (Obsolete 1927)

23. Prohibition. This classification covers complaints received concerning bootlegging activities and other violations of the alcohol tax laws. Such complaints are referred to the Bureau of Alcohol, Tobacco and Firearms, Department of the Treasury, or the field representatives of that agency.

24. Profiteering. 1920-42. (Obsolete 1945)

25. Selective Service; Selective Training and Service Act.

26. Interstate Transportation of Stolen Motor Vehicles; Interstate Transportation of Stolen Aircraft.

27. Patent Matters.

28. Copyright Matters.

29. Bank Fraud and Embezzlement.

30. Interstate Quarantine Law. 1922-25. (Obsolete 1925)

31. White Slave Traffic Act.

32. Identification (Fingerprint Matters).

33. Uniform Crime Reporting.

34. Violation of Lacy Act. (Obsolete 1927)

*35. Civil Service. This classification covers complaints received by the FBI concerning Civil Service matters which are referred to the United States Civil Service Commission in Washington or regional offices of that agency.

36. Mail Fraud.

*37. False Claims Against the Government. 1921-22. (Obsolete 1928)

*38. Application for Pardon to Restore Civil Rights. 1921-35. (Obsolete 1936) Subjects allegedly obtained their naturalization papers by fraudulent means. Cases later referred to Immigration and Naturalization Service.

**39. Falsely Claiming Citizenship.

40. Passport and Visa Matters.

41. Explosives. (Obsolete)

42. Deserter; Deserter, Harboring.

43. Illegal Wearing of Uniforms; False Advertising or Misuse of Names, Words, Emblems or Insignia; Illegal Manufacture, Use, Possession, or Sale of Emblems and Insignia; Illegal Manufacture, Possession, or Wearing of Civil Defense Insignia; Miscellaneous, Forging or Using Forged Certificate of Discharge from Military or Naval Service; Miscellaneous, Falsely Making or Forging Naval, Military, or Official Pass; Miscellaneous, Forging or Counterfeiting Seal of Department or Agency of the United States; Misuse of the Great Seal of the United States or of the Seals of the President or the Vice President of the United States; Unauthorized Use of *"Johnny Horizon"*

Symbol; Unauthorized Use of *Smokey Bear* Symbol.

44. Civil Rights; Civil Rights, Election Laws, Voting Rights Act, 1965; Overseas Citizens Voting Rights Act of 1975.

45. Crime on the High Seas (Includes stowaways on boats and aircraft).

46. Fraud Against the Government; Anti-Kickback Statute; Dependent Assistance Act of 1950; False Claims, Civil; Federal Aid Road Act; Lead and Zinc Act; Public Works and Economic Development Act of 1965; Renegotiation Act, Criminal; Renegotiation Act, Civil; Trade Expansion Act of 1962; Unemployment Compensation Statutes; Economic Opportunity Act. [See also classifications "206-10" — authors' comment.]

47. Impersonation.

48. Postal. Violation (Except Mail Fraud). This classification covers inquiries concerning the Postal Service and complaints pertaining to the theft of mail. Such complaints are either forwarded to the Postmaster General or the nearest Postal Inspector.

49. National Bankruptcy Act.

50. Involuntary Servitude and Slavery.

51. Jury Panel Investigations.

52. Theft. Robbery. Embezzlement. Illegal Possession or Destruction of Government Property. Interference With Government Communications.

53. Excess Profits on Wool. 1918. (Obsolete 1925)

54. Customs Laws and Smuggling. Complaints are referred to the nearest district office of the U.S. Customs Service or the Commissioner of Customs, Washington, D.C.

55. Counterfeiting. Complaints are referred to either the Director, U.S. Secret Service, or the nearest office of that agency.

56. Election Laws.

57. War Labor Dispute Act. (Obsolete 1951)

58. Bribery; Conflict of Interest.

59. World War Adjusted Compensation Act 1924-44. (Obsolete 1928)

60. Anti-Trust.

**61. Treason or Misprision of Treason.

*62. Miscellaneous: including Administrative Inquiries; Misconduct Investigations of Officers and Employees of the Department of Justice and Federal Judiciary; Domestic Police Cooperation; Eight-Hour-Day Law; Fair Labor Standards Act of 1938 (Wage and Hours Law); conspiracy. [Sometimes used for security cases particularly miscellaneous ones such as "National Security Electronic Surveillance File" and "[Joseph P.] McCarthy Control File" — authors' comment.]

*63. Miscellaneous — Nonsubversive. This classification concerns correspondence from the public which does not relate to matters within FBI jurisdiction. [Formerly included many of the investigations now included in 62 — authors' comment.]

**64. Foreign Miscellaneous. This classification is a control file utilized as a repository for intelligence information of value identified by country. More specific categories are placed in classifications 108-113.

**65. Espionage; Attorney General Guidelines on Foreign Counterintelligence; Internal Security Act of 1950; Executive Order 11905.

66. Administrative Matters. This classification covers such items as supplies, automobiles, salary matters and vouchers. [Frequently used as an informer file — authors' comment.]

*67. Personnel Matters. This classification concerns background investigations of applicants for employment with the FBI. [Also used for investigations of "attacks against the FBI" — authors' comment.]

68. Alaskan Matters. (Obsolete 1956)

69. Contempt of Court.

70. Crime on Government Reservation.

71. Bills of Lading Act.

72. Obstruction of Criminal Investigations.

*73. Application for Pardon After Completion of Sentence and Application for Executive Clemency.

74. Perjury.

75. Bondsmen and Sureties.

76. Escaped Federal Prisoner; Escape and Rescue; Probation Violator; Parole Violator; Mandatory Release Violator.

*77. Applicants (Special Inquiry, Departmental and Other Government Agencies, except those having special classifications).

78. Illegal Use of Government Transportation Requests.

79. Missing Persons.

80. Laboratory Research Matters. In field office files this classification covers the FBI's public affairs matters and involves contact by the FBI with the general public, Federal and State agencies, the Armed Forces, corporations, the news media and other outside organizations.

81. Gold Hoarding 1933-45. (Obsolete 1952)

82. War Risk Insurance (National Life Insurance). (Obsolete 1967)

83. Court of Claims.

84. Reconstruction Finance Corporation Act. (Obsolete 1953)

85. Home Owner Loan Corporation. (Obsolete 1952)

86. Federal Lending and Insurance Agencies.

87. Interstate Transportation of Stolen Property (Fraud by Wire, Radio or Television).

88. Unlawful Flight to Avoid Prosecution, Custody, or Confinement; Unlawful Flight to Avoid Giving Testimony.

89. Assaulting or Killing a Federal Officer. Congressional Assassination Statute.

90. Irregularities in Federal Penal Institutions.

91. Bank Burglary; Bank Larceny; Bank Robbery.

92. Anti-Racketeering.

93. Ascertaining Financial Ability. This classification concerns requests by the Department of Justice for the FBI to ascertain a person's ability to pay a claim, fine or judgment obtained against him by the United States Government.

94. Research Matters. This classification concerns all general correspondence of the FBI with private individuals which does not involve any substantive violation of Federal law. [Contains "records of leaks to sycophantic writers and the FBI's arranging for publication of books favorable to it" according to Harold Weisberg in an *Affidavit* (7/20/79) filed in *AFSC* v. *Webster*. — authors' comment.]

95. Laboratory Cases (Examination of Evidence in Other Than Bureau's Cases).

96. Alien Applicant. (Obsolete 1944)

**97. Foreign Agents Registration Act. [Frequently used for investigation of organizations — authors' comment].

**98. Sabotage.

99. Plant Survey. (Obsolete 1944) This classification covers a program wherein the FBI inspected industrial plants for the purpose of making suggestions to the operators of those plants to prevent espionage and sabotage.

**100. Domestic Security. This classification covers investigations by the FBI in the domestic security field, e.g. Smith Act violations. [The most common classification by far for "subversive" investigations. Up to 1978 listed as "Subversive Matter (individuals); Internal Security (organizations); Domestic Security investigations."—authors' comment.]

101. Hatch Act. (Obsolete 1941) [Seems to be a catch-all classification used for investigations of alleged subversive activities by government employees — authors' comment.]

**102. Voorhis Act.

103. Interstate Transportation of Stolen Cattle.

104. Servicemen's Dependents Allowance Act of 1942. (Obsolete 1957)

**105. Foreign Counterintelligence Matters. Attorney General Guidelines on Foreign Counterintelligence. Executive Order 11905. [Frequently used as a "subversive matter" file, similar to "100;" for investigations purporting to determine whether a person or group is subject to foreign influence, control or financing — authors' comment.]

106. Alien Enemy Control; Escaped Prisoners of War and Internees. 1944-45. (Obsolete 1963) Suspects were generally suspected escaped prisoners of war, members of foreign organizations, failed to register under the Alien Registration Act. Cases ordered closed by Attorney General after alien enemies returned to their respective countries upon termination of hostilities.

107. Denaturalization Proceedings. (Obsolete 1952)

108. Foreign Travel Control. (Obsolete 1944) This classification concerns security-type investigations wherein the subject is involved in foreign travel.

**109. Foreign Political Matters. This classification is a control file utilized as a repository for intelligence information concerning foreign political matters broken down by country.

**110. Foreign Economic Matters. This classification is a control file utilized as a repository for intelligence information concerning foreign economic matters broken down by country.

**111. Foreign Social Conditions. This classification is a control file utilized as a repository for intelligence information concerning foreign social conditions broken down by country.

**112. Foreign Funds. This classification is a control file utilized as a repository for intelligence information concerning foreign funds broken down by country.

**113. Foreign Military and Naval Matters. This classification is a control file utilized as a repository for intelligence information concerning foreign military and naval matters broken down by country.

114. Alien Property Custodian Matters. (Obsolete 1972)

115. Bond Default; Bail Jumper.

*116. Department of Energy Applicant; Department of Energy, Employee. [Formerly Atomic Energy Commission. Many investigations of atomic scientists were conducted under this classification — authors' comment.]

**117. Department of Energy, Criminal.

*118. Applicant, Intelligence Agency. (Obsolete 1952) [Formerly this classification was listed as "Applicant-Central Intelligence Agency" — authors' comment.]

119. Federal Regulations of Lobbying Act.

120. Federal Tort Claims Act.

*121. Loyalty of Government Employees. (Obsolete) Executive Order 9835.

122. Labor Management Relations Act, 1947.

*123. Special Inquiry, State Department, Voice of America (U.S. Information Center). (Obsolete 1963) This classification covers loyalty and security investigations on personnel employed by or under consideration for employment for Voice of America.

*124. European Recovery Program (Int'l Cooperation Administration), formerly Foreign Operations Administration, Economic Cooperation Administration or E.R.P., European Recovery Programs; A.I.D., Agency for International Development. (Obsolete 1963) This classification covers security and loyalty investigations of personnel employed by or under consideration for employment with the European Recovery Program.

125. Railway Labor Act; Railway Labor Act — Employer's Liability Act.

*126. National Security Resources Board, Special Inquiry. (Obsolete 1950) This classification covers loyalty investigations on employees and applicants of the National Security Resources Board.

*127. Sensitive Positions in the United States Government. (Obsolete 1950)

*128. International Development Program (Foreign Operations Administration). (Obsolete)

129. Evacuation Claims. (Obsolete 1966)

*130. Special Inquiry, Armed Forces Security Act. (Obsolete 1951)

131. Admiralty Matters.

*132. Special Inquiry, Office of Defense Mobilization. (Obsolete 1951)

*133. National Science Foundation Act. Applicant. (Obsolete 1963)

**134. Foreign Counterintelligence Assets. This classification concerns individuals who provide information to the FBI concerning Foreign Counterintelligence matters. [Up to 1978 listed as "Security Informants" — authors' comment.]

135. PROSAB (Protection of Strategic Air Command Bases of the U.S. Air Force). (Obsolete) This classification covered contacts with individuals with the aim to develop information useful to protect bases of the Strategic Air Command.

136. American Legion Contact. (Obsolete)

137. Informants, Other than Foreign Counterintelligence Assets. This classification concerns individuals who furnish information to the FBI concerning criminal violations on a continuing and confidential basis. [Up to 1978 listed as "Criminal Informants" — authors' comment.]

*138. Loyalty of Employees of the United Nations and Other Public International Organizations. This classification concerns FBI investigations based on referrals from the Civil Service Commission wherein a question or allegation has been received regarding the applicant's loyalty to the U.S. Government as described in Executive Order 10422.

139. Interception of Communications (Formerly, Unauthorized Publication or Use of Communications).

*140. Security of Government Employees; S.G.E., Fraud Against the Government. Executive Order 10450.

141. False Entries in Records of Interstate Carriers.

142. Illegal Use of Railroad Pass.

143. Interstate Transportation of Gambling Devices.

144. Interstate Transportation of Lottery Tickets.

145. Interstate Transportation of Obscene Matter; Broadcasting Obscene Language.

146. Interstate Transportation of Prison-Made Goods.

147. Department of Housing and Urban Development Matters.

148. Interstate Transportation of Fireworks.

149. Destruction of Aircraft or Motor Vehicles.

150. Harboring of Federal Fugitives, Statistics. (Obsolete)

*151. (Referral cases received from CSC under Pub. L. 298). Agency for International Development; Department of Energy (Civil Service Commission); National Aeronautics and Space Administration; National Science Foundation; Peace Corps; Actions; U.S. Arms Control and Disarmament Agency; World Health Organization; International Labor Organization; U.S. Information Agency. This classification covers referrals from the Civil Service Commission wherein an allegation has been received regarding an applicant's loyalty to the U.S. Government. These referrals refer to applicants from Peace Corps, Department of Energy, National Aeronautics and Space Administration, Nuclear Regulatory Commission, United States Arms Control and Disarmament Agency, and the United States Information Agency.

152. Switchblade Knife Act.

153. Automobile Information Disclosure Act.

154. Interstate Transportation of Unsafe Refrigerators.

*155. National Aeronautics and Space Act of 1958.

156. Employee Retirement Income Security Act. [Formerly Welfare & Pension Plans Disclosure Act.]

**157. Civil Unrest. This classification concerns FBI responsibility for reporting information on civil disturbances or demonstrations. [Up to 1978 listed as "Extremist Matters; Civil Unrest." Used for files on so-called "racial matters," e.g. COINTELPRO operations against the Black Panther Party — authors' comment.]

**158. Labor-Management Reporting and Disclosure Act of 1959 (Security Matter). (Obsolete 1966)

159. Labor-Management Reporting and Disclosure Act of 1959 (Investigative Matters).

160. Federal Train Wreck Statute.

*161. Special Inquiries for White House, Congressional Committee and Other Government Agencies.

162. Interstate Gambling Activities.

**163. Foreign Police Cooperation. This classification covers requests by foreign police for the FBI to render investigative assistance to such agencies.

164. Crime Aboard Aircraft.

165. Interstate Transmission of Wagering Information.

166. Interstate Transportation in Aid of Racketeering.

167. Destruction of Interstate Property.

168. Interstate Transportation of Wagering Paraphernalia.

169. Hydraulic Brake Fluid Act. (Obsolete 1966)

**170. Extremist Informants. (Obsolete) This classification concerns individuals who provided information on a continuing basis on various extremist elements.

171. Motor Vehicle Seat Belt Act. (Obsolete 1965)

172. Sports Bribery.

173. Public Accommodations, Civil Rights Act of 1964 Public Facilities, Civil Rights Act of 1964 Public Education, Civil Rights Act of 1964 Employment, Civil Rights Act of 1964.

174. Explosives and Incendiary Devices; Bomb Threats (Formerly, Bombing Matters; Bombing Matters, Threats).

175. Assaulting the President (or Vice President) of the United States.

176. Anti-riot Laws.

177. Discrimination in Housing.

178. Interstate Obscene or Harassing Telephone Calls.

179. Extortionate Credit Transactions.

180. Desecration of the Flag.

181. Consumer Credit Protection Act.

182. Illegal Gambling Business; Illegal Gambling Business, Obstruction; Illegal Gambling Business, Forfeiture.

183. Racketeer-Influenced and Corrupt Organizations.

184. Police Killings.

**185. Protection of Foreign Officials and Official Guests of the United States.

186. Real Estate Settlement Procedures Act of 1974.

187. Privacy Act of 1974, Criminal.

188. Crime Resistance. This classification covers FBI efforts to develop new or improved approaches, techniques, systems, equipment and devices to improve and strengthen law enforcement as mandated by the Omnibus Crime Control and Safe Streets Act of 1968.

189. Equal Credit Opportunity Act.

190. Freedom of Information/Privacy Acts. This classification covers the creation of a correspondence file to preserve and maintain accurate records concerning the handling of requests for records submitted pursuant to the Freedom of Information — Privacy Acts.

**191. False Identity Matters. This classification covers the FBI's study and examination of criminal elements' efforts to create false identities.

192. Hobbs Act — Financial Institutions.

193. Hobbs Act — Commercial Institutions.

194. Hobbs Act — Corruption of Public Officials.

195. Hobbs Act — Labor Related.

196. Fraud by Wire.

197. Civil Actions or Claims Against the Government. This classification covers all civil suits involving FBI matters and most administrative claims filed under the Federal Tort Claims Act arising from FBI activities.

198. Crime on Indian Reservations.

**199. Foreign Counterintelligence (country abbreviation—Terrorism).

**200. Foreign Counterintelligence Matters. [In 1978 listed as "Foreign Counter-intelligence—China" — authors' comment.]

**201. Foreign Counterintelligence Matters. [In 1978 listed as "Foreign Counter-intelligence—Satellite" — authors' comment.]

**202. Foreign Counterintelligence Matters. [In 1978 listed as "Foreign Counterintel-ligence—Cuba" — authors' comment.]

**203. Foreign Counterintelligence Matters. [In 1978 listed as "Foreign Counterintelligence—all other countries" — authors' comment.]

204. Federal Revenue Sharing. This classification covers FBI investigations conducted where the Attorney General has been authorized to bring civil action whenever he has reason to believe that a pattern or practice of discrimination in disbursements of funds under the Federal Revenue Sharing statute exists.

205. Foreign Corrupt Practices Act of 1977.

206. Fraud Against the Government — Department of Defense.

207. Fraud Against the Government — Environmental Protection Agency.

208. Fraud Against the Government — General Services Administration.

209. Fraud Against the Government — Dept. of Health, Education and Welfare.

210. Fraud Against the Government — Department of Labor.

CHAPTER II

THE FBI AND THE FREEDOM OF INFORMATION AND PRIVACY ACTS

Introduction

This Chapter is divided into four sections. The first section briefly describes the major provisions of the Freedom of Information Act (FOIA) and Privacy Act (PA). It is followed by a discussion of the attacks directed at the FOIA by the FBI. This law, which has begun to show its usefulness in keeping the public informed about what the government does, is seen as a major threat by those agencies which — the FBI in the forefront — prefer to operate behind a curtain of secrecy. The next section explains how an FOIA request is processed by the FBI. The final section discusses another form of attack on the FOIA — how the FBI plays statutory exemptions "games" — and offers suggestions for overcoming the FBI's maneuvers.

The Freedom of Information and Privacy Acts

A people denied the right to scrutinize the operations of government and hold government officials accountable for their actions is powerless to control the direction of government and to make informed choices. The FOIA provides the means of increasing public knowledge about the operations and decision-making processes of the federal bureaucracy.

First passed in 1966, and amended and strengthened in 1974 (over President Ford's veto), the Freedom of Information Act provides access to many government records, including an individual's own files, compiled and possessed by any branch, agency or subdivision of the Executive Branch of the federal government, including all federal regulatory agencies and government-controlled corporations. The 1974 amendments (effective Feb., 1975) made the investigative files of the FBI, the CIA and other intelligence and police agencies available to the public for the first time.

Access to these records is not confined to U.S. citizens. The law allows "any person" to request records, including resident aliens and citizens of other countries wherever they reside. The FBI wants the FOIA amended to give aliens access to FBI records only at the agency's discretion. (Some agencies already claim this discretion.) In addition to individuals, groups of all sorts are entitled to make requests: universities, the press, corporations, unincorporated associations, public interest groups, state and local governments.

The FOIA requires agencies to respond promptly to requests and sets specific time limits. It requires that fees charged (for search and copying) be reasonable and permits agencies to reduce or waive fees if release of the information primarily benefits the public. Agencies are *permitted but not required* to withhold information if it falls within one or more of the nine specific exemptions spelled out in the law. The principal grounds for withholding records in whole or in part are protection of privacy, confidentiality of sources, and national defense and foreign relations.

If, in the opinion of the requester, an agency improperly withholds records, delays in responding, charges excessive fees, or fails to make a complete search for the records requested, the FOIA allows a requester to appeal the agency's actions administratively. An appeal which is not wholly successful may be challenged by the requester in federal court. Recognizing that legal action is costly, the FOIA provides that the court may award attorneys' fees to an FOIA requester who "substantially prevails" (for example, convinces a judge that the records sought should have been released by the agency in the first place). This provision is obviously meant to deter agencies from simply refusing to release material and forcing requesters to sue in order to get the records they want.

Perhaps the most important fact about the FOIA is that it does not require you to have a reason for requesting government records. Under the FOIA you need not *have or give* a reason. You have an absolute (within the nine exemptions) right to know.

The Privacy Act (PA), adopted in 1974, provides access to and allows for inspection, correction, or destruction of *personal* records in the possession of the executive branch of the Federal government (with the exception of the CIA and certain other agencies) which can be retrieved through a person's name or social security number. This law provides access to a smaller body of documents, both because of its concern only with personal records and because its exemptions are much more extensive than those of the FOIA. In addition, there is no provision for an administrative appeal of an agency's denial of records under the PA so that it is necessary to sue in federal court in order to challenge an agency's decision. Nonetheless, many important benefits are derived from the PA. It requires agencies to publish each year descriptions of their records system in the *Federal Register*. It also provides a set of restrictions on what kind of information about an individual an agency can collect, record, and disseminate. Information on a U.S. citizen must be *both relevant* and *necessary* to the agency in carrying out a specific authorized purpose. For example, the FBI is prohibited from recording personal information about an individual or his or her activities if that person is not connected in some way with an official, legitimate FBI investigation. In addition, the information must be "necessary to the successful completion of the investigation" as well as relevant.[1]

Information describing how an individual exercises First Amendment rights may be collected or recorded *only* where it is authorized by statute or if the individual consents, or if the information is "pertinent to *and* within the scope of an authorized law enforcement activity."[2] An FBI report states that:

> Such information could encompass membership in organizations, public pronouncements and/or political activity of individual citizens. The law enforcement activity must be authorized and the information must be both pertinent to and within the scope of such activity in order to record it in our files.[3]

Finally, the PA requires that any information used by a federal agency to make a determination about an individual must be accurate, relevant, timely and complete. For example, the FBI must see to it that information it gathers, records, and disseminates when it conducts background investigations on applicants for federal jobs meets this test.

Approximately 70,000 requests for files have been made to the FBI by private citizens, organizations, scholars, journalists, businesses, etc., the great part of them since the FOIA was strengthened in 1975. Many of these requests have resulted in revelations about the government's illegal but too frequently successful efforts to disrupt, destroy and otherwise interfere with the lawful political actions of organizations and individuals. The police and intelligence agencies' use of political spies and informers, these agencies' burglaries, thefts, and character assassinations, their programs to pit liberal and progressive organizations against each other and to "neutralize" their effectiveness, the extensive illegal wiretaps, microphones, mail and trash covers, and mail openings for a period of forty years — all this has been partially exposed because of the FOIA.

As important as revealing past illegalities and abuses is the awareness on the part of government agencies that, as long as there is a Freedom of Information Act, their actions may be made public. This knowledge is a deterrent to government officials, helping to ensure that their conduct will be within the law and the Constitution.

Considering the public's right to know and its need to hold the government accountable, the FOIA still has serious weaknesses. But from the FBI's standpoint — that of increasing its autonomy and reducing public scrutiny — the FOIA is far too strong. It is not surprising, then, that during the last few years the FBI, joined by other intelligence agencies, has conducted a campaign to eviscerate or destroy the FOIA.

Attacks on the FOIA

Destruction of Files[4]
Shortly after World War II the FBI asked the National Archives and

Records Service (NARS) to approve destruction of FBI field office files covering the period 1910-1938. The request was justified on the ground that the files were of no further use to the FBI and were of no historical, research, legal, or other value (the standards the law required NARS to apply) because their contents were duplicated in counterpart files kept at FBI Headquarters in Washington. In approving and in *inducing Congress to approve* this request, NARS did not seek to verify these assertions by physically inspecting the FBI files. (Until recently, Congressional approval of destruction was required.) In 1945 and 1946 the FBI made further requests to NARS for authority to destroy field office files. Although NARS approved the requests (without inspecting the files) the FBI seemed in no hurry to exercize the granted authorization. Instead, it placed closed field office files on retention schedules of 20 to 30 years.

Shortly after the amendments to the Freedom of Information Act went into effect (February 1975), giving the public wider access to FBI investigatory files, the FBI stepped up the actual destruction of its field office files whose destruction had been authorized by NARS in 1945-6 and sought NARS approval for even more extensive destruction of its records. For example, in May 1975 the FBI asked for authority to destroy all field office files, index cards and other related materials in three kinds of closed cases: (a) investigation led to no prosecution; (b) investigation failed to find the perpetrator; and (c) investigation showed the charge was unfounded or was "not within the jurisdiction of the FBI." This latter category includes the "preliminary inquiry" files which are overwhelmingly domestic security intelligence files. In "preliminary inquiries" *the field office files are the only files,* since no counterpart files are even created at Headquarters. Nonetheless, without ever physically reviewing any documents, NARS again certified these files as valueless and approved their destruction.

During 1977 the FBI succeeded in getting NARS authority to accelerate the pace of destruction by shortening the retention periods for "closed" files in field offices: NARS gave authority to destroy noncriminal (including security) cases 10 years after closing; criminal cases 5 years after closing, and material in auxiliary field offices six months after closing. (However, since this authorization, several moratoriums on destruction have been imposed, as explained below.) The most startling move came in May of 1977 when the FBI asked NARS for authority to destroy FBI Headquarters files on a massive scale. These are the very files whose alleged completeness and permanence the FBI has used from *1946 to 1977* to justify the destruction of field office files. Again without any physical inspection, NARS appraisers certified these files as "valueless" and appropriate for destruction. But this time, objections were raised by public interest groups, by some professionals within NARS itself, and by the Congressional committees NARS felt compelled to consult. Out of this protest came an extraordinary event.

For the first time NARS felt constrained to ask to inspect some FBI files and the FBI felt constrained to grant that request.[5] Even then what occurred was a sham "inspection." In the spring of 1977 two NARS appraisers (one totally inexperienced), accompanied by an FBI agent at all times, made a spot check of some 76 files in three field offices. Furthermore, the 76 files, out of the millions in existence, were not read in their entirety and the parts read were selected by the accompanying FBI agent.

Inadequate as this "study" may have been, the NARS appraisers discovered what anyone who has looked at both field office and Headquarters files has discovered — that for some field office files there are no counterpart files at Headquarters and that where there are counterpart files the two files do not contain the same material. The field office files contain the original investigative material — agents' notes, correspondence, interviews, ELSUR logs, working drafts of memos and reports, notes of illegal actions not reported officially to Headquarters, informer reports, signed statements, and the like. While none of this kind of material is in the Headquarters files, unique and important material appears in Headquarters files — communications with other branches and agencies of government and with nongovernment bodies and individuals. (See Ch. I, Appendix B.)

Though it reported this factual finding, NARS concluded that since summaries of everything important were sent to Headquarters, the certification of the field offices' files for destruction was justified and should be approved.

These NARS-FBI maneuvers alarmed a wide variety of individuals and groups. Whatever the intention — and the timing gave rise to grave suspicions — the effect of this destruction program would have been to effectively "repeal" the Freedom of Information Act so far as FBI files were concerned. It was to prevent implementation of this program that a disparate group of historians, publishers, socially concerned church groups, writers, journalists, researchers, scientists, trade unionists, teachers, and political activists brought suit in federal court to enjoin the FBI and NARS from all further destruction of FBI files pending the development, under court supervision, of a rational plan to identify and preserve all valuable material (*AFSC* v. *Webster*, 485 F. Supp. 222).

It was learned in the suit that among the field office files no longer available to scholars because they have been destroyed are most of the files concerning the internment of Japanese-Americans during World War II, the American Protective League (a vigilante group that worked closely with the FBI in the 1920s), and the American Legion (1950-1954). In an FBI document dated August 2, 1976, which discusses possibilities for further destruction of files, an FBI official states:

Because of social-political factors, files relating to World War II activities could be considered for destruction. Files relating to internal security-extremist matters without foreign involvement such as Klan, Minutemen, Nation of Islam, Black Panther Party, and antiriot and bombing matters should be considered for destruction after they are 10 years old.[6]

The FBI testified that a voluntary (and therefore revokable) moratorium on the destruction of security-related files was in effect because former top FBI officials require such documents in preparing their defense in various pending criminal actions against them (the officials concerned are John J. Kearney, L. Patrick Gray III, Mark Felt, and Edward Miller). In addition, Senator Church's committee investigating intelligence activities placed a moratorium on the destruction of a limited number of files. (Files in the FBI's criminal classifications are not subject to the moratorium and some of these may contain material from domestic security investigations).

On January 10, 1980, federal District Court Judge Harold H. Greene handed down a precedent-setting opinion in support of his decision in *AFSC* v. *Webster* cited above. Evidence presented at a five-day hearing on the plaintiffs' application for a preliminary injunction convinced the judge to issue a sweeping order restraining NARS and the FBI from destroying or approving the destruction of any FBI files until a plan for meeting their statutory responsibilities with respect to FBI files is approved by the court.

Judge Greene agreed with the plaintiffs' contention that NARS had violated the law and completely defaulted in meeting its duty to assure the preservation of FBI files having historical, legal, and research value. He wrote that the evidence showed that:

. . . the Archivist and those under his supervision have failed for a period of over thirty years adequately to carry out these statutory and regulatory responsibilities with respect to the records of the Federal Bureau of Investigation.

* * *

[Never] [d]uring that entire period . . . did a single employee of the Archives see a single FBI file. All decisions were made on the basis of representations of the FBI . . .

As the judge noted, some of these representations were incorrect. For example, the judge said that while NARS proceeded on the assumption that the FBI's files at Headquarters and in the field offices were "to all intents and purposes identical, the evidence clearly shows this to be erroneous." Judge Greene suggested in his opinion that the late FBI Director J. Edgar Hoover's policy of refusing access to FBI files to anyone outside the Bureau accounts for NARS failure to demand access to those files. However, that suggestion does not account for the fact that none of the FBI Directors or Attorneys

General since Hoover's death in 1972 has granted access to NARS either. This suggests a resistance to outside inspection that, coupled with what the judge called "a bias, on impermissible grounds, in favor of the destruction rather than the preservation" of records, constitutes a fundamental and unchanged FBI policy.

The judge did recognize, however, that the stepped-up destruction program in 1975 was motivated "at least in part" by the desire of both NARS and the FBI "to escape the burdens of the Freedom of Information Act by disposing of some . . ." files.

With respect to the FBI and the significance of its files the judge wrote that:

> [t]he files of such an agency contain far more of the raw materials of history and research and far more data pertaining to the rights of citizens than do the files of bureaus with more pedestrian mandates. The public interest demands that great care be taken before such records are committed to destruction.

* * *

> . . . the FBI's relationship to this country's history and the legal rights of its citizens is unique, and the intensity of the scrutiny to which its files should be subjected before they are authorized to be destroyed must reflect that uniqueness.

Because of this uniqueness, Judge Greene ordered that no FBI records can be destroyed until

> . . . qualified historians and archivists have had a chance to sort them out so as to ascertain which ones are of genuine historical value and which ones may be disposed of without damage to anyone.
>
> Some, or many, of the FBI's records presently destined for disposal deserve to be preserved, not only for the benefit of plaintiffs and others like them but as part of the national heritage. George Santayana taught us that "those who cannot remember the past are condemned to repeat it." The lessons of history can hardly be learned if the historical record is allowed to vanish.

At a hearing before Judge Greene on February 15, the FBI and NARS advised the court that a plan would not be ready earlier than January 1981. The judge indicated that his injunction will remain in force until a plan is submitted and carefully scrutinized.

As this book goes to press, the plaintiffs, with the assistance of the Fund for Open Information and Accountability, Inc., are organizing historians, archivists, journalists, civil libertarians, and others to assure that the plan will provide for the integrity of the FBI files so they may be made available to the public under the FOIA.

Before Judge Greene halted all destruction the only way an

39

individual could protect FBI documents from destruction was to submit an FOI/PA request since the FBI says it will not destroy files that are the subject of *pending* FOI/PA requests. We still strongly recommend this step to any readers who anticipate needing FBI documents. For example, if a request had been made in late 1977 for records on what the FBI and NARS referred to as "sex offenders and sex perverts" in the federal government, 99 cubic feet of irreplaceable records dealing, in all likelihood, with the investigation, harassment, and job loss of "sex offenders" and "homosexuals" could have been saved and made available for historical, legal, and social science use with due protection of individual privacy.[7] Or if a request had been filed early in 1978 for FBI records of investigations of Selective Service Act violations, an important body of material on the draft and resistance to it from World War II through the Vietnam era could have survived, and with privacy safeguarded, been opened to research.[8]

Proposed FBI Charter (S1612/HR5030)

That the FBI was deadly serious about getting free of the FOIA and its requirement for public disclosure and public accountability became absolutely clear with the introduction in July 1979 of a proposed FBI Charter. Even before proposing this Charter, FBI Director William Webster was publicly recommending similar limitations on the release of FBI files. The Charter (Sec. 533(c)) allows the FBI to place a ten-year moratorium on the release of all investigative files after an investigation is "closed." At the expiration of the moratorium the FBI at *its own discretion* may decide whether to send the file to the National Archives or to destroy it. (So much for the Freedom of Information and Privacy Acts!)

The Charter, none will be surprised to learn, was drafted by the FBI and the Justice Department. What is shocking is that it is supported by President Carter, Senator Kennedy, and Congressman Peter Rodino. Kennedy and Rodino chair the Judiciary Committees in their respective houses and can be expected to have considerable influence on the outcome of the proposed Charter.

As one would expect from a Charter that authorizes unreviewed destruction of records by the agency that creates the records, the other provisions of the Charter expand the FBI's powers and in general legalize the abusive practices revealed to the public by the congressional investigations of the mid-seventies. No one can be blamed for concluding that the FBI's call for unreviewed power to destroy documents indicates that the FBI expects to have much in its files that it would prefer to keep hidden from the public.

Proposed Amendments to the FOIA

If there could be any remaining doubt that what the FBI is after is total exemption from the Freedom of Information Act, the proposed amendments to the FOIA submitted to Congress in June, 1979, would eliminate it.[9]

These amendments, if adopted by Congress, would exempt a great portion of the FBI's records from disclosure under FOIA. Changed to suit the FBI, the FOIA would permit the agency to decide whether or not to disclose three kinds of records:

1. records the FBI considers "the most sensitive" — investigations of foreign intelligence, foreign counterintelligence, terrorism, and organized crime;

2. manuals, guidelines and other noninvestigatory records to the extent to which producing them would (in the agency's judgment) cause specified harm; and

3. records concerning ongoing investigations.

These proposed exemptions from mandatory disclosure leave very little, if anything, of public interest subject to release under FOIA. Evidence of the abuses of power and illegal acts the agency has consistently resorted to could easily be hidden from public scrutiny since "domestic security" political investigations would likely be within the "most sensitive" categories. We know — and we know in large part because the FOIA as it now reads requires the FBI to release such documents — that during the 1960s and 1970s the FBI often "justified" political investigations by claiming that the purpose of investigating various dissidents — antiwar, civil rights, or women's liberation groups and activists — was to determine whether they had "terrorist" connections or were financed or infiltrated by foreign intelligence agents.

The proposed withdrawal of records concerning ongoing investigations provides another hiding place for illegitimate activities. A security investigation of an individual is likely to be terminated only by his or her death. Investigations of organizations also tend to be nearly interminable. Security investigations rarely lead to criminal prosecutions. Three investigations in which Congressional inquiries and court proceedings have shown that the FBI used the most abusive and illegal techniques are also three of the longest investigations: the Communist Party, USA (still under investigation); the Socialist Workers Party; and the National Association for the Advancement of Colored People (NAACP).

The FBI asks that the FOIA be amended to provide for a seven-year moratorium (after an investigation is closed or prosecution occurs) on the release of all law-enforcement investigative records. The FBI claims that the requested moratorium is part of its need for increased ability to protect "confidential sources" or, in the words of FBI Director William Webster, "to reestablish the essential free flow of information from the public to the FBI." The FBI states that a moratorium is needed in order to prevent easy identification of "confidential sources" by a requester analyzing FBI records "while names, dates, places, and relationships are relatively fresh in his mind." Two other proposed

41

amendments are related to increasing "protection" for informers. One seeks to extend the protection from disclosure which the FOIA presently permits for "confidential sources" explicitly to include agencies or employees of state, municipal, or foreign governments who supply information to the FBI. Another amendment changes the standard for withholding information from "that which would identify" to "that which would *tend* to identify."

seeks to decrease the ability of some of its targets to use the FOIA at all. For example, it wants authority to deny FBI files to all aliens who are not permanent residents and to all felons (or those acting on their behalf). These restrictions do not violate the spirit of FOIA, the agency argues, because neither group is part of the citizenry that needs to obtain information in order to be "an informed electorate." It hardly seems faithful to the spirit of the FOIA to turn one of its noble purposes — to keep the electorate informed — into a means for restricting access to voters *only*. FBI documents obviously have an important bearing on more than electoral issues. The FBI — the agency whose records are a long chronicle of invasions of privacy (and worse) of living persons — also proposes to revise the FOIA so as to extend privacy protection for "25 years after death." Under such a provision it would be well into the 21st century before the FBI's recent misdeeds with respect to many antiwar and civil rights protesters could be discovered.

These proposals for change — the amendments to the FOIA, the FBI Charter, and the NARS/FBI destruction plan — appear to have a common purpose. They seek to reestablish the FBI as a virtually autonomous agency with limited, if any, accountability for its actions. By authorizing more extensive withholding of documents from disclosure and by permitting unreviewed destruction of documents, these various proposals effectively repeal the FOIA as it applies to the FBI.

Alleged Interference with Informers

Webster's major argument in support of his moratorium proposal is that government informers need protection from reprisals. He claims that the FBI has been losing a significant number of informers, "the single most important investigative tool in law enforcement," because they fear their identities will be revealed in released documents. Attorney General Bell's intransigence in the Socialist Workers Party civil damage suit against the FBI[10] (where he refused to turn over informer files although ordered to do so by the court) shows the growing importance the FBI places on this issue. However, the General Accounting Office concluded in its 1978 study of the *Impact of the Freedom of Information and Privacy Acts on Law Enforcement Agencies* that while

42

[law] enforcement officals almost universally agree that the Freedom of Information and Privacy Acts have eroded their ability to collect and disseminate information . . . the extent and significance of the information not being gathered because of these acts cannot be measured.[11]

With few exceptions, FBI informants have always understood that their identities could be revealed at the FBI's discretion (see below on the (b) (7) (d) exemption). The FOIA has never required the identity of legitimate confidential informers to be released. The FBI carefully conceals informers' identities under the (b) (7) (d) exemption provided in FOIA. There is no evidence that the safety of any security informer was ever jeopardized by an FOIA release. As FBI Director William Webster himself has testified before a Congressional Subcommittee: "To our knowledge no informant has suffered physical harm as a result of an FOIAPA disclosure."[12]

Alleged General Interference with Law Enforcement

The FBI sometimes cites the number of "law trained" FBI agents diverted from "real" law enforcement work and speculates on the resulting number of criminals that escape detection. But the FBI now has regularly budgeted slots for FOI/PA personnel and should not need to divert agents from investigative work as was done temporarily during the crash program in 1976-77 known as "Project Onslaught." Much of the work involved in processing FOIA is done by clerks, not agents. Agent time in FOI/PA work could be dramatically reduced if the agency were less intransigent in resisting requests.

The FBI has argued that in some cases, because of the FOIA

. . . it has taken the FBI longer to apprehend a criminal, that the FBI has had to spend additional agent hours collecting and/or verifying information, that the public has been increasingly reluctant to cooperate, and that some criminals are using the acts to try to obtain sensitive information from law enforcement agencies.[13]

However, the General Accounting Office Study referred to above found that such cases do not show that the FBI has been unable to fulfill its investigative responsibilities. Moreover,

[the] FBI had difficulty determining whether the impact on its operations resulted solely from the FOI/PA. Other laws or regulations, administrative policies, and a general distrust of law enforcement agencies may have had as much or more to do with the FBI's difficulties as the FOI/PA. Therefore, it was not possible to accurately document the total impact these two laws have had on the investigative operations of the FBI.[14]

Allegedly Excessive Costs

Yet another argument against the FOIA focuses on the cost of the 400 staff members and 45 attorneys working full time on FOI/PA requests and appeals. The annual cost at FBI Headquarters for 1978 is alleged to be 7.8 million dollars.[15] The FBI alleges that despite these large expenditures, it cannot keep current with FOI/PA requests.[16] It particularly blames its backlog on such larger requests as those in the Rosenberg and Hiss cases and downgrades the public importance of such requests.

While agency resistance to the FOI/PA may have unnecessarily added to the cost, it is true that implementing the FOI/PA costs money. However, Congress has determined that public funds should be spent in order to achieve the purposes of the FOI/PA.

How FBI Headquarters Responds to FOIA Requests[17]

Introduction

The basic organizational units of the FBI are called Divisions. There are two investigative divisions at Headquarters — intelligence and criminal. These are the units that direct the operations which generate the information available to the public under FOI/PA.

The work of responding to FOI/PA requests, however, is handled by a special FOI/PA Branch which is part of the Records Management Division, one of the six administrative divisions.

According to the FBI, each FBI Field Office has two Special Agents who have received some training in FOI/PA work. In the smaller offices these agents work part-time processing requests. In the larger offices (New York, Los Angeles, San Francisco) the agents work full-time and also have clerical help.

Chart I depicts the steps followed in processing an FOI/PA request addressed to FBI Headquarters. The request, received in the mail room of the Records Management Division, is directed to the Initial Processing Unit (IPU) where a clerk inspects it and sends a letter of acknowledgment.

Search

If there is insufficient information to start searching for the files or records requested (this is known in Bureauese as an "unperfected" request) the papers are forwarded to the Initial Correspondence Team which sends out a form letter indicating what material is missing and holds the request open for 60 days. If no response is received within that time, the "case" is "administratively closed" but can be reopened if the requester responds subsequently. (Cases will also be "administratively closed" when a requester fails to respond within 60 days when the FBI asks that a signature be notorized or that fees be remitted.)

In practice, we know that the FBI calls a letter "unperfected" even

44

Chart I: How FBI Headquarters Processes an FOIA/PA Request

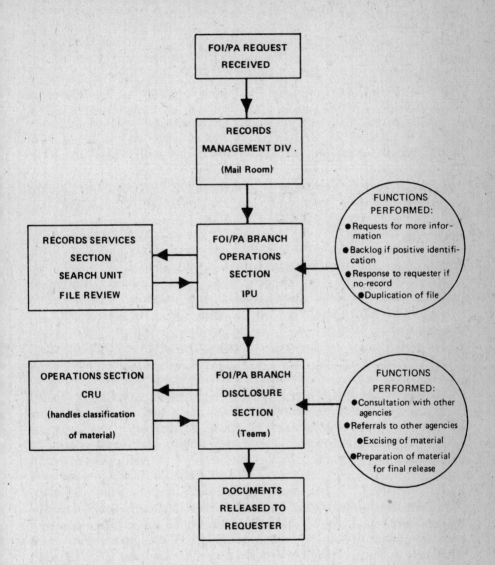

Source: GAO, *Timeliness*, p. 20 (see Bibliography).

when there is adequate information to begin and complete a search for the files and documents requested. The letters sent out by the FBI are often very broadly worded so that it appears to requesters that extensive biographical information — which they are reluctant to provide — is demanded. For common names, some means must be provided for telling whether the "Jane Smith" in the file index is the Jane Smith who is requesting the documents. The FOIA searcher may require, for example, an address or a school attended during the relevant time period, or, especially if the files requested are at Headquarters, the city of residence at the relevant time. However, a requester should insist that the information to "perfect" a request be reasonable and specific.

A "perfected" request is given to a clerk to search the General Index for the requested files or records. (Other indices, such as the ELSUR index, are searched only if specifically requested.) There are three possible outcomes of this General Index search:

1. *"No-record":* No record is found; Initial Correspondence Team sends a letter stating that the FBI has "no-record" corresponding to (or, in Bureauese, "identifiable with") the request.

2. *"No-record main-file":* This response means that while the General Index to the Central Records System contains no indication of a "main" file on the subject requested, it does show some "see references" (see Ch. I) which may pertain to the subject. In order to decide if the "see references" are pertinent, additional information is needed. The information needed is asked for in the letter sent the requester.

FBI policy regarding "see references" is to search for "see reference" documents only when those documents are in files relating to organizations or incidents identified in the request letter. According to a General Accounting Office report, "The see reference files would be reviewed only if the requester specifically identified records associated with a particular organization or incident covered in an investigation."[18] Because "see ref." documents may contain only a cursory mention of the individual, unlike "main" files, the FBI clerks often do need more extensive background information for deciding whether a "see ref." pertains to the same individual. Though a "main" file is apt to include such identifying information as birthdate, social security number, etc., a "see ref." will often indicate no more than (to take a common example) that an individual having a certain name was at a particular meeting. Thus, the fact that an individual was affiliated with an organization may help the FBI tell whether a "see ref." does indeed refer to that individual. But additional information is not invariably needed to check "see refs." If the FBI does demand additional information, try to pin down the precise nature of the problem and the specific information needed.

3. *"Main" files* (and perhaps also "see references") on the subject of the request are found.

Disclosure and Nondisclosure

Requested records uncovered are duplicated by the Initial Processing Unit, and assigned a place on the waiting list, until an analyst in the Disclosure section is available to start a new case. (There is always a backlog but its size seems to be diminishing.) If the request is a Project request, defined by the FBI as a request in which 15 or more volumes (roughly 200 pages per volume) exist on the subject requested, it will be assigned by a Unit Chief (Unit D, E, or F) to a Team Captain who, in turn, assigns it to an analyst. Similarly, a Non-Project Request (defined as "any other") is routed to Unit A, B, or C, assigned by the Unit Chief to a team and assigned by the Team Captain to an analyst. Project Units were established to enable large requests to be processed without interfering with smaller ones.

The analyst performs three tasks in "processing" the documents:

1. *Referring Classified Material:* Material in the files that is now classified or that the analyst thinks may be classifiable is referred to the Classification Review Unit. (About 35% of all FOIA cases at FBI Headquarters require referrals to the CRU.) The CRU reviewer examines the material in light of the operative classification order — at present, Executive Order 12065 — and returns it to the analyst indicating which documents or segments are classified "confidential," "secret," or "top secret." The analyst withholds all classified information from release. If the classified documents are over twenty years old, the Department Review Committee of the Department of Justice normally reviews them to determine whether they warrant continued classification. (Exemption (b) (1) of the FOIA enables agencies to withhold classified information.)

2. *Referring Other Agency Material:* Documents in FBI files that originated with another agency (e.g., a memo from the State Department or Post Office) or FBI documents that incorporate information obtained from another agency are sent to that agency for its decision concerning what may be released.

3. *Excising:* All material not referred to other agencies or to the Classification Review Unit is read line by line by the Disclosure section analyst to determine what material is to be excised. When other agencies or the CRU do not object to release, the FBI analysts still read every line and make their own deletions. No actual "cutting" is done, although this method was formerly used. At present, a special marking pen is wiped over the material to be deleted. This procedure leaves the text visible on the page actually marked, but produces a concealing black area on the photocopies of the marked documents which are released to the requester. In addition to "blacking out" portions of documents (words, lines, paragraphs, symbols, markings, file numbers, file titles, etc.) the analyst may determine that whole documents are to be withheld. Analysts keep track on inventory sheets of which exemption applies to which withheld information; but these inventories

are normally not supplied to the requesters, but should be. In deciding what to excise, the analyst supposedly applies the exemptions allowed in the FOI/PA as interpreted by the Attorney General's directives and guidelines. Initial decisions are reviewed by Team Captains, who are usually responsible for what is finally disclosed or withheld. Only the most "complex" cases are referred to the Unit Chief for review and final determination. Occasionally a case is sent to the Section Chief for review.

When this processing step is completed, the requester receives a letter that announces the outcome and explains where to direct appeals. There are essentially three possible outcomes:

1. *Request granted in full:* This response indicates that the FBI released all records it found which pertained to the request, and made no withholdings or excisions. It is almost unheard of for a substantial request to be granted in full.

2. *Request denied in part:* This indicates that the FBI withheld some material as falling under one or more of the exemptions to the FOI/PA. Denials involve excising passages or withholding whole pages or documents.

3. *Request denied in full:* This indicates that the FBI used one or more FOI/PA exemptions to completely refuse to release any information contained in its records.

Even if your request is granted in part or in full, you may be asked to pay a fee before receiving any documents. (At present, the FBI automatically waives fees on requests costing $25 or less since it costs more than that to collect payment.)

Appeals

Under FOIA, a dissatisfied requester has the right of administrative appeal. (While the PA does not provide for administrative appeal, agency decisions may be challenged in federal court.)

Appeals involving exemptions other than (b) (1) go to the Department of Justice's Office of Privacy and Information Appeals (OPIA). The Department Review Committee of the Department of Justice is responsible for determining the appropriateness of FBI classification decisions when such decisions are administratively appealed.

About 20 percent of the appeals of FBI withholdings involve (b) (1), and these are considered by the Review Committee. Appeals involving (b) (1) as well as other exemptions go to both the Review Committee *and* the OPIA.

In theory, the Review Committee will not uphold the classification of information dealing with the use of illegal techniques in domestic security cases. However, it does affirm the FBI's right to classify evidence of illegal activity involving a "foreign establishment." Whether or not the Review Committee is right to permit classification of information concerning this sort of illegal activity, one can only hope that the Committee has a firmer grasp of the differences between "foreign" and "domestic" matters than the FBI has had. (Many FBI investigations were, and are, "justified" by a claimed search for foreign influence or control. Years of intensive investigations which revealed no foreign ties only convinced the FBI to look harder.)

The Exemptions "Games"

Introduction

The FOIA permits, but does not require, government agencies to exempt from disclosure information which falls into one or more of nine categories. Because the FOIA has a strong, built-in presumption in favor of disclosure, courts have consistently held that the burden of proof is on the agency which is attempting to withhold information, not on the requester who seeks its release. Moreover, the official Department of Justice policy is to favor release *even when* material is technically exemptible. In a May 1977 letter to all federal departments and agencies, the Attorney General held that:

> The government should not withhold documents unless it is important to the public interest to do so, even if there is some arguable basis for the withholding.[19]

The FBI should, of course, be adhering to this admirable policy. Unfortunately, as many groups and individuals seeking access to FBI records have discovered, the FBI not only uses the exemptions to the fullest extent allowed by the FOIA, it mercilessly stretches these exemptions to cover up vast amounts of material which it has no legal right to withhold.

The FOIA, as amended in 1974, provided that "any reasonably segregable portion of a record shall be provided to any person requesting such record after deletion of the portions which are exempt under this subsection." This means, of course, that if only part of a document is exempt, the rest must be released. The Attorney General, in a memorandum of February 1975, set this policy:

> In order to apply the concept of "reasonably segregable," agency personnel should begin by identifying for deletion all portions of the requested document which are to be withheld in order to protect the interest covered by the exemption or exemptions involved. The remaining material (assuming it constitutes information that is responsive to the request) must be released if it is at all intelligible — unintelligibility indicating, of course, that it is not "reasonably" segregable from the balance. There is language in the legislative history of the "reasonably segregable" provision which indicates that even unintelligible matter remaining after the

deletion process must be released. (See S. Rept. pp. 31-32.) It does not seem that this sentence, contained in a report on the bill in its earlier stages, should outweigh the plain language of the provision. Conjunctions, prepositions, articles, and adverbs are almost always technically "segregable" without disclosing material which must be protected. Unless the qualification "reasonably" means that such unintelligible excerpts need not be provided, it seems meaningless. Of course, doubts about the intelligibility or responsiveness of remaining nonexempt material should be resolved in favor of release to the requester.[20]

Note that the Attorney General does permit agencies to withhold otherwise nonexempt material if such material is "unintelligible." This policy is questionable: if the material is "unintelligible," and was not deleted by the agency when the agency applied the various FOIA exemptions, what possible harm could come of letting the requester see the material? Why should agency personnel waste time deleting material which does not fall within any of the FOIA exemptions and which might possibly be of interest to a requester?

Even before passage of the amended FOIA in 1974, the Department of Justice (in 28 Code of Federal Regulations 50.8, 1973) held:

Persons outside the Executive Branch engaged in historical research projects will be accorded access to information or material of historical interest contained within the Department's investigatory files compiled for law enforcement purposes that are more than fifteen years old and are no longer substantially related to current investigative or law enforcement activities, subject to deletions to the minimum extent deemed necessary to protect law enforcement efficiency and the privacy, confidences, or other legitimate interests of any person named or identified in such files.

However, the FBI does not construe this regulation as in any way mitigating its power to invoke FOIA exemptions. In FOIA releases the FBI does not seem to process requests more liberally when the records are 15 years old or older. The FBI's resistance to releasing the Rosenberg/Sobell files is a case in point.

The standard names of the nine exemptions — "(b) (1)," "(b) (2)" . . . "(b) (9)" — are derived from the subsection of the FOIA in which these exemptions are enumerated. Exemption "(b) (1)," for example, is so called because it is stated in subsection (b) (1) of the act. (b) (1) (the "national security" exemption) and (b) (7) (the "law-enforcement records" exemption) are the two most often employed by the FBI in hiding "sensitive" and embarrassing information maintained in its files. The Privacy Act exemptions, used much less frequently by the FBI, are similarly named after the subsections of the Privacy Act in which they appear: (J) (1)-(J) (2), (K) (1)-(K) (7).

The Privacy Act exemptions, though potentially far broader than those of the FOIA, are of less importance, since they are infrequently cited by the FBI. The FBI, in accordance with Department of Justice policy, processes requests under whichever of the two acts permits the most disclosure. The only PA exemption discussed in this chapter will be (K) (5). (K) (5) primarily concerns investigations of applicants for federal employment. The Privacy Act also permits withholding of some information in categories such as: records kept by the CIA; by criminal law enforcement agencies; records maintained in providing protection to the President or other federal officials; records relating to investigations of applicants for federal or military employment or contracts; and examination material for federal appointment or promotion.

On most of the releases in the Rosenberg case, exemptions used by the FBI were written next to the deleted material. (See the documents reproduced in Ch. IV.) The FBI processed the documents this way because of a court order requiring it. Often, requesters are told that certain exemptions were invoked but do not find out which exemption applies to which deleted passage or passages. Yet the FBI always keeps track internally of which exemptions apply to which passages, using an inventory sheet for this purpose. The GAO has suggested that instead of such sheets, "the FBI could mark on each page of a document which exemption was used to withhold information, allowing requesters to determine on what basis information was excised."[21] This suggested system of marking — in effect, the same as the one used on the Rosenberg documents — would be worthwhile, but would hardly constitute a full explanation of the basis on which material was withheld. The GAO also expressed the view that "requesters should be told how many pages are in their files and how many are denied entirely, so that they will have an idea of the file's size."[22] In request letters, one should ask that the FBI provide this information. The policy (but not the invariable practice) at FBI Headquarters since June 1978 has been to follow both these GAO recommendations in processing all FOIA requests.

Preferable to a mere listing of the number of pages denied, and of the exemptions cited for each withholding, is an inventory of all documents contained in a file, with *detailed, factually based* justifications for every withholding. Such detailed refusal justifications are known as "Vaughn Indices."[23] Document 27 in Ch. IV is the FBI's poor excuse for a "Vaughn Index" (see Glossary). Even an index as inadequate as Document 27 will not be prepared without a court order, if then, though requesters ought to receive adequate "Vaughn Indices" as a matter of course whenever records are withheld.

We hope that the discussion of the exemptions which follows will provide some insight into the FBI's reasons for employing exemptions. It is also hoped that when the FBI has not specified which exemption is being applied to a particular piece of information, our discussion will help requesters determine which exemption was in all likelihood relied upon.

One fact in the requester's favor in the exemptions game, particularly where a large number of documents is involved, is that information denied in one document may well slip through in another. Different FBI analysts assigned to the "processing" of FOIA requests vary widely in the amount of information they allow the public to receive. The FBI often keeps copies of the same document in several files, and the information denied in one file may be released *on the same document* from another file. For an example of this, see Documents 30 and 31, Ch. IV. Bear in mind also that FBI agents, under constant pressure to turn out reports during an investigation, rehash the same scraps of information over and over. This repetitiveness can work to the requester's advantage since information denied in one document may be deemed releasable on another.

It is in part because of these frequent processing inconsistencies that the present authors are able to report with confidence on the sorts of material the FBI denies under which exemption. Ingenious or devious sleuthing was not necessary, since the information carefully concealed in one place is often freely released in another. Demonstrating the irrationalities and inconsistencies in the FBI's withholdings strengthens one's ability to successfully contest the appropriateness and necessity of the exemptions invoked.

However, despite wild variations in the processing of documents, certain areas are very carefully concealed. Some files relating to the Rosenberg case are still considered so "sensitive" that the FBI has refused to reveal, and researchers have been unable to determine, even the *titles* of these files. (File "65-58068," mentioned in Ch. IV, Doc. 27, and on scores of other documents in the Rosenberg files, is a prime example of this.) But it can be useful to spot those topics which are most sedulously concealed, in order to focus on those topics when appealing withholdings or when suing the government for release of withheld material. Moreover, the capricious and inconsistent use of exemptions in so many documents casts grave doubt on their use, even in those documents where information is so well hidden one cannot positively establish that the exemptions are being abused.

A warning: Our discussion of the FOIA exemptions pertains to the FOIA as amended in 1974. The situation will be entirely different if the FBI succeeds in its campaign to amend and thereby gut the FOIA. It is impossible to predict what amendments, if any, will be passed, but we mention in the course of the discussion below a few of the FBI's proposals.

Though our treatment of the exemptions necessarily focuses on the sorts of information which are difficult to obtain, our negative tone should not be taken to deprecate the value of the material which the

FBI has released and continues to release. While in many instances only a lawsuit will pry the records from the FBI, a simple FOIA request (perhaps followed by an administrative appeal) often results in the release of information which is of considerable interest to the requester.[24]

National Security Information: The (b) (1) Exemption

Exemption (b) (1) states that the FOIA does not apply to matters that are:

(A) specifically authorized under criteria established by an Executive order to be kept secret in the interest of national defense or foreign policy and (B) are in fact properly classified pursuant to such Executive Order.

Congress, in passing the FOIA, did not challenge the prerogative of the executive branch to establish criteria for the classification of information to be kept secret in the interests of "national security." However, in its 1974 amendments to the FOIA, Congress unambiguously gave to the district courts the power to review documents *in camera* to determine whether such documents have been properly classified, that is, whether the procedural and substantive criteria set by Executive Order have been followed.

The courts have shown reluctance to exercise their new power. Too often, despite notorious abuses by many agencies of the power to classify documents, courts have accepted at face value an agency's allegation that information has been properly classified, and have refused to examine the documents for themselves.

When the amended FOIA went into effect in February 1975, the Executive Order governing classification was E.O. 11652, signed by Richard Nixon. (37 FR 5209, March 8, 1972, effective June 1, 1972.)[25] The Nixon order was superseded on December 1, 1978, by Jimmy Carter's E.O. 12065. (43 FR 28950, July 3, 1978.) Each order was supplemented by an implementing directive: the Nixon order by a National Security Council (NSC) Directive of May 17, 1972 (37 FR 10053), and the Carter order by an Interagency Classification Review Committee (ICRC) Directive of October 2, 1978 (43 FR 46280). In addition, agencies develop their own directives for implementing the orders.

The Carter order, Section 1-101, provides that "if there is a reasonable doubt which designation [that is, "top secret," "secret," or "confidential"] is appropriate, or whether the information should be classified at all, the less restrictive designation should be used, or the information should not be classified." The NSC implementing directive for the Nixon order contained a similar provision. This means that the relevant Executive Orders, like the FOIA, express a presumption in favor of openness — a presumption that the FBI continually violates.

Until 1975, the FBI did not classify internal documents (documents not meant for dissemination outside the various offices of the FBI). But many documents in FBI files are not internal in this sense. These include documents sent by other agencies to the FBI, or from the FBI to other agencies. Also not truly internal are reports and letterhead memos (LHMs) since documents of these sorts (excluding the "Administrative pages" of reports) are considered suitable for dissemination. (See Documents 4 and 6, Ch. IV, for examples of a report and an LHM.) It appears that, at least in "security" cases, pre-1975 LHMs and reports were classified as a matter of course, and are released under FOIA only to the extent that they have become declassified. Nevertheless, it remains true that most documents denied under (b) (1) were not classified before the FOIA request for them was received. Documents may sit unclassified in FBI files for many years, never to become classified until a member of the public asks to see them.

The two most important pre-Nixon Executive Orders on classification were Dwight D. Eisenhower's E.O. 10501 (18 FR 7050, November 10, 1953) and Harry S. Truman's E.O. 10290 (16 FR 9795, September 26, 1951). The Truman order was the first to formally extend the classification system to nonmilitary agencies involved in "national security."[26]

The Truman order authorized four classifications: "Security Information — Top Secret," "Security Information — Secret," "Security Information — Confidential," and "Security Information — Restricted." Eisenhower's order developed the threefold system which has remained in effect to the present: "Top Secret," "Secret," and "Confidential."

The three classifications of the Eisenhower order have been the *only* classifications authorized by Executive Order, from 1953 on. However, the Atomic Energy Act of 1954 does authorize one other classification: "Restricted Data," not to be confused with Truman's "Restricted." "Restricted Data" applies only to material classified under the Atomic Energy Act. If such material happens to have found its way into FBI files, it should be exempted under (b) (3) (the "statutory" exemption) rather than (b) (1) (the "national security" exemption). (b) (3) is explained below.

The FBI, like most agencies, has its own markings and catch phrases designed to restrict the internal flow of sensitive information. "Strictly Confidential," "Sensitive," "JUNE," "Do Not File" — these phrases may function like classification markings or look like classification markings, but most likely they are not. Though agencies have always had such "special access programs," Carter's classification order was the first to make any formal provision for them (Sec. 4-2).

The Attorney General's February, 1975, memo on the amended FOIA ruled that requested classified records must be reviewed in accordance with the *currently* applicable Executive Order, no matter what the age of the records.[27] Decisions to declassify or to continue classification must be based on the Executive Order in effect when the FOIA request is being processed. Thus, while a knowledge of earlier orders helps in understanding classification markings on pre-1972 documents, only the Nixon and Carter orders have directly affected the release of records under the amended FOIA.

Carter's E.O. 12065 — the current basis for classification — is, on paper, a step toward government openness and accountability. Unfortunately, its apparent improvements over the Nixon order (E.O. 11652) seem to be more in the nature of public relations gimmicks than of substantive gains for the public. Its "liberalizing" provisions may in the end prove to be little more than excuses to crack down on "leakers," on the theory that Carter's reasonable provisions ensure that classified information deserves strict protection. As the Interagency Classification Review Committee wrote in its implementing directive, E.O. 12065 "is intended to increase openness in Government by limiting classification and accelerating declassification but, at the same time, providing improved protection against unauthorized disclosure for that information that requires such protection in the interest of national security."[28]

One apparent improvement is its definition of "Confidential," the lowest classification. Under Nixon's order, the test of "Confidentiality" had been whether "unauthorized disclosure could reasonably be expected to cause damage to the national security." The standard set by Carter is more stringent: " 'Confidential' shall be applied to information, the unauthorized disclosure of which reasonably could be expected to cause identifiable damage to the national security" (Section 1-104). ("National Security" is defined as "the national defense and foreign relations of the United States" — Sec. 6-104). Its standards for "Secret" and "Top Secret," however, are virtually the same as those set under Nixon. "Top Secret" applies, under Carter's order, "only to information the unauthorized disclosure of which reasonably could be expected to cause exceptionally grave damage to the national security" (Sec. 1-102). "Secret" is defined in the same way as "Top Secret" except that "exceptionally grave" is transformed into the weaker term "serious" (Sec. 1-103). Absurdly vague as these definitions are, they do set some limits to the types of information which are properly classifiable. But even if the limits set were broader still, they would fail to encompass the records of political surveillances routinely classified by the FBI, records having no bearing whatever on national security.

Though within the government much is made of the distinctions between "Confidential," "Secret," and "Top Secret," the differences have little significance for the general public. "Confidential" information is no more accessible under the FOIA than "Top Secret." Thus, the standards for invoking "Confidential" — the minimum classification — are the most relevant to a member of the general public seeking records under the FOIA. But all the same, the improved definition of "Confidential" in Carter's order is unlikely to have much practical effect. The FBI has argued, with requesters seeking to have previously classified information reviewed under the newer Carter order, that the change from "damage" to "identifiable damage" is no change at all. Worse, officials of intelligence agencies tend to define crucial terms in total disregard of the applicable Executive Orders. Classification officers, in explaining their decision to classify, have been known to appeal to such vague justifications as that release "might affect" the national security. Often, they appear entirely unaware of the criteria established by Executive Order. In determining whether a document was properly classified, the courts may consider it relevant to know whether the classification officer had in mind the appropriate criteria.

Perhaps more promising than the new test of "Confidentiality" is the unprecedented policy on declassification embodied in Carter's E.O. 12065. This E.O. holds that information which *is* properly classified under the standards we cited *should nevertheless be declassified* when the public interest in disclosure outweighs the need for classification (Sec. 3-303). Previous orders did not take into account the public's interest in disclosure. If information "required" protection, no amount of legitimate public interest could dislodge it from agency files unless an agency employee cared to "leak" it. The catch in Carter's policy is that normally it will be up to an agency official, and no one else, to weigh the public's interest against the need for secrecy. Given the FBI's long history of scorn for the public, it is unlikely that the public interest will often be found to outbalance the alleged requirement of secrecy. A somewhat more realistic prospect for improvement under this new "balancing" rule is if the *courts* take it upon themselves to perform this sort of balancing when they review the propriety of a claim of classification.

One indication of the FBI's resistance to this new rule is its intriguing suggestion (made to an FOIA requester) that the rule requires *no* modification of FBI practices since, even prior to the Carter order, FBI classification officers weighed public interest against probable damage to national security. Since prior orders made no provision for the balancing of public interest, the FBI's claim amounts to the confession that, in its devotion to openness in government, the FBI deliberately disregarded Presidential orders and risked damage to the national security. This confession rings false, especially since it is being used as an excuse to prevent liberalization of the FBI's disclosure policy.

The Carter order, like Nixon's before it, speaks of a rare and wonderful phenomenon known as "automatic declassification." Actually, both orders create the impression that "automatic declassification" is, with a handful of exceptions, the normal fate of classified material. However, the "exceptions" turn out to be so unexceptional that, where FBI records are concerned, "automatic declassification" is no more normal than spontaneous generation.

The Nixon order arranged for a seemingly straightforward "general declassification schedule" (GDS), under which information was to be "automatically declassified" within six to ten years from the year it originated. The order simultaneously negated the GDS with a list of four exemptions from the GDS (the FBI calls these "XGDS Categories"). Four may not sound like many exemptions, but the second one *alone* exempts "classified information or material specifically covered by statute, or pertaining to cryptography, or disclosing intelligence sources or methods." This "XGDS Category" was the FBI's favorite. (See E.O. 11652, Section 5(A), 5 (B)) However, there was some provision for classification review (by the agency, of course) after ten years from the date of the document, to determine whether the document warranted continued classification (Sec. 5(C)). There was also a rule for "automatic declassification" after 30 years. The "XGDS Categories" weren't applicable to the "30-year rule" but the E.O. still left it easy enough for 30-year-old material to be kept classified. (Sec. 5 (E)).

The FBI claims to have classified (under the Nixon order) 95,000 pages of documents on the Rosenberg case alone. Of these 95,000 — extending from the forties to the seventies, with the bulk in the fifties — not one has been deemed subject to "automatic declassification."

The Carter order calls for "automatic declassification" no more than six years after original classification — but, of course, with so-called "exceptions" which are proving to be the rule (Sec. 1-401). Though no categories of exemptions from declassification are specified, Carter *seems* to limit the potential for indefinite classification by ordering that:

> Only officials with Top Secret classification authority and [certain specified] agency heads . . . may classify information for more than six years from the date of the original classification. This authority shall be used sparingly. In such cases, a declassification date or event, or a date for review, shall be set. This date or event shall be as early as national security permits and shall be no more than twenty years after original classification, except that for foreign government information the date or event may be up to thirty years after original classification. (Section 1-402).

But FBI classification officers all have "Top Secret" authority. And when they extend classification beyond six years, as they invariably seem to do, they are under no compulsion to set *any* date for automatic declassification. Instead, they set a date or event for "review" — that is, a time when the document will be examined to determine whether it should continue to be classified. Though Section 1-502 of the order demands that some justification be listed on the document for continuing classification beyond six years, the justifications (which agencies are allowed to decide for themselves) can be as broad as — or even broader than — the "XGDS Categories" of the Nixon order. It is unclear what happens if, at the appointed time, a classified document is not "reviewed." Though it may be technically "declassified," it is not released to the public. If a member of the public somehow has enough information to be able to make a request for the document, the agency apparently still has the authority to *reclassify* it.

Even if classified material is not due for "review," agencies are required to review it if a member of the public requests and reasonably describes it. (Section 3-501). However, a few exceptions to this mandatory review requirement are granted in Section 3-503.

The order permits up to 30 years to elapse before classified "foreign government information" is reviewed or automatically declassified. The maximum otherwise is 20 years. Given the chimerical nature of "automatic declassification," the extended protection accorded "foreign government information" seems largely a symbolic gesture. But the fact is that classifications involving foreign relations are harder to challenge than those relating solely to domestic matters. While FBI classification officers freely wield their stamps on domestic matters, they are even more likely to prevent disclosure of foreign information.

However, the phrase, "foreign government information" does not encompass *all* information provided by or related to foreign governments. Section I.F. of the Interagency Classification Review Committee Directive (1978) is clear on this point. It defines "foreign government information" as:

a. Information provided to the United States by a foreign government or international organization of governments in the expectation, expressed or implied, that the information is to be kept in confidence; or

b. Information produced by the United States pursuant to a written joint arrangement with a foreign government or international organization of governments requiring that either the information or the arrangement, or both, be kept in confidence.

The mere fact that information was received from a foreign government should not be sufficient to exempt it from "automatic declassification," or to classify it in the first place. Still less sufficient is the fact that the information pertains to a foreign government. The ICRC implementing directive requires that, except where doing so would reveal intelligence information:

. . . foreign government information incorporated in the United States documents shall, whenever practicable, be identified in such manner as to ensure that the foreign government information is not declassified prematurely or made accessible to nationals of a third country without consent of the originator. (Section I.G. 12)

The declassification of requested information does not necessarily lead to its release. The FBI's position is that declassification renders only the (b) (1) exemption unavailable. This leaves all the other FOIA exemptions, exemptions which the FBI uses freely to withhold declassified information. This practice, while technically permissible, suggests that the FBI is not adhering to the Justice Department policy that "the Government should not withhold documents unless it is important to the public interests to do so." After all, if information has been declassified (non-automatically), then a specific judgment has been made that release could not reasonably be expected to cause damage (or identifiable damage) to the national security. Given the FBI's tendency to overuse its power to classify, one would imagine that, when a judgment is made to declassify, the information must be innocuous indeed. It is therefore odd that the FBI should often take such care to keep declassified information from the public.

Like earlier E.O.'s, Carter's 12065 sets definite requirements for the marking of classified information. Indeed, the stamping of a document "Confidential," "Secret," or "Top Secret" is usually taken to be a minimal necessary condition for a document's being classified. It is therefore surprising that the FBI should frequently invoke (b) (1) on documents which bear no classification markings. When this occurs, there is some reason for thinking that such documents have not been properly classified. (See, for example, Ch. IV, Documents 11 and 30).

The ICRC implementing directive requires that:

The overall classification of a document shall be marked, stamped, or affixed permanently at the top and bottom of the outside of the front cover (if any), on the title page (if any), on the first page, and on the outside of the back cover (if any). Each interior page of a classified document shall be marked or stamped at the top and bottom either according to the highest classification of the content of the page, including the designation "Unclassified" when appropriate, or according to the highest overall classification of the document. In any case, the classification marking of the page shall not supersede the classification marking of portions of the page marked with lower levels of classification. (Section I.G. 7)

If documents are classified only in part, this fact must also be clearly marked:

Classifiers shall identify the level of classification of each classified portion of a document (including subjects and titles), and those portions that are not classified. Portion marking shall be accomplished by placing a parenthetical designator immediately preceding or following the text that it governs. The symbols "(TS)" for top secret, "(S)" for secret, "(C)" for confidential, and "(U)" for unclassified shall be used for this purpose. If individual portion marking is impracticable, the document shall contain a description sufficient to identify the information that is classified and the level of such classification. (Section I.G. 9)

However, in some cases a waiver of the portion-marking requirement may be granted. Declassification, like classification, must be clearly marked.

Not only is the FBI required to mark the classification a document or portion has, it must also mark certain facts about the classification. All classified documents should show on their face:

(1) The identity of the classifier;

(2) Date of classification and office of origin;

(3) Date or event for automatic declassification or for review to determine whether continued classification is warranted;

(4) Date, if any, for automatic "downgrading" (lowering of classification);

(5) If the date for automatic declassification or review is more than six years from the date of classification, the identity of the official authorizing the extension. (In FBI documents, this will normally be the same as the classifier; and, if so, requirement (5) does not apply.);

(6) Reason for extended classification past six years. This is to be stated in narrative form, or by reference to an agency regulation stating the reason in narrative form. (See Section 1-5 of the Carter order).

The Nixon order (and the NSC implementing directive) required conspicuous marking of the overall classification of a document on the top and bottom of the first and last page, and, where practicable, each interior page of documents which are not permanently bound. (FBI documents, including reports, are normally not permanently bound.) Marking of classified sections of documents was also required where practicable. In addition, classified documents were to be stamped indicating either when they would be automatically declassified or what category of exemption from the General Declassification Schedule (GDS) was applicable. (As mentioned earlier, the FBI routinely exempted its classified documents from the GDS.) Also, the identity of the classifier is to be stamped if the classifier is other than the person approving or signing the document. (It seems that normally the classifier of FBI documents is not the signer or approver. FBI classifiers are identified by number; strangely, the FBI occasionally deletes these "classification officer" numbers.) If the document is inadvertently not stamped as to its inclusion in or exemption from the GDS, the documents is to be deemed subject to the GDS. This "inadvertence" is common, and hence many documents classified under the Nixon order have "inadvertently" become declassified.

Because the burden of proof is on the agency to justify its withholdings, the requester has a right to know the facts of the classification of requested documents, to determine whether these documents were properly classified pursuant to Executive Order. If the document is released in part, one can verify for oneself whether the marking requirements have been met, and from the markings one can determine some of the critical facts about the document's classification. (See Ch. IV, Documents 29-32.) Often, but not invariably, classification markings on released documents will be crossed out, but still readable. This indicates that *as released* the documents contain no classified information. If classified information has been deleted, the FBI should write "(b) (1)" next to the deletion. The crossing-out of classification markings means either that the page is completely declassified, or else that the classified sections have been deleted. The FBI has also been known to "white" out classification markings entirely, so that the reader cannot tell whether the markings had ever been made. This is an unjustifiable practice unless — as is quite unlikely — the markings *themselves* are exempt under the FOIA.

Document 28 of Chapter IV shows the way the FBI keeps track internally of which information coming under an FOIA request is classified. Memos such as Document 28 should be provided to FOIA requesters because these memos are not exempt and they contain many of the facts relevant to determining whether procedural criteria for invoking (b) (1) have been met. However, it is only by "mistake" that the public ever gets to view such memos.

If a document is withheld *in toto*, one will sometimes know nothing whatever about the document — not even that it exists. This is one reason why the GAO's recommendation that requesters be told how much material is being denied is so important. However, even if the FBI does withhold entire documents under (b) (1), and fails to inform the requester *how many* documents or pages are involved, it will tell the requester that (b) (1) was invoked in processing the request. One therefore will at least have a basis for asking the FBI to provide further information about the classification of documents denied. If the requirements of the applicable Executive Order and implementing directive have not been met — including the procedural requirements such as proper marking — one has a basis for arguing that the documents are not properly classified and cannot be denied under (b) (1).

Remember that the FOIA requirement that reasonably segregable portions be released applies as much to classified documents as to any other. Classified sections of otherwise unclassified pages are bracketed and marked with a "C," "S," or "TS" ("Confidential," "Secret," or "Top Secret"). Remaining sections should be released unless they fall into an FOIA exemption other than (b) (1).

As we have seen, Carter's E.O. 12065 defines "national security" as "the national defense and foreign relations of the United States." In a similar spirit, the second paragraph of Nixon's E.O. 11652 speaks of classified information as "official information and material which, because it bears directly on the effectiveness of our national defense and the conduct of our foreign relations, must be subject to some constraints for the security of our Nation, and the safety of our people and our allies." The FOIA exemption (b) (1) eschews the phrase "national security" altogether, preferring to speak simply of "national defense" and "foreign policy." Eisenhower's E.O. 10501, in effect (with some amendments) from 1953 to 1972, protected "defense information and material."

These facts need to be emphasized to fully appreciate the outrageousness of the FBI's incessant appeals to the (b) (1) exemption. The FBI regularly uses the (b) (1) exemption to hide information that has no bearing whatever on national defense or foreign relations. (b) (1) is often used to shield evidence of the disruptive and frequently illegal activities and strategies taken by the FBI in its war against domestic advocates of political and social change. The concern for avoiding possible embarrassment to the Bureau accounts for more (b) (1) exemptions than does any interest in national defense or foreign relations. In many cases the use of (b) (1) appears to serve no purpose whatever, and is simply the residue of years of habitual secrecy. Carter's order explicitly sets down that "classification may not be used to conceal violations of law, inefficiency, or administrative error, to prevent embarrassment to a person, organization, or agency, or to restrain competition." (Section 1-601.) But since the FBI would never admit to having exercised the power to classify for any reason other than "national security," Carter's prohibitions are unlikely to do any good except perhaps when a classification decision is challenged in an administrative appeal or lawsuit.

The continued insistence on classifying evidence of past, politically motivated harassment and surveillance belies claims that the FBI has reformed. To classify, as the FBI often does, the fruits of operations directed against domestic activists, is to affirm that these operations were lawful and were justified in the interests of "national security." Some sense of the FBI's bogus appeals to "national security" can be derived from Chapter IV, Documents 24, 30, 31, and 32. See also Documents 4, 5, 6, 8, 11, 12, 20, 23, and 29 — all documents either currently or formerly classified in whole or in part.

The FBI is surprisingly careless in keeping track of which information is classified. Sometimes, a document withheld entirely under (b) (1) in one file will be released unexpurgated in another. The FBI notifies other appropriate agencies, and other offices of the FBI itself, when a decision is made to classify or declassify. The fact of this notification is usually recorded right on the face of the document. But slipups are frequent, and FBI Headquarters is sometimes unaware that it has itself classified certain information. However, the FBI probably uses (b) (1) less inconsistently than it does the other exemptions. Those topics on which no information whatever is allowed to escape are more likely to be blanked out under (b) (1) rather than the other exemptions.

One solution — not as radical as it sounds — to the various problems surrounding the FBI's use of (b) (1) is simply to put the classification system out of the reach of agencies such as the FBI, and to restrict it once again to the military. As we shall see below, the FOIA (b) (7) group of exemptions protects law-enforcement records, including records of such "security-related" cases as espionage and sabotage. What more does the FBI need? The answer, from the FBI's point of view, is that the FBI has "national security" responsibilities beyond its responsibilities to enforce federal law.[29]

The FBI, of course, has another solution to what it sees as the problems surrounding the control of "national security" information. Instead of the page-by-page review required by the FOIA, the FBI would like a blanket exemption for all information in its most "sensitive" categories, including foreign intelligence, foreign counter-intelligence, organized crime, and terrorism. Since much of what used to be called domestic intelligence has been rechristened "foreign counterintelligence" or "terrorism investigation" by the FBI, the possibility of such a blanket exemption is most alarming.

Law Enforcement Records: The (b) (7) Exemptions

(b) (7), the other FOIA exemption frequently used and abused by the FBI, permits agencies to withhold:

> investigatory records compiled for law enforcement purposes, but only to the extent that the production of such records would (A) interfere with enforcement proceedings, (B) deprive a person of a right to a fair trial or an impartial adjudication, (C) constitute an unwarranted invasion of personal privacy, (D) disclose the identity of a confidential source and, in the case of a record compiled by a criminal law enforcement authority in the course of a criminal investigation, or by an agency conducting a lawful national security intelligence investigation, confidential information furnished only by the confidential source, (E) disclose investigative techniques and procedures, or (F) endanger the life or physical safety of law enforcement personnel.

(b) (7) applies only to records which are both investigatory and compiled for law enforcement purposes. For the (b) (7) exemptions to be legitimately invoked, the compilation of records must have a basis in criminal, civil, judicial, or administrative enforcement proceedings. Political surveillance, still less disruption of lawful political activity, cannot properly be hidden under (b) (7). Moreover, in a memorandum of June 2, 1977, the Department of Justice explicitly prohibited the use of (b) (7) (a), (b) (7) (d), or (b) (7) (e) to conceal unlawful activities.[30]

In determining whether the (b) (7) ("law enforcement records") exemptions are applicable to certain FBI records, it helps to know whether the FBI obtained those records as part of a "criminal" or a "security" investigation. Although this may now be changing, the FBI in the past has drawn a firm line between the two sorts of investigations. An FBI clerk checking the "General Index" can in principle determine, simply by the classification number of the file in which an individual is mentioned, whether the reference to the individual contains "security" or "criminal" data. (These file classification numbers are listed in Appendix C, Ch. I.) If the clerk had been instructed to list only criminal references, he would, for example, include "91" (bank robbery) files and neglect "100" ("subversive matter") files.

The point is that the (b) (7) exemptions are inherently more dubious when invoked on material from "security," rather than "criminal," case files. Of course, some security files do relate to the FBI's law enforcement responsibilities. Espionage, for example, is illegal. However, even in those security cases where the FBI at least makes some pretense of "law enforcement," much of the information it collects has no perceptible bearing on law enforcement, and hence is not exemptible under any of the (b) (7) group. "Security" investigations are often initiated and continued more for the purpose of stifling lawful dissent than for any law enforcement purpose, and even the pretense of law enforcement is apt to be lacking. Security cases lacking even the outer trappings of law enforcement investigations are likely to be filed under "100," "157," and "134." Unfortunately, while released FBI files prove that many FBI investigations were unrelated to law enforcement, some courts in FOIA cases have chosen to assume that all FBI investigatory records are compiled for law-enforcement purposes.

The third variety of FBI cases is the "applicant" investigation. These are investigations of applicants for federal employment or of persons already employed by the federal government. These investigations have an arguable basis in the FBI's "law enforcement" responsibilities. (Executive Order 10450, 4/27/53, and other E.O.s ordered that the appointment of civilian federal employees be made subject to investigation.) However, in gathering information for "applicant" cases, the FBI often far exceeded any reasonable interpretation of its "law enforcement" responsibilities.

The FBI has been seeking to amend the (b) (7) exemptions by extending their protection of investigatory records to encompass guidelines, directives, and manuals as well. In addition, its proposed Charter provides for a ten-year moratorium enabling the FBI to refuse (with some exceptions) any request for records in a case ten years after the termination of an investigation without prosecution, or ten years after prosecution. (The FBI's proposed amendments to the FOIA contain a similar provision with the moratorium reduced to seven years.) Since domestic security cases have a way of getting reopened every few months until the target's death, without any prosecution ever being brought, such a moratorium could effectively hide almost all FBI political files, even if the FBI failed in its overt attempts to have all "security"-related cases explicitly exempted.

The FBI formerly used (b) (7) (a) as a blanket exemption for any information on pending cases. Since 1976, the FBI has released some such information when, in its opinion, release would not "affect" the investigation. However, the FBI does not restrict (b) (7) (a) to pending cases. Information from inactive or closed cases is sometimes withheld when there is a "reasonable possibility" for prosecution or where release would interfere with the investigation of another, open case. As with all the FOIA exemptions, the burden of proof is on the agency attempting to deny records. Although (b) (7) (a) is the broadest of the (b) (7) exemptions, it is worth challenging and is particularly vulnerable where the FBI investigation has been "ongoing" for many years, is politically motivated, and has resulted in no "enforcement proceedings."

The FBI keeps careful track of whether an investigation is "pending," "pending inactive," or "closed." (A fourth "status" of cases, "RUC," is explained in the Glossary in Ch. V.) That "status" of an individual's case will normally be indicated on the documents pertaining to him/her, and if the case is "pending inactive" or "closed," the use of (b) (7) (a) is less defensible than if the case is "pending." Remember also that the FBI keeps cases technically "pending" when there is no prospect — imminent or distant — that law enforcement proceedings will be initiated. In such cases, (b) (7) (a), and indeed all the (b) (7) exemptions, should be inapplicable.

One excuse offered by the FBI for never wanting to inform requesters which exemptions apply to their records is, in effect, that the applicability or inapplicability of (b) (7) (a) is *itself* information which is exempt under (b) (7) (a). The Bureau's argument is that to give away the fact that (b) (7) (a) applies is to tip the requester off to the existence of a current investigation. To let the requester know that (b) (7) (a) is not usable in his/her case is to let the requester continue criminal activity secure in the knowledge that the FBI is not on to him/her yet. However, the use of (b) (7) (a) only implies that the requested records in some way bear on a current investigation. It does not establish that the *subject* of the request has the FBI on his/her trail. And the failure to use (b) (7) (a) is not a sure sign that the subject's recent activities have escaped the FBI's watchful gaze. Even on extremely recent records, the FBI often uses (b) (7) (c), (b) (7) (d), and (b) (1) in preference to (b) (7) (a), and these other exemptions seem to do the job of preventing disclosures. Moreover, on older cases, the claim that it would damage current interests to inform requesters of which exemptions apply is absurd.

(b) (7) (c) is similar in language to exemption (b) (6), and the two are sometimes used interchangeably or in tandem. (b) (6) exempts "personnel and medical files and similar files the disclosure of which would constitute a clearly unwarranted invasion of personal privacy." The precise distinction between "clearly unwarranted" in (b) (6) and simply "unwarranted" in (b) (7) (c) is clear to no one. The rationale behind the different language apparently was that law enforcement records are potentially even more embarrassing than personnel and medical files, and require somewhat more careful protection. The FBI relies predominantly on (b) (7) (c), not (b) (6), even in cases where the information was obtained in the course of a political ("domestic intelligence") investigation, and has no bearing on law enforcement.

The overall thrust of the FOIA, and of the court cases under it, is that information must be revealed, *regardless* of who the requester is, and *regardless* of his/her motives for wanting the information, unless the information falls under one or more of the nine specific exemptions. But (b) (7) (c) [along with (b) (6)] is a partial exception to this overall thrust, since the question of whether an invasion of privacy is "unwarranted" (and even of whether released information would violate privacy at all) depends on the identity of the person to whom the information will be released. When an individual requests records that pertain to him, and only to him, clearly there is no basis for a (b) (7) (c) exemption. A third party (say a historian or journalist) requesting these same records, however, might be denied them under (b) (7) (c). But if these records have public interest, the agency maintaining the records may decide that release to the historian or journalist — while admittedly an invasion of privacy — is warranted.

One might imagine that records on oneself would be released with only the slightest touches of (b) (7) (c). Yet the FBI has considered it an "unwarranted invasion of personal privacy" to disclose to an individual such information as the names of his/her spouse, parents, siblings, housemates, political coactivists, fellow workers, and neighbors. The Department of Justice, in a memorandum of May 25, 1977, directed that some of these preposterous overuses of (b) (7) (c) should cease. In the words of the memo:

> ... if the FBI has a file on John Doe — our requester — and information has been deliberately placed in that file which pertains to Richard Roe, that Roe information is presumptively information about Doe as well and should not ordinarily be

withheld from him on 7 (c) grounds. If it does not pertain to Doe, one may well ask, why it is in the Doe file at all? If the information is intimate or very personal, and does not actually involve Doe, it may be appropriate for continued denial of access on privacy grounds. These cases should be carefully reviewed by you, however, and the routine excising/denial of all "third-party information" is to cease. The test under the statute is *unwarranted* invasion of personal privacy, not simply invasion of privacy. The burden under the statute and our regulations is on the one who would deny access. These concepts are to be applied strictly in reviewing cases on administrative appeal.[31]

This memo appears to concern principally the "main" file on an individual, more than the "see refs." (that is, references to an individual which occur in files on other individuals or groups). (On the distinction between a "main" file and a "see ref.," see Ch. I.) And indeed, the Justice Department's argument against using (b) (7) (c) to withhold any part of a requester's "main" file is powerful. But the memo unmistakably implies that, even with mere "see refs.," the burden is on the FBI to show why (b) (7) (c) should be invoked, and that third-party information should not be routinely excised.

In "third party requests" (that is, requests for information on individuals other than oneself) the balancing of the public interest becomes paramount. The Department of Justice memo previously quoted holds that:

> . . . the "reason" for making or considering release of requested records on a third party can arise from the historical nature of the material in a file, the public figure status or other notoriety of the subject, etc. But, if the balancing test does not produce a result where the "reason" outweighs the protectable privacy interest — however slight it may be — the privacy interest will be asserted. This will also continue to be our position as to requests "without reasons" seeking to rummage around in other persons' personnel files.

The more important the information from the public's point of view, the more powerful the argument that possible invasions of privacy are warranted. Yet even in the Rosenberg case — called by J. Edgar Hoover himself "the crime of the century" — (b) (7) (c) was at first invoked to keep ancient but significant information on principal figures in the case from the public. (b) (7) (c) continues to be invoked on the Rosenberg case files, though on a smaller scale than at first. Moreover, the FBI — against the judgment of professional historians — has decided on its own that certain cases are of little historical interest and that information on these cases is exempt under (b) (7) (c).[32] The FBI, which has for so long devoted obsessive care both to violating personal privacy and to distorting the historical record, seems ill-equipped to appreciate and to balance the claims of history and of personal privacy.

There is, of course, an irony in the FBI's use of (b) (7) (c) to "protect" the privacy of the very people whose privacy its political surveillance and disruption have massively invaded. In fact, some of the FBI's (b) (7) (c)s have little relation to the protection of privacy. For example, the FBI will sometimes release considerable intimate information about an individual, yet keep back under (b) (7) (c) the classification number of the individual's files — protecting, not personal privacy, but the FBI's investigative interest. As with the FBI's use of the other exemptions, the element of sheer inexplicable irrationality plays a large role. Individuals have had their own zip codes withheld from them, apparently under (b) (7) (c). The arbitrariness of the FBI's use of (b) (7) (c) is probably even greater than that evidenced in its use of the other exemptions. Depending on which FBI analyst happens to be processing an FOIA request, (b) (7) (c) will be used for occasional excisions or for wholesale withholdings.

As might be expected, the FBI is somewhat more careful to protect the privacy of Bureau "friends" and employees than of the victims of FBI surveillance. Though (b) (7) (d) explicitly authorizes the withholding of the names only of certain confidential sources, the FBI attempts to get around this restriction by sometimes using (b) (7) (c) to conceal the names of nonconfidential sources. In a similar spirit, the names of sympathetic media contacts, to whom information or misinformation is supplied by the FBI, may be deleted. And the names of FBI employees (including agents) lower in rank than Section Heads are routinely exempted on documents originating after 1960.

The FBI's solicitude for the personal privacy of its targets even extends past a target's lifetime. It has taken the unfounded position that (b) (7) (c) protects both living and dead. Perhaps recognizing that this position has no basis in current law, the FBI is attempting to amend (b) (7) (c) so as to explicitly protect any "natural person" up to 25 years after death.

The FBI also finds it convenient to use (b) (7) (c) to keep back information which it considers "outside the scope" of the FOIA request being processed, whether or not the information would invade privacy. This practice is indefensible. See also the discussion of "outside scope" below.

(b) (7) (d) is the most overused of the (b) (7) exemptions. "Source" in (b) (7) (d) applies not merely to regular, paid informers, but more generally to all human suppliers of information. But the FOIA does not provide any authority for withholding the names of *all* sources, not even of all *confidential* sources. (b) (7) (d) speaks not of sources generally, but of confidential sources. The widely accepted standard is that a source is confidential only if he/she has received an express or implied promise of confidentiality. As the Congressional Conference Committee on the 1974 FOIA Amendments put it, a source's identity "may be protected if the person provided information under an express assurance of confidentiality or in circumstances from which such an assurance could be reasonably inferred."[33] Even if a source is confidential under this standard, his/her name is not necessarily exemptible. Several courts have held that the mere promise of confidentiality to a source is insufficient to defeat the public's right to know.

The (b) (7) group, including (b) (7) (d), applies to "investigatory records compiled for law enforcement purposes." Congress did include in the (b) (7) (d) exemption a provision not found in the other (b) (7)s, a provision covering certain information supplied by confidential sources in "lawful national security intelligence investigations." The Congressional Conference Committee on the 1974 FOIA amendments stressed in its report that "national security" is to be strictly construed to refer to military security, national defense, or foreign policy.[34] Thus, no more than its fellow members of the (b) (7) group can (b) (7) (d) properly be used to conceal the fruits of political monitoring. The lawfulness of a "national security investigation" has often been an irrelevant consideration to the FBI. Many investigations were initiated without any basis in the FBI's legal responsibilities and were conducted by illegal methods. Moreover, most "national security" investigations had no connection to any national security interest. Investigations other than "criminal" and "applicant" were most often called "*subversive*," not "national security" cases. Such cases were conducted under such headings as "domestic intelligence," "internal security," "subversive matter," "racial intelligence," or "extremist." These cases concerned domestic dissenters almost exclusively, with no connecting strand to national defense or foreign relations. Yet these investigations are now, for purposes of concealment under FOIA exemptions, being justified in the name of "national security." The very term "investigation" is a euphemism when, as has often been the case, it denotes a program to suppress lawful political action and speech.[35]

The FBI alleges that with few exceptions its sources supply information under an expressed or implied promise of confidentiality. Hence, the right is asserted to excise the name of virtually anyone who provides information. However, there is considerable evidence that the claim of almost universal, presumed confidentiality was dreamed up recently by the FBI solely to prevent disclosure. A former agent, M. Wesley Swearingen, has contended that during his 25 years with the FBI, agents were instructed to make certain informers understand that they might have to testify in open court on the Bureau's behalf.[36]

Swearingen's charges are confirmed by no less an authority than J. Edgar Hoover, who wrote in a 1968 memo that "as a general rule, all of our security informants are considered available for interview by Department Attorneys and for testimony if needed."[37] The "potential witness" rule — accepted by many, though unfortunately not all, the courts — holds that a person is not a confidential source if he might later be called to testify by the agency.[38]

The FBI files released to date amply support the position that informers do not receive automatic promises of confidentiality. Agents are careful to differentiate sources which require protection from those which do not. Expressions such as "conceal," or "whose identity requires protection," or "who requested that his identity be protected" are regularly used by agents when they feel a source requires protection, and the need to protect a given source will normally be noted in *every* document presenting information identifiable as coming from that source. Thus, if a source was considered confidential when the document was written, that fact will be noted *right on the document*. These contemporaneous written comments by the agents are the only basis the FBI FOIA analysts have for determining whether a source was confidential. These FOIA analysts rarely if ever have any first-hand knowledge of the case they are processing, and have no way of determining — apart from the documents in front of them — whether a source was confidential. Even if the informer's name is legitimately deleted, the note that the informer was considered confidential is not itself exemptible information and should be released. In innumerable documents, it is apparent that sources which the agent who had written the document did not consider confidential have been deleted under (b) (7) (d).

Claims of (b) (7) (d) are particularly suspect when made on documents intended for dissemination outside the FBI. Letterhead memos (LHMs) and reports (exclusive of the administrative pages) are written so as to be suitable for dissemination to other government agencies. This holds even when they are not in fact disseminated. LHMs, usually much shorter than reports, are drawn up expressly for dissemination outside the FBI (see Ch. IV Documents 4-6). On reports, sources which the writer believes should be protected are identified only by "T" symbols. That is, the source will be called "T-1," "T-2," etc., and identified more fully only in the "administrative pages" which are supposed to be kept within the Bureau.[39] Even on the administrative pages, a particularly "sensitive" source will not be precisely identified. (Incidentally, information which is genuinely "administrative," rather than "investigative," would seem not to be exemptible under (b) (7) (d), or under any of the (b) (7) exemptions.)

The apparatus of "T" symbols, explicitly designed to protect confidential sources, should mean that in most instances the bodies of reports are releasable without the need to invoke (b) (7) (d). However, the FBI freely uses (b) (7) (d) to delete large portions of the bodies of reports. Moreover, the "T" sources (identified on the administrative pages accompanying reports) are frequently not confidential sources, at least not in the sense intended by the FOIA. They may be mail covers, trash covers, microphone surveillances, burglaries — in short, any of the

70

sources of information specified in this book. The fact, for example, that a mail cover was placed on an individual should not be exempted under (b) (7) (d) *even if* (as is highly unlikely) the name of the person performing the mail cover is exemptible.

An official FBI case report is *not* an informer's report; the two are easily distinguished. (See Ch. IV, Documents 4, 5, 10, 12, 32) The FBI manual requires that informers submit written reports or sign transcriptions of oral reports (an exception is that of "extremist" informers reporting on imminent violence).[40] Informer reports are rarely transmitted from the field offices to FBI Headquarters, let alone shown to other government agencies. But from these informer reports, and from whatever other information is available, the agent will draw up an official FBI investigative report (usually called simply a "report") which conceals anything the FBI would rather not have outside agencies know. Even such major FBI programs as Detcom, Comsab, Security Index, or Communist Index could not be mentioned in any investigative report.[41] So despite the phenomenal volume of reports pouring out of the FBI, much crucial information is deliberately excluded. Since the crucial information — including informers' reports — is often never disseminated even to FBI Headquarters, it is essential that FOIA requests be directed to field offices as well as Headquarters.

One type of document particularly helpful in determining whether a source was a "potential witness" is the "prosecutive summary." Not often written for "security" cases, these summaries set out the evidence of illegal activity marshalled in a particular investigation, list the sources of information, and explain which sources are available for testimony. Even if a file does not contain a "prosecutive summary," the type of information such summaries typically contain may be present in other forms. The fact that such information is *not* present in a file is extremely revealing in itself, in that it suggests that the file was not compiled for law enforcement purposes and hence that the (b) (7) exemptions are inapplicable.

The fact that a file concerns an "applicant" case may possibly be relevant in determining whether sources were confidential. According to a 1977 report of the House Committee on Government Operations, "it is not customary for agencies to grant pledges of confidentiality in collecting information concerning employment, Federal contracts, and security clearances."[42] Unless an explicit promise of confidentiality was made, and recorded in the file, there is little reason to think that the source in an "applicant" case — or perhaps in any case — was confidential. (See also the discussion of Privacy Act exemption (k) (5) below.)

The FBI's own manual indicates that federal employees cannot be considered confidential sources. However, the manual also states that if the employee provides information beyond his official authority — even in violation of regulations — (b) (7) (d) can be invoked. The appeals of-

71

fice upholds the FBI's position on this issue.[43] The FBI does frequently delete names of federal employees under (b) (7) (d). It also regularly conceals state and local employees, including police officers, who provide information. It is unclear whether (b) (7) (d) can legitimately be used for sources who are government employees. The FBI wants the (b) (7) (d) exemption amended so that municipal and state agencies which furnish information "on a confidential basis" are unambiguously protected by (b) (7) (d).

It must be stressed again that (b) (7) (d) is not necessarily applicable just because the author of the document considered the source a "confidential" one. Many factors come into play: are the FBI records in question investigatory? Were they compiled for law enforcement purposes? Was the information supplied only by the source? Was the deleted information gathered for a lawful national security investigation? Was the source a potential witness? Was he/she later exposed publicly, e.g., at a trial or in a book? Would deleted information supplied by the source identify him/her if it were released? Is the source still alive? Still active? Was the "source" simply a provider of information, or an active influence on his/her targets? The questions which are perhaps the hardest are also the oddest: Was the source a human being? Did the source exist at all?

These last two questions are not always easy to answer — even for the FBI analyst reviewing the documents for possible release. Even in many FBI documents intended solely for internal use, the agents attempt to conceal hard evidence of illegality. Thus, a burglary (or "black bag") is often called an "anonymous source." Electronic Surveillances (ELSURs) and burglaries are often given "S*" numbers (e.g., "NY 603-S*"), and are spoken of as if they were live informers. The nature of these "sources" is often deducible from the nature of the information supplied. For example, a "confidential source" who supplies photographs of personal papers maintained in an individual's apartment or of the membership lists of an organization may well be a burglary performed by FBI agents. A "confidential source" providing both sides of telephone conversations is almost surely a wiretap (a "TESUR"). An analyst who deletes a source number under (b) (7) (d) may nevertheless have enough information available to realize that the source is not human, and hence that (b) (7) (d) is improperly invoked.

Permanent numbers are assigned to "sensitive" sources of information — for example, "CSNY 1020-S*" (a "Confidential Source, New York") or "CNDI 5" (a "Confidential National Defense Informant"). Source numbers followed by an "S" are "security" sources; by a "C," "criminal"; by an "R," "racial." Asterisked sources are unavailable to testify and are likely to be illegal investigative techniques. However, unasterisked sources are not necessarily legal or available for testimony either. The FBI often considers source numbers exempt from disclosure on the principle that releasing the number reveals that certain

72

information is all coming from the same source, and thereby tends to pinpoint the source. The FBI has sometimes informed requesters that a (b) (7) (d) deletion involves a source number rather than a source name, though normally it will not make this admission. It is sometimes useful to know that a number — and not a name — has been excised, even if one does not know what the number is, since one will at least know that the source is a "sensitive" one.

One of the most difficult questions in determining whether (b) (7) (d) was legitimately invoked is whether the informer actually existed. Agents, under pressure to supply "derogatory information," would occasionally make it up — sometimes inventing imaginary informers and pocketing the informer's pay themselves. Sometimes, the "informer" may be an actual individual, but the information allegedly supplied a fabrication by the agent.[44] Needless to say, the documents drawn up by the agent will not reflect that the sources are fictitious. Though wildly inaccurate information *may* indicate that the informer did not exist (or did not supply the information in question), it is much more likely to indicate that the informer made up the "information" out of whole cloth. FBI informers are generally paid on a "C.O.D." basis and are far more "unreliable" than agents.

We have been speaking primarily of the FBI's deletion of informers' names. But at least equally important is its use of (b) (7) (d) to delete information supplied by an allegedly confidential source. The FBI originally misused (b) (7) (d) to withhold all or most of the information supplied by an allegedly confidential source, whether or not the information would reveal the source's identity. Starting in 1977, the FBI slightly liberalized its policy, releasing more of the information provided by its sources. Yet wholesale and often absurd deletions of informer information continues. Information concerning large public meetings is still sometimes deleted, even when there would be no possibility of tracing the source of the information. Occasionally, public information supplied by a supposedly confidential source will be excised.

The General Accounting Office (GAO) wrote that the FBI's use of (b) (7) (d) to withhold information in a particular case

> . . . is affected by the case's type, circumstances and age, and by the requester's type. For example, in an organized crime case officials would be restrictive with the information released because identifying informants may result in the informants' being murdered. In a domestic security case which is 10 or 15 years old, a more liberal release would be made because of the age and type of material and the number of sources that could have provided the information.[45]

This "more liberal" release policy in older, so-called "domestic security" cases, might better be called a "less illiberal" policy. Even in "domestic security" cases which were conducted 30 or more years ago, (b) (7) (d) is often freely used. (See, for example, Ch. IV, Document 27.)

In discussing (b) (7) (c), it was mentioned that this exemption is sometimes used to conceal an informer's identity. A variant of this procedure is the simultaneous application of (b) (7) (c) and (b) (7) (d) to the same information. When the two are applied together to delete an informer's name, the FBI's reasoning often seems to be that even if the source turns out not to be confidential, the privacy exemption — (b) (7) (c) — provides a back-up method for keeping his/her identity secret. Another use of the combination (b) (7) (c)-(b) (7) (d) is to delete the information supplied by the source. In this use, the FBI implies that the information would not only reveal the identity of the confidential source, it would reveal personal information about the informer's targets or about the informer him/herself. Commonly, the list of files to which an informer's report is channeled is blacked out under (b) (7) (c)-(b) (7) (d). (See Ch. IV, Document 10.)

(b) (7) (e), though abused less often than (b) (7) (c) or (b) (7) (d), is used with some frequency by the FBI. The FBI manual prohibits the use of (b) (7) (e) for well-known techniques, discontinued techniques, or unlawful techniques. The Department of Justice Guidelines call for it to be applied only where disclosure would impair future effectiveness in law enforcement proceedings. Among the most frequent uses of (b) (7) (e) are to conceal pretext telephone calls and interviews, and "security flashes." Other techniques sometimes hidden under (b) (7) (e) include trash covers, stop notices, and photo albums.[46]

Other Exemptions: (b) (2), (b) (3), (b) (5), Privacy Act (k) (5), and "Outside Scope"

Between them, (b) (1) and (b) (7) cover an incredible quantity and variety of information; or, at least, as interpreted by the FBI they do. However, the FBI finds them insufficient and resorts with some regularity to three other FOIA exemptions, and one Privacy Act exemption: (b) (2) ("internal personnel" matters); (b) (3) (matters exempted by laws other than the FOIA); (b) (5) (certain current "opinion" documents); and PA (K) (5) (confidential sources in "applicant" investigations). Another basis for withholding information is the notion that information falls "outside the scope" of a given FOIA/PA request. "Outside scope" is often used by the FBI as if it were a kind of statutorily authorized exemption, though neither of the two access acts mentions it.

(b) (2) permits the withholding of information "related solely to the internal personnel rules and practices of an agency." The Senate Report on the 1966 FOIA listed as examples of such rules "personnel's use of parking facilities or regulation of lunch hours, statements of policy as to sick leave, and the like." This interpretation has been upheld by the courts, which have rejected the broader reading of (b) (2) taken by the House Report.[47]

The FBI at first took the unfounded position that (b) (2) authorized the Bureau to place all "administrative markings" off limits to the public. Such exempted material included markings referring to file numbers, agents' initials, notes synopsizing information within a document, case leads, markings referring to type of investigation, and records of dissemination of information. Such excisions clearly rested on a bizarre interpretation of "internal personnel rules and practices."

A Department of Justice memorandum of May 25, 1977, ended the routine deletion of "administrative markings," but authorized the continued use of (b) (2) when some harm would result from release. The memo instructed that, when a document contains nothing releasable *except* "administrative markings," the document not be released unless the requester desires it.[48]

Though it may seem foolish to ask for a bunch of "administrative markings" on an otherwise blacked-out page, requesters are well advised to insist on it. One can sometimes learn a great deal simply by seeing such information as the date ("What was I up to then?"), the type of document ("What could have been so urgent that the FBI had to send a teletype?"), or the dissemination of information ("Why did they send copies to so many field offices? Did anybody outside the FBI get the information?").

The same Department of Justice memo also noted that if "administrative markings" are appropriately withheld under (b) (2), there will ordinarily be another exemption applicable as well. In other words, it should be quite rare for the FBI to have to rely solely on (b) (2) to exempt "administrative markings."

The FBI has continued to use (b) (2) to excise "sensitive" information unrelated to personnel rules and practices. For example, (b) (2) is sometimes used to delete the code word "JUNE." "JUNE" files, maintained in special locations, deal with electronic surveillances and surreptitious entries (see Ch. I). The "JUNE" system is of legitimate interest to the public, and in any case concerns much more than internal personnel rules and practices, if it concerns such rules and practices at all. The FBI's practice of taking the trouble, in documents being released, to excise certain segments of the documents under (b) (2) is especially strange, given the Supreme Court's statement that the "general thrust of the exemption is simply to relieve agencies of the burden of assembling and maintaining for public inspection matters in which the public could not reasonably be expected to have an interest."[49]

The FBI distinguishes "low 2" from "high 2" material. "Low 2" consists of routine instructions and "administrative markings"; "high 2" consists of such things as manuals and directives. The courts have not been clear on whether manuals and similar material are properly exemptible under (b) (2). The FBI has been trying to resolve the issue by having (b) (7) amended from "investigative records" to "records maintained, collected, or used" for law enforcement or certain other purposes. This amendment of (b) (7) would make it unnecessary to invoke (b) (2) to protect law enforcement manuals and the like. In any case, the FBI has released some portions of its manuals but would like the right not to release any more.

(b) (3) (as amended in 1976) exempts from disclosure any material which any statute specifically exempts, "provided that such statute (A) requires that the matters be withheld from the public in such a manner as to leave no discretion on the issue, or (B) establishes particular criteria for withholding or refers to particular types of matters to be withheld." (Prior to 1976, (b) (3) simply exempted matters "specifically exempted from disclosure by statute.")

The FBI has little opportunity to wield (b) (3). When it does invoke (b) (3), it should inform the requester which statute it is appealing to. Perhaps the (b) (3) material most commonly withheld by the FBI is Grand Jury testimony.

Agencies other than the FBI — particularly the CIA — make less restrained use of (b) (3). However, the FBI often has information in its files which originated with other agencies. The FBI will in such cases consult the other agencies, and will abide by the other agencies' decision to exempt material. For CIA-originated information found in FBI files, (b) (3) (or a combination of (b) (3) and (b) (1)) is often invoked, based on the National Security Act of 1947 or the CIA Act of 1949. The National Security Act provides that "the Director of Central Intelligence shall be responsible for protecting intelligence sources and methods from unauthorized disclosure." The CIA Act exempted the agency from any law requiring disclosure of an agency's internal structure.

Tax information received by the FBI from the IRS is generally exempted under (b) (3) if the information concerns someone other than the individual making the request.[50] Remember that if material is classified on the basis of the Atomic Energy Act of 1954, rather than pursuant to Executive Order, it can be exempted under (b) (3) instead of (b) (1).

If an FBI statutory charter becomes law, it might include language which would offer more scope to the FBI's employment of (b) (3). But if no charter is passed, or if one is passed which in no way exempts the FBI from the FOIA's disclosure provisions, then the FBI will probably continue to be sparing in its use of (b) (3).

(b) (5) permits the exemption of "inter-agency or intra-agency memoranda or letters which would not be available by law to a party other than an agency in litigation with the agency." This exemption applies primarily to attorney work products, and to memos which contain agency opinions prepared in the course of decision-making. It does not apply to material which simply interprets a decision already made.

The FBI apparently no longer makes extensive use of (b) (5). The Department of Justice policy is not to use (b) (5) when the release of material is unlikely to affect law enforcement concerns and does not involve major policy decisions. According to a 1978 GAO Report, the FBI formerly used (b) (5) to exempt:

- Secret Service forms delineating the potential threat of the individual to the President.

- Agents' opinions and recommendations.

- Internal memos between headquarters and field offices recommending certain actions.

- Conference material from a strategy meeting with an assistant United States attorney.

- Interagency communications.

- Instructions to the field office on when to interview a subject.

- Decision to put an individual in a particular index.[51]

The FBI claims now to use (b) (5) only for the Secret Service form, and sometimes for "sensitive" opinions and recommendations of agents.[52] The exemption of the Secret Service form is evidently not done as a matter of course, since some such forms (FD-376s) have been released uncensored. (See Ch. IV, Document 8.) (k) (3) of the Privacy Act specifically exempts Secret Service records from disclosure. However, the FBI's official policy is such that material exempt under the PA is not to be withheld unless it is also exempt under the FOIA.

Only one Privacy Act (PA) exemption is claimed with much regularity by the FBI. (The FBI's stated policy, which is in keeping with the FOIA and the PA, is to process all requests under whichever act permits the most disclosure.) Exemption (k) (5) of the PA applies to

... investigatory material compiled solely for the purpose of determining suitability, eligibility, or qualifications for Federal civilian employment, military service, Federal contracts, or access to classified information, but only to the extent that the disclosure of such material would reveal the identity of a source who furnished information to the Government under an express promise that the identity of the source would be held in confidence, or, prior to the effective date of this section [9/27/75] under an implied promise that the identity of the source would be held in confidence.

On files predating 1975, (k) (5) is used for all sources contacted during an "applicant" investigation. Our remarks on the myth of implied confidentiality with respect to (b) (7) (d) are applicable here, and need not be repeated. It seems that any information properly exempted under (k) (5) is also exempt under (b) (7) (d). On documents originating in 1975 or later, the FBI claims to use (k) (5) only where it sees a notation that a source requested confidentiality. We have already indicated that, even on pre-1975 documents, the FBI notes all sources whom it considers confidential.

One more "exemption" must be considered: one which, though not mentioned by the FOIA or the PA, enables the FBI to keep significant information from requesters. The FBI normally refuses to provide, or inform the requester of, information unilaterally determined to be "outside the scope" of or "not pertinent" to a request. Unfortunately for the requester, information kept back as "outside the scope" may be highly pertinent to a request. Yet this information will not be released and its existence will be difficult to discover.

Department of Justice guidelines seem to require that when a particular document falls in part within the scope of a request, then the entire document should be considered within the scope and deletions made only on the basis of FOIA/PA exemptions. However, the fact that a file contains one or more documents which are pertinent to a request does not, for the Department of Justice, mean that the entire file is pertinent.

A carefully formulated request letter may help forestall some of the more preposterous "outside scope" withholdings. Once some documents have been released, it is often possible to ascertain the existence of others which have been withheld as "outside scope" (or as statutorily exempt). FBI documents contain numerous references to other FBI documents. Also, the "administrative markings" show to which files copies of a given document were sent. These files are often closely related to the file from which the released document was taken, but they are generally considered "outside scope" by the FBI.

CHAPTER III

HOW TO SEND FOR FBI FILES

Introduction

This chapter begins with a discussion of the much asked question: "Should I send for my FBI files?" Even though people know they have a legal right to such files, many have fears and doubts about the safety, wisdom, or usefulness of exercising that right. Despite the fact that, as someone put it, "It must be the first time in history that we get to see the files of the secret police *before* the revolution," just over 70,000 people have asked for a look. To encourage the fulfillment of the people's right and need to know, we address the most commonly expressed concerns that keep people from sending for files.

After encouraging the reader to request files, this chapter next provides practical instructions and materials to assist in initiating and persevering in such a request. Among the materials are sample request and appeal letters, a map locating all FBI field offices and resident agencies, and the addresses and phone numbers of FBI Headquarters and field offices and of Congressional oversight committees.

Should I Send for FBI Files?

"Why should I bother?"

"Let sleeping dogs lie. If I send for my files, they'll start in on me again."

"I'll just get back blank pages for ten cents a page."

"What if I'm not in the files? Then they'll start one on me if I ask them to look."

These are among the common reactions to the idea of making an FOIA request to the FBI.

The existence of widespread fear of asking for files is itself strong evidence that the FBI is viewed by the American people as the nation's secret police. It was precisely to prevent the growth of such secret government that the Freedom of Information Act was enacted by Congress. It was designed to give citizens a tool to make government agencies accountable, to keep them within the law and the Constitution. As columnist Garry Wills has said, " . . . sending for one's files is a patriotic duty."[1]

The public's fears, based on the past conduct and the future potential of the FBI, are far from irrational. But such agencies grow and thrive on popular fear. They depend on it to immobilize the public. One way to overcome fear is to assert our rights, to become informed and to join with others in resisting the FBI's illegal, abusive, and indecent practices.

It is important for scholars, journalists, and other writers to use FBI and other government files in preparing material for public education. But those who are not professional public educators also have a role to play. Some individuals' files are quite rich and contain stories that should be rescued from the FBI and made available to the public. In addition, many people did not really feel the danger of an uncontrolled secret police until they saw their own or a friend's or relation's file. The reality of and potential for repression is made vivid when you realize that it was your garbage being ransacked, your employer or minister being asked insinuating questions, your bank, telephone company, or hospital records being perused, or your license plate being recorded and checked. Each person's/organization's file, even if it does not contain a frontpage story, can move us to a determination to fight back.

FBI files are a valuable national resource. They contain the history of a critical agency of government. They warn us about the dangers of an uncontrolled police agency. And they also tell us the story of the people's struggles over many decades to bring about important social changes. It is a story that historians, political scientists, journalists, broadcasters, other researchers and writers, as well as ordinary citizens, can tell only if they have the documents.

As Judge Harold Greene wrote in *AFSC* v. *Webster*, 485 F. Supp. 222 (1980), the FBI files

> . . . perhaps more than those of any other agency, constitute a significant repository of the record of the recent history of this nation, and they represent the work product of an organization that has touched the lives of countless Americans.

How to Make an FOI/PA Request

General Remarks

The sample letter in Appendix A can be used to request personal files as well as files on other individuals (called "third-party" requests), organizations, or publications, and any kind of subject matter or event. We have indicated on the letter the places where different types of information must be supplied, depending on which kinds of files are being requested.

This section and those that follow provide general instructions and discuss the purposes served by the main parts of the letter.

The Freedom of Information Act (FOIA) allows any "person" — U.S. citizen, resident alien, foreign national, private organization, even governmental body — to obtain records held by agencies (including the

FBI) in the executive branch of government. (The Privacy Act (PA) permits access only to certain records on oneself held by executive agencies.)

As you proceed with your request to the FBI, be sure to date and retain copies of all correspondence. Dated notes should be taken during or immediately after all telephone conversations which you have with the FBI in connection with your request. It can speed up the processing of your request if, in your initial letter, you instruct the FBI to call you if additional information is needed in order to find the records you requested. Nor should you be reluctant about calling the FBI yourself. Letters from the FBI, not always models of clear prose style, are replete with Bureauese and may leave you puzzled about what exactly is meant. A phone conversation with a person in the FBI's FOI/PA Unit may save many weeks of frustrating and unenlightening correspondence. The job of the staff of the FOI/PA Unit is to serve you — they are paid to see that you get all the documents you are entitled to.

Remember that under the law you needn't *have* or *give* any reason whatsoever for requesting government records. You have a right to them without any showing of need, so there is no reason to be defensive. However, some remarks about need might have a desirable effect — for example, in getting fees waived or in hurrying things along, or in overcoming FBI objections that release would violate others' personal privacy.

Where to Write

As explained in Chapters I and II, FBI field offices house most of the raw data of investigations. On any given investigation, FBI Headquarters (in Washington, D.C.) is likely to have less information than the appropriate field offices, provided of course the field office files on the investigation have not been destroyed. But if you address your request only to FBI Headquarters, only Headquarters records systems will be searched. It is essential, therefore, to write *separately to Headquarters* and *to each field office* in whose territory you have lived, worked, or traveled, or which you think is likely to have records on the subject of your request. You may also want to direct requests to the generally smaller FBI "resident agencies." Resident agencies normally amalgamate their files with those of the local field office at the close of an investigation, but there are instances of resident agencies' retaining files longer than this. (It was papers from the files of the Media, Pa. resident agency which in 1971 first alerted the public to the scope of the FBI's political operations, though these papers may have been in the resident agency for only a short time.) Addresses of Headquarters, the various field offices, and foreign liaison offices are listed in Appendix D of this chapter. The map indicates the location of the resident agencies.

The sample letter takes into account the possibility that files will be destroyed by asking that "do not destroy" notices be sent to all relevant FBI units with copies to the requester. It is true that FBI regulations prohibit the destruction of documents and files pertaining to *pending* FOI/PA requests, but there have been instances of destruction in violation both of these regulations and even of court injunctions.

Personal Records

Although many people request personal records under both the Privacy Act and the FOIA, we advise against citing the PA. Much FBI material, which can be withheld under the far broader PA exemptions, is available under FOIA, whereas anything available under PA can almost certainly be obtained equally well under FOIA. The FBI's stated policy is to process requests under whichever act permits the maximum disclosure. However, using only the FOIA may eliminate delaying tactics that the FBI has employed when the Privacy Act is cited alone or in conjunction with the FOIA.

The following response to a request based on both FOIA and PA illustrates the difficulties that can arise from citing the PA:

The investigative activity involved [in your request] has been previously reported to Federal Bureau of Investigation Headquarters, Washington, D.C. Pursuant to Title 28, Code of Federal Regulations, 16.57 (C), records maintained at Federal Bureau of Investigation Headquarters will be processed for your client and Headquarters will correspond directly with your client, if it has not done so already, and the information released will include documentation from the investigation in New York.

"Previously reported" here simply means that summaries of investigative matters, not the primary data, were sent from the field office to Headquarters. Although the requester certainly has a right to the field office files under the FOIA (and perhaps even under the PA), the FBI uses the federal regulation cited (which concerns the PA) to delay and discourage the requester.

The following information is necessary to the processing of your request and we have therefore incorporated it into the sample letter: date and place of birth; social security number; variations of your name (including nicknames, married names, stage names, etc.); variations in the name(s) of the organization(s) pertinent to your request (including branch locations and dates, where applicable).

It may ensure a more thorough search if you give the FBI additional information to help distinguish you from others with the same or similar name. This is particularly true where information on you is contained in a file which does not have your name in its title. Such additional information may include: names of organizations whose files you think might contain information about you, public events which might have come to the notice of the FBI, employment positions held, and previous addresses. Remember that this information is not required. If for any reason you are hesitant, don't provide it.

Other Records

Requests for records other than those on yourself should be made under FOIA. You may want to request records on other persons ("third-party requests"), or organizations, publications, events, or subject matters you think the FBI may have investigated. Since requests of this sort often raise more serious privacy problems than requests for personal records (see discussion of (b) (7) (c) exemption, Ch. II), it may help to explain what interest you and/or the general public have in release of the files.

"Third-party" requests may be made on prominent persons from such areas as labor, journalism, academia, sports, politics, law, arts, etc., or on members of your own family. It is unlikely that records on living persons will be released without their consent, except perhaps in cases that have received widespread public attention. The chances of getting files on currently existing organizations are enhanced if the request comes from an official representative of the organization. Examples of subject matter or event files might include COINTELPRO, the 1964 Democratic Convention, an anti-war or anti-Klan demonstration in your town, or the Ghetto Informants Program.

If you are interested in records other than or in addition to those on yourself, try to describe the scope of your request with reasonable clarity. However, you should avoid too narrow a description of your interest, since this gives the FBI an excuse to limit its search to a smaller area. If the FBI feels that you have made a broader request than you realized, it will contact you and ask if you would like to limit your request to what the FBI feels is a more manageable size. You may find, once you learn the actual volume involved, that you do not want as much as you unknowingly requested; but do not be intimidated into asking for less than you want. If your initial request was too narrow, you can make additional requests, though this can be time consuming.

FBI Search

FBI standard procedure at both Headquarters and field offices is to search only the "General Index" for the "main" files. (On the FBI's search procedure, see Ch. II.) But a substantial amount of information gathered by the FBI on a person, group, or subject matter often resides outside the "main" file devoted to that person, group, or subject matter. Much of this information is obtainable through what the FBI calls "see references." (See Ch. I and Ch. IV, Document 20.) Similarly, the ELSUR Index cards on individuals who were the subject of microphone or telephone surveillance will only be searched if the FBI is specifically asked to do so. (See Ch. I.) We have included in the "optional" section of the letter a request for the tapes of monitored conversations. The sample letter is worded to indicate that you want information pertaining to your request to be produced wherever it happens to be.

There are other places where material is kept and although we can't be certain that they will be searched, even when you specifically request it, you may want to specify some of them in your letter. The sample letter requests that "JUNE" files be searched. An optional paragraph includes a request that "Do Not File" files, SAC safes, special file rooms, and offices of FBI officials be searched. You may also want to ask for a search of the special indices you think might contain information you desire. (See Ch. I.)

Sometimes the FBI will find references in its indices to a file which it cannot locate. If any file pertaining to your request is "missing," you may ask that it be put on "special locate." We have incorporated such a request into the sample letter. Having a file on "special locate" alerts FBI personnel that it is missing and such files do occasionally turn up.

Withholding

Records must be released unless they fall into one of the FOIA or PA exemptions, and even "exemptible" material may be released at the agency's discretion. (The exemptions are permissive, not mandatory.) Agencies must release all nonexempt portions of documents which can be reasonably segregated from the exempt information. The FBI often abuses its power to exempt, relying in this chiefly on the "national security" (b) (1) exemption and the "law enforcement" (b) (7) exemption. The FBI's use of the exemptions is explained at length in Ch. II.

The sample request letter specifies that when the FBI denies material, it should explain the reason for the denial and indicate which exemption applies to which deleted passage. The FBI has been more willing to inform requesters which of the various FOIA exemptions have been used to deny which passages or documents than to supply explanations of *why* the exemptions were invoked. Many of the documents printed in Chapter IV (for example, Documents 5 and 6) illustrate the way the FBI can indicate which exemption applies to which passages. Documents 24-26 illustrate ways the FBI has attempted, when denying documents in full, to inform requesters which exemptions it considered applicable. The information which the sample letter suggests you request about classified documents is no more than President Carter, by Executive Order, has required to be marked on the face of all classified documents. (See Ch. IV, Document 29) When deleted material is "blacked out," rather than "whited out" or cut out, it is easier to tell that information has been deleted. The FBI seems now generally to "black out" deleted material.

We also recommend that you specifically request certain material which may appear trivial, but experience has shown that file covers, search slips, "see reference" cards, abstracts, administrative markings, and even multiple copies of the same document can be valuable. (The FBI has sometimes withheld this material as being of no interest to the public.) Administrative markings may show that information from a file was supplied to another government agency, or may indicate that a copy of the document in the file you received was placed in another file, a file which you would also like to receive. Though a single file (or a number of files pertaining to a request) may contain several copies of the same document, there may be markings on one copy that do not appear on others. In the Rosenberg releases, the FBI "presumed" (often falsely) that certain documents were duplicative, and it was only with great difficulty that some of these "presumptive duplicates" were wrested from the FBI. Thus, while it can add to the cost, it is not senseless to demand that all copies of documents within the files be produced. (Chapter IV, Document 3 is an example of a "file cover"; Document 20 illustrates the "see reference" cards; Documents 21 and 22 are "search slips"; Document 5 shows what "administrative pages" of FBI reports are likely to contain. "Abstracts" are explained in Ch. I.)

Fees and Fee Waivers

The FBI takes advantage of the FOIA's provision that agencies be allowed to charge search and copying fees. Its rates for copying are ten cents a page, but it automatically waives copying charges when the total amount is less than twenty-five dollars, since it costs more than twenty-five dollars to collect that amount. The FBI cannot charge for the time it spends reviewing to see if it wants to withhold portions of the records. To protect yourself against a large copying fee, ask to be consulted if the total fee is going to surpass some amount you specify in your request letter. If you do not wish to pay the full fee, you may review the records at the FBI office and select those you want copied. If you wish to review documents without paying a fee, say so in your initial request letter. (The sample letter does *not* contain language to this effect.)

The FOIA directs agencies to reduce fees, or to waive fees entirely, when the agencies determine that reduction or waiver is in the public interest because furnishing the information primarily benefits the general public. Ask for a fee waiver if your request is in the public interest. Relevant factors which you may mention include the noncommercial use intended for the material (writing books and articles is not commercial), the public education purposes the material will advance, or the tax-exempt or nonprofit status of the organization under whose auspices you are writing. Indigency also is a recognized basis for waiver or reduction of fees. Bear in mind, however, that the FBI has not been generous about fee waivers.

Delays in Response

The FOIA requires an agency to respond to your initial request within 10 business days after receiving it. Under unusual circumstances, 10 additional days are allowed. However, the FBI rarely meets these time requirements. Instead, it simply sends an acknowledgment that the request has been received and is being processed. Delays past the statutory 10-day deadline are grounds for taking an administrative appeal, which is explained below.

Administrative Appeals

The FOIA gives the right to appeal any denial of records. This is a so-called "administrative appeal" to the head of the agency. It costs nothing but stamps and paper and does not involve bringing a lawsuit. Besides denial of records, other reasons for appealing include: excessive delay by the agency, excessive fee charged, refusal to waive fee, or inadequacy of agency search for records. All appeals are handled by the same Department of Justice office whose address appears on our sample appeal letters. Sample letters in Appendix B illustrate the way to make an appeal. The FOIA requires that appeals be answered within 20 business days, although this limit is rarely met.

Though this book should help you to decide whether an appeal is worth the effort and to argue cogently in any appeal you do take, you may need to rely on your own knowledge of the subject of your request when you attempt to decide whether the FBI has failed to release significant information.

Though appeals often help one obtain additional information, the appeals process frequently fails to result in as full a release as one would like. At this point you have the option of bringing a lawsuit.

Whatever you decide about going to court, you should also consider reporting attempts to frustrate your efforts to get the material you seek (enclosing copies of your correspondence with the FBI) to your congressional representatives and to members of the House and Senate Oversight Committees (see Appendix F). An inquiry from a member of Congress to the FBI concerning your difficulties may help. But even if it does not, giving the Oversight Committees concrete examples of an agency's failure to comply with the FOI/PA helps the Committees protect and strengthen this important and beleaguered law.

Amending Your Records Under the Privacy Act

The Privacy Act enables individuals to have agency records on themselves corrected or expunged when those records are not accurate, relevant, timely, or complete. A sample letter requesting such amendments is printed in Appendix C.

A handbook on the FOI/PA published by the House Committee on Government Operations and listed below advises that:

While you should have no trouble in determining whether or not the information contained in your file is accurate, complete, and up-to-date, it might be somewhat more difficult to ascertain whether it is "relevant" to the agency's purpose. However, if you have doubts about anything you find in your records, you should challenge the information and force the agency to justify its retention in your file. There is one thing in particular you might look for: the Privacy Act prohibits the maintenance of information concerning how an individual exercises his first amendment rights unless (1) the maintenance is authorized by statute or the individual to whom it pertains, or (2) unless it is pertinent to and within the scope of an authorized law enforcement activity. In most instances, you would be on solid ground in challenging any information in your file describing your religious and political beliefs, activities, and associations, unless you have voluntarily given this information to the agency.

Requests for amendment must be acknowledged within 10, and action on the request completed within 30, working days.

If your request is denied, the FBI must explain its refusal and tell you how to appeal that decision. Appendix C contains a sample appeal letter.

A decision on appeals must be made within 30 days (an additional 30 days applies only in "unusual circumstances"). If your appeal is denied, you have a right to write a brief statement disputing the records for insertion in your files. This is probably not a useful way to deal with unwanted material in FBI files.

The FBI alleges that almost all its records are exempt from the amending provisions of the PA. However, the FBI's policy is to consider requests for record amendment as a matter of "discretion," and some amendments and destructions of FBI files have been *ordered* by courts.

Records of Other Agencies

Readers who want to secure records from government agencies other than the FBI should send for one of the following guidebooks:

Using the Freedom of Information Act: A Step by Step Guide (published by Center for National Security Studies, 122 Maryland Avenue, N.E., Washington, D.C. 20002). Available for $1.50 prepaid. A guide for intelligent laymen through the bureaucratic thicket. Includes index, sample letters, addresses of agencies, and detailed information to help you plan an effective strategy.

Getting Your Government Files (Published by the Grand Jury Project, 853 Broadway, New York, N.Y. 10003). Available for a donation. Contains information about FOIA, instructions for requesting documents and appealing denials, names and addresses of selected government agencies.

A Citizen's Guide on How to Use the Freedom of Information Act and the Privacy Act in Requesting Government Documents, House Committee on Government Operations. (Published by Government Printing Office, Washington, D.C., 1977, 59 pp., $3.00)

APPENDIX A: Sample Letter for Requesting Records
(The areas in **Bold Type** explain how to use this sample letter to write your own.)

Name
Address
Daytime Phone Number
Date

FOI/PA Unit
Federal Bureau of Investigation
[INSERT NAME AND ADDRESS
OF FBI OFFICE — SEE APPENDIX D OF THIS CHAPTER]

Dear   :

This is a request under the Freedom of Information Act as amended (5 U.S.C. 552).

I request a complete and thorough search of all filing systems and locations for all records maintained by your agency pertaining to **(me/name of organization (s)/or description of subject matter)**, including but not limited to files and documents captioned in, or whose captions include **(my name/the organization's name/or the subject matter)** in the title. This request specifically includes "main" files and "see references," including but not limited to numbered and lettered subfiles, 1A envelopes, enclosures behind files (EBFs), Bulky Exhibits, control files, and "JUNE" files. I want all records to be produced with the administrative markings and all reports to include the administrative pages.

[OPTIONAL: I wish to be sent copies of "see reference" cards, abstracts, search slips including search slips used to process this request, file covers, multiple copies of the same document if they appear in a file, and tapes of any electronic surveillances. Please search, "DO NOT FILE" files, SAC safes, special file rooms, and offices of FBI officials. I want all pages released regardless of the extent of excising, even if all that remains are the stationery headings or administrative markings.]

In addition to a search of the General Index, please search the ELSUR Index.

Please search for records under the following names:

[FOR PERSONAL RECORDS, list all names — married names, nicknames, stage names, etc. Also list variations of your name, e.g., John Doe, J.R. Doe, John R. Doe, J. Richard Doe, John Richard Doe, and Richard Doe or R. Doe.]

[FOR ORGANIZATIONS, list variants of organization's name and indicate whether this organization has (or has had) chapters and other offices in other locations.]

Please place any "missing" files pertaining to this request on "special locate" and advise me that you have done this.

[If request is for records other than your own, it may help to add an explanation of your interest in the files, e.g., your connection to the organization, your relation to the subject of the request, the prominence of the subject, your journalistic or scholarly interest, and the like.]

If documents are denied in part or in whole, please specify which exemption(s) is (are) claimed for each passage or whole document denied. Please provide a complete itemized inventory and a detailed factual justification of total or partial denial of documents. Specify the number of pages in each document and the total number of pages pertaining to this request. For "classified" material denied please include the following information: the classification (confidential, secret, or top secret); identity of the classifier; date or event for automatic declassification, classification review, or downgrading; if applicable, identity of official authorizing extension of automatic declassification or review past six years; and, if applicable, the reason for extended classification past six years.

In excising material, please "black out" the material rather than "white out" or "cut out." I expect, as provided by the Freedom of Information Act, that the remaining nonexempt portions of documents will be released.

As I expect to appeal any denials, please specify the office and address to which an appeal should be directed.

I believe my request qualifies for a waiver of fees since the release of the requested information would primarily benefit the general public and be "in the public interest."

[USE ANY APPLICABLE ARGUMENT FOR THIS CLAIM, e.g., that the files will be used for the preparation of educational materials to be distributed through a school, church, or other organization or group, particularly if the group is a not-for-profit, tax-exempt research or educational organization.]

If a fee waiver is not granted, please consult me before proceeding if the fee is in excess of $. I reserve all rights to recover any money paid for fees not waived.

Please send a memo (copy to me) to the appropriate units in your office to assure that no records related to this request are destroyed. Please advise of any destruction of records and include the date of and authority for such destruction.

[FOR REQUESTS TO FIELD OFFICES: I wish to make it clear that I want all records in your office "identifiable with my request" even though reports based on those records have been sent to FBI Headquarters and even though there may be duplication between the two sets of files. Please do not refer me to Headquarters.]

I can be reached at the phone listed above. Please call rather than write if there are any questions or if you need additional information from me.

I expect a response to this request within 10 working days as provided for in the Freedom of Information Act.

Sincerely yours,

Sworn to on the

Name   [notarize   signature],   Social
day of   Security number, date and place of
                                         birth.

before me   Your title, if writing on behalf of an
          Notary Public   organization.

MARK ENVELOPE: ATTN FOI/PA UNIT
REMEMBER TO SEND A SEPARATE LETTER TO FBI HEADQUARTERS AND
TO EACH RELEVANT FBI FIELD OFFICE

APPENDIX B: Sample Appeal Letters

Note: This Appendix contains three appeal letters. Each of the letters applies to a different ground for an FOIA appeal. If you are appealing on more than one ground, you may wish to combine items from more than one letter into a single appeal.

We have not included a sample letter on inadequacy of the FBI's *search* for records in response to your request. If you feel the search has been incomplete because of references in the documents (e.g., references to wiretaps or other surveillances the logs of which are not among the documents released), because there are gaps in the files that cannot be accounted for by claimed exemptions, or for any other reason, you may send a separate appeal letter setting forth your evidence or add an appeal on inadequacy of search to whichever other appeal letter you send.

These appeal letters are slightly altered versions of letters developed by the Center for National Security Studies (122 Maryland Ave., N.E., Washington, D.C. 20002), and printed in *Using the Freedom of Information Act: A Step By Step Guide.* They are reproduced here with the permission of the Center.

(The areas in **Bold Type** explain how to use this sample letter to write your own letter.)

Appeal Where FBI Does Not Meet FOIA Time Limits

> Name
> Address
> Daytime Phone Number
> Date

Assoc. Attorney General
Office of Privacy & Information Appeals
Dept. of Justice
Washington, D.C. 20530

Re: Request Number
[Add this if the FBI has given your request a number.]

Dear   :

This is an appeal pursuant to subsection (a) (6) of the Freedom of Information Act, as amended (5 U.S.C. 552):

[Use this paragraph if the FBI has made no response to your request, and if more than ten working days, plus time in the mails, have elapsed.]

On (date), I sent the FBI a letter requesting records under the FOIA, To date, I have received no response.

[Use this paragraph if you have received a letter advising you of delays in processing your request.]

On **(date)** I received an acknowledgment from **(name of official signing the letter)**, that my FOIA request of **(date)** had been received, but that I would have to await the results of "processing."

As you know, the FOIA provides that an agency must make an initial determination of whether to comply with an FOIA request within ten working days of receiving the request. The agency may take an additional ten working days in unusual circumstances. Since I have allowed more than a reasonable amount of time for compliance, I am treating your agency's failure to respond as a denial. This letter is a formal appeal of that denial.

I am enclosing a copy of our exchange of correspondence so that you can see exactly what materials are under request.

As provided for in the amended Act, I will expect to receive a reply to this appeal within twenty working days.

Sincerely,

Name
[No need to have signature notarized.]

[Mark your envelope clearly:
"Attention Freedom of Information Appeals"]

Appeal of Deletions or Withholdings

Name
Address
Daytime Phone Number
Date

Assoc. Attorney General
Office of Privacy & Information Appeals
Dept. of Justice
Washington, D.C. 20530

Re: Request Number
[Add this if the FBI has given your request a number.]

Dear   :

This is an appeal pursuant to subsection (a) (6) of the Freedom of Information Act, as amended (5 U.S.C. 552).

On **(date)**, I received a letter from **(name of official)** of your agency denying my request for **(describe briefly the information you are after)**. This reply indicated that an appeal letter could be sent to you. I am enclosing a copy of my exchange of correspondence with your agency so that you can see exactly what files I have requested and the insubstantial grounds on which my request has been denied.

[Here we include sample paragraphs which you may want to adapt to your own case. These lay out additional arguments for release. Use them only if they apply to your case. For help in framing other arguments, see Ch. II.]
[Optional paragraph, to be used if the agency has withheld all or nearly all the material which has been requested]:
You will note that your agency has withheld the entire [or nearly the entire]

document [or file, or report, or whatever] that I requested. Since the FOIA provides that "any reasonably segregable portion of a record shall be provided to any person requesting such record after deletion of the portions which are exempt," I believe that your agency has not complied with the FOIA. I believe that there must be [additional] segregable portions which do not fall within the FOIA exemptions and which must be released.

[Optional paragraph, to be used if the agency has used the (b)(1) exemption for national security to withhold information which is of importance to public debate] :

Your agency has invoked the (b) (1) exemption to withhold information which I believe is of importance to public debate. As you know, section 3-303 of Executive Order 12065 states that, in order to withhold information, a senior agency official must "determine whether the public interest in disclosure outweighs the damage to national security that might reasonably be expected from disclosure." In this case, the importance of the information requested outweighs such possible damage.

[Here you should add some additional explanation of the important public interest in the material you are requesting. If possible you should include sample newsclips or cite reports which demonstrate public interest. You should also state your intention to make the information available to the public.]

[Sample optional arguments to be used if the exemption which is claimed does not seem to make sense; you should cite as many specific instances as you care to of items withheld from the documents that you have received. We provide two examples which you might want to adapt to your own case.]

"On the memo dated   the second paragraph withheld under the (b) (1) exemption appears to be describing a conversation at an open meeting. If this is the case, it is impossible that the substance of this conversation could be properly classified." Or, "The memo dated   refers to a meeting which I attended, but a substantial portion is deleted because of the (b) (6) and (b) (7) (c) exemptions for unwarranted invasions of personal privacy. Since I already know who attended this meeting, no privacy interest is served by the withholding."

I trust that upon examination of my request, you will conclude that the records I have requested are not properly covered by exemption(s)

[Here repeat the exemptions which the agency's denial letter claimed applied to your request] of the amended FOIA, and that you will overrule the decision to withhold the information.

[Use if an itemized inventory is not supplied originally]

If you choose instead to continue to withhold some or all of the material which was denied in my initial request to your agency, I ask that you give me an index of such material, together with the justification for the denial of each item which is still withheld.

As provided in the Act, I will expect to receive a reply to this administrative appeal letter within twenty working days.

If you deny this appeal and do not adequately explain why the material withheld is properly exempt, I intend to initiate a lawsuit to compel its disclosure. **[You can say that you intend to sue, if that is your present inclination; you may still decide ultimately not to file suit.]**

Sincerely yours,

Name
[No need to notarize signature on appeals.]

**[Mark clearly on envelope
"Attention: Freedom of Information Appeals"]**

Appeal of Refusal to Waive or Reduce Fees

[If request for fee waiver in your initial request letter is refused, send this appeal letter. If you are appealing deletions or withholdings you can combine this material on the fee waiver in the same letter, or you can write two separate appeal letters.]

Name
Name of your organization, if any
Address
Daytime Phone Number
Date

Assoc. Attorney General
Office of Privacy & Information Appeals
Dept. of Justice
Washington, D.C. 20530

Dear   :

This letter constitutes my appeal of the FBI's refusal to waive fees in connection with my request of **(date)** under the FOIA for the **[briefly describe the documents requested.]** As you know, you have provided me with portions of the requested items and assessed a cost of $.

I have requested and here repeat my request that you waive these fees on the grounds that "furnishing the information can be considered as primarily benefiting the general public."

The language of the FOIA makes clear that Congress intended that the assessment of fees not be a bar to private individuals or public interest groups seeking access to government documents. At the same time, it permitted the charging of fees so that corporations or individuals using the Act for private gain could be charged the cost of the services provided.

The legislative history of the FOIA's provision calls for a liberal interpretation of the phrase "primarily benefitting the public." This suggests that all fees should be waived whenever the release of the information contributes to public debate on an important policy issue and when the person requesting the information is doing so for the purposes of contributing to the "uninhibited, robust and wide-open" debate on public issues.

This approach means that all fees should be waived if two criteria are met: (1) the information will contribute to the public debate on important policy issues, and

(2) the information was requested so that it could be used for that purpose.

The release of this information would benefit the public because [here add explanation of the benefits to the public that would follow from the release. Take however much space you need. If you are writing on behalf on an organization, add something about your group's service to the public. If it is a tax-exempt nonprofit organization you should say so, and you may want to include your tax exemption number. If you are a member of the press, or writing a book or article, say so, and then omit the next paragraph].

No financial benefit would follow from the release of this information and I intend to make the information available to the general public.

[Add details of how you would make the material public, such as plans to give it to a library or make it available to the media. If possible, support this claim by attaching copies of letters from such institutions expressing interest in the documents.]

[If possible, add a paragraph here citing specific cases of identical or similar requests which were granted a fee waiver and that your case likewise merits a fee waiver.]

[Use this paragraph if search fees are charged:]

Finally, since this request is for material which is clearly of benefit to the public, other persons will undoubtedly also request these records. It would be unfair if the first requester were to bear the full financial cost of the initial search.

Since the information that is the subject of this letter fits the criteria spelled out by Congress for a waiving of fees in the public interest, I believe that your agency should waive such fees, or, at the very least, reduce them substantially.

Sincerely yours,

Name
[No need to notarize signature on appeals.]

[Mark clearly on envelope
"Attention: Freedom of Information Appeals"]

APPENDIX C: Sample Letters for Amending Records Under the Privacy Act

The texts of the request and appeal letters printed in this section are taken from the sample letters provided in *A Citizen's Guide on How to Use the Freedom of Information Act and the Privacy Act in Requesting Government Documents*, House Committee on Government Operations, 1977.

(The areas in **Bold Type** explain how to use the sample letters to write your own letters.)

Request to Amend Records

Name
Address
Daytime phone number
Date

Director,
Federal Bureau of Investigation
Washington, D.C. 20535
Re: Privacy Act Request to Amend Records

Dear   :

By letter dated   , I requested access to **(use same description as in request letter).**

In viewing the information forwarded to me, I found that it was **(inaccurate) (incomplete) (outdated) (not relevant to the purpose of your agency).**

Therefore, pursuant to the Privacy Act of 1974, 5 U.S.C. 552a, I hereby request that you amend my record in the following manner: **(Describe errors, new information, irrelevance, etc.)**

In accordance with the Act, I look forward to an acknowledgment of this request within 10 working days of its receipt.

Thank you for your assistance in this matter.

Sincerely,

Sworn to on the   Name [notarize signature]
                                   Social Security number
day of   Date and place of birth

before me
          Notary Public

                                                  Name
                                                  Address
                                                  Daytime phone number
Assoc. Attorney General   Date
Office of Privacy & Information Appeals
Dept. of Justice
Washington, D.C. 20530

Re: Privacy Act Appeal

Dear   :

   By letter dated   to Mr.   (official to whom you addressed your
amendment request), I requested that information held by your agency concerning
me be amended. This request was denied, and I am hereby appealing that denial.
For your information i am enclosing a copy of my request letter along with a copy
of Mr.   's reply. (If you have any additional relevant information, send it
too.)
   I trust that upon consideration of my reasons for seeking the desired changes,
you will grant my request to amend the disputed material. However, in the event
you refuse this request, please advise me of the agency procedures for filing a
statement of disagreement.
   [Optional] I plan to initiate legal action if my appeal is denied.
   Thank you for your prompt attention to this matter.

                                          Sincerely,

                                          Name
                                          [No need to notarize signature on
                                          appeals]

[Mark clearly on envelope:
"Attention Privacy Act Appeals"]

APPENDIX D: FBI Offices — Addresses and Phone Numbers

FBI Headquarters	J. Edgar Hoover Bldg., Washington, D.C. 20535	202-324-5520 (FOI/PA Unit)

Field Office

Albany, NY 12207	U.S. Post Office and Courthouse	518-465-7551
Albuquerque, NM 87101	Federal Office Bldg.	505-247-1555
Alexandria, VA 22314	300 N. Lee St.	703-683-2680
Anchorage, AK 99510	Federal Bldg.	907-272-6414
Atlanta, GA 30303	275 Peachtree St. NE	404-521-3900
Baltimore, MD 21207	7142 Ambassador Rd.	301-265-8080
Birmingham, AL 35203	Room 1400, 2121 Bldg.	205-252-7705
Boston, MA 02203	J.F. Kennedy Federal Office Bldg.	617-742-5533
Buffalo, NY 14202	111 W. Huron St.	716-856-7800
Butte, MT 59701	U.S. Courthouse and Federal Bldg.	406-792-2304
Charlotte, NC 28202	Jefferson Standard Life Bldg.	704-372-5485
Chicago, IL 60604	Everett McKinley Dirksen Bldg.	312-431-1333
Cincinnati, OH 45202	400 U.S. Post Office & Crthse Bldg.	513-421-4310
Cleveland, OH 44199	Federal Office Bldg.	216-522-1401
Columbia, SC 29201	1529 Hampton St.	803-254-3011
Dallas, TX 75201	1810 Commerce St.	214-741-1851
Denver, CO 80202	Federal Office Bldg.	303-629-7171
Detroit, MI 48226	477 Michigan Ave.	313-965-2323
El Paso, TX 79901	202 U.S. Courthouse Bldg.	915-533-7451
Honolulu, HI 96850	300 Ala Moana Blvd.	808-521-1411
Houston, TX 77002	6015 Fed. Bldg. and U.S. Courthouse	713-224-1511
Indianapolis, IN 46202	575 N. Pennsylvania St.	317-639-3301
Jackson, MS 39205	Unifirst Federal and Loan Bldg.	601-948-5000
Jacksonville, FL 32211	7820 Arlington Expressway	904-721-1211
Kansas City, MO 64106	300 U.S. Courthouse Bldg.	816-221-6100
Knoxville, TN 37919	1111 Northshore Dr.	615-588-8571
Las Vegas, NV 89101	Federal Office Bldg.	702-385-1281
Little Rock, AR 72201	215 U.S. Post Office Bldg.	501-372-7211
Los Angeles, CA 90024	11000 Wilshire Blvd.	213-272-6161
Louisville, KY 40202	Federal Bldg.	502-583-3941
Memphis, TN 38103	Clifford Davis Federal Bldg.	901-525-7373
Miami, FL 33137	3801 Biscayne Blvd.	305-573-3333
Milwaukee, WI 53202	Federal Bldg. and U.S. Courthouse	414-276-4681
Minneapolis, MN 55401	392 Federal Bldg.	612-339-7846
Mobile, AL 36602	Federal Bldg.	205-438-3674
Newark, NJ 07101	Gateway I, Market St.	201-622-5613
New Haven, CT 06510	170 Orange St.	203-777-6311
New Orleans, LA 70113	701 Loyola Ave.	504-522-4671
New York, NY 10007	26 Federal Plaza	212-553-2700
Norfolk, VA 23502	870 N. Military Hwy.	804-461-2121
Oklahoma City, OK 73118	50 Penn Pl. NW	405-842-7471
Omaha, NB 68102	215 N. 17th St.	402-348-1210
Philadelphia, PA 19106	Federal Office Bldg.	215-629-0800
Phoenix, AZ 85004	2721 N. Central Ave.	602-279-5511

Pittsburgh, PA 15222	Federal Office Bldg.	412-471-2000
Portland, OR 97201	Crown Plaza Bldg.	503-224-4181
Richmond, VA 23220	200 W. Grace St.	804-644-2631
Sacramento, CA 95825	Federal Bldg.	916-481-9110
St. Louis, MO 63103	2704 Federal Bldg.	314-241-5357
Salt Lake City, UT 84138	Federal Bldg.	801-355-7521
San Antonio, TX 78296	Federal Bldg.	512-225-6741
San Diego, CA 92188	Federal Office Bldg.	714-231-1122
San Francisco, CA 94102	450 Golden Gate Ave.	415-552-2155
San Juan, PR 00918	U.S. Courthouse and Fed. Bldg.	809-754-6000
Savannah, GA 31405	5401 Paulsen St.	912-354-9911
Seattle, WA 98174	915 2nd Ave.	206-622-0460
Springfield, IL 62702	535 W. Jefferson St.	217-522-9675
Tampa, FL 33602	Federal Office Bldg.	813-228-7661
Washington, DC 20535	9th and Pennsylvania Ave. NW	202-324-3000

Liaison Offices [Legats]

Legal Attache [AH c/o the American embassy for the cities indicated]:
  Bern, Switzerland
  Bonn, Germany [Box 310, APO, New York 09080]
  Buenos Aires, Argentina
  Caracas, Venezuela [APO, New York 09893]
  Hong Kong, BCC [FPO, San Francisco 96659]
  London, England [Box 40, FPO, New York 09510]
  Manila, Philippines [APO, San Francisco 96528]
  Mexico City, Mexico
  Ottawa, Canada
  Paris, France [APO, New York 09777]
  Rome, Italy [APO, New York 09794]
  Tokyo, Japan [APO, San Francisco 96503]

APPENDIX E: Map of FBI Field Offices and Resident Agencies

FBI FIELD OFFICES

PACIFIC TIME ZONE

MOUNTAIN TIME ZONE

ALASKA

BERING TIME ZONE

FAIRBANKS

4

ALASKA-HAWAII
TIME ZONE

JUNEAU

YUKON
TIME ZONE

GUAM

NOTE WHEN IT IS 6:00 P.M. MONDAY
IN EASTERN TIME ZONE, IT IS 9:00 A.M.
TUESDAY IN GUAM.

PACIFIC TIME ZONE

20

HAWAII

ALASKA HAWAII
TIME ZONE

FIELD OFFICES

1 ALBANY	7 BIRMINGHAM	13 CINCINNATI	19 EL PASO	25 KANSAS CITY
2 ALBUQUERQUE	8 BOSTON	14 CLEVELAND	20 HONOLULU	26 KNOXVILLE
3 ALEXANDRIA	9 BUFFALO	15 COLUMBIA	21 HOUSTON	27 LAS VEGAS
4 ANCHORAGE	10 BUTTE	16 DALLAS	22 INDIANAPOLIS	28 LITTLE ROCK
5 ATLANTA	11 CHARLOTTE	17 DENVER	23 JACKSON	29 LOS ANGELES
6 BALTIMORE	12 CHICAGO	18 DETROIT	24 JACKSONVILLE	30 LOUISVILLE
				31 MEMPHIS

‎SIDENT AGENCIES

EASTERN TIME ZONE

ATLANTIC TIME ZONE

ATLANTIC TIME ZONE

PUERTO RICO

VIRGIN ISLANDS
(SAN JUAN OFFICE)

ST. THOMAS
CHARLOTTE AMALIE

ST CROIX

☆ FBI Headquarters
㊶ State Capital & Field Office Hq. City
⊙ State Capital & RA
⊙ State Capital & RA - No Office Space
50 Field Office Hq. City
● Resident Agency
▪ Resident Agency - No Office Space
— Field Division Boundaries
- - State Lines Overlapped by Field Division Districts
⋯⋯ Time Zone Boundaries *

*NOTE: ARIZONA, HAWAII AND PORTIONS OF INDIANA DO NOT OBSERVE DAYLIGHT SAVING TIME

JULY 10, 1975

NEW YORK   46 PORTLAND   53 SAN FRANCISCO
NORFOLK   47 RICHMOND   54 SAN JUAN
OKLAHOMA CITY   48 SACRAMENTO   55 SAVANNAH
OMAHA   49 ST. LOUIS   56 SEATTLE
PHILADELPHIA   50 SALT LAKE CITY 57 SPRINGFIELD
PHOENIX   51 SAN ANTONIO   58 TAMPA
PITTSBURGH   52 SAN DIEGO   59 WASHINGTON, D.C.

101

APPENDIX F: Congressional Committees With FOI/PA and FBI Oversight Functions

Senate	Jurisdiction
Committee on the Judiciary	Includes FBI programs and budget; FOI/PA matters
Subcommittee on Adm. Practices and Procedures	FOI/PA matters
Select Committee on Intelligence	All counterintelligence and foreign intelligence matters and budgets
Governmental Affairs Committee	FOI/PA matters are occasionally referred to this committee

House of Representatives	
Judiciary Committee	Includes FBI programs and budget
Subcommittee on Civil and Constitutional Rights	Includes FBI programs and budget
Permanent Select Committee on Intelligence	Counterintelligence and foreign intelligence matters and budgets
Government Operations Committee	Includes FOI/PA matters, National Archives, and record keeping matters
Subcommittee on Government Information and Individual Rights	FOI/PA and National Archives matters are referred to this subcommittee

Address for Senate Committees: U.S. Senate, Washington, D.C. 20510

Address for House Committees: U.S. House of Representatives, Washington, D.C. 20515

Phone for House and Senate Committees: (202) 224-3121

CHAPTER IV

TYPICAL FBI DOCUMENTS DEMYSTIFIED

Introduction

If their release is to be more than a symbolic victory over the FBI's bureaucratic sanctity, documents must be read and understood by members of the public. The documents annotated in this chapter were chosen primarily because of their heuristic value and not because of any intrinsically notable content. (The bibliography should help the reader locate particularly significant FBI documents.) There are three barriers to interpreting released FBI records:

1. *Bureauese.* Documents are written for the eyes of FBI personnel. An unfamiliarity with FBI investigative and administrative practices, and with the jargon in which such practices are reported, can make a document impenetrable. The documents below, and the information contained in other parts of the present book should help considerably in deciphering "bureauese."

2. *Censorship.* Extensive unjustifiable deletions and witholdings are the rule when the FBI processes an FOI/PA request. A careful examination of the documents printed here and of Ch. II on FOI/PA exemptions should provide a rough guide to the sort of information that is likely to lie beneath the censor's deletion, and should also suggest which challenges to raise against illegitimate withholdings.

3. *Deception.* The authors know of no verifiable instance in which phony documents ("notional records") have been concocted and released in order to fool FOI/PA requesters. We do know that even on documents intended never to escape the confines of the Bureau, candor is commonly lacking. As former agent Anthony Villano has written:

> . . . as an agent I had to break almost every rule in the book in order to do my job. The Bureau never wanted to know about such transgressions, so, in the reports we filed, they were either not mentioned or else covered by lies. We also spent a good part of our time distorting the truth in administrative accounts our supervisors received. The system, with all of its cumbersome recordkeeping, forces a premium to be put on fakery.[1]

Though Villano justifies his "fakery" by the need to fight crime, other ex-agents have testified to less noble motivations. Some agents invent imaginary informants, or else make up "information" which they can attribute to actual informants, in some cases pocketing the payments authorized for the supposed informants.[2] But agents are probably more truthful than their informants, who are liable not to be paid at all unless they tell the FBI what it wants to hear.

It goes without saying that deliberate deception is hard, if not impossible, to detect, although a close familiarity with FBI practices and with the facts of a case often help. Moreover, there are some instances which can be characterized as midway between "bureauese" and "deception" and which are interpretable with some probability. For example, an agent may "report" that a landlord "changed his mind" about renting an auditorium to a targeted organization. In such a case it is likely that the landlord's apparent fickleness is attributable to FBI coaxing, but though FBI personnel and knowledgeable members of the public can read this probable fact between the lines, the document may not explicitly mention any reason for the landlord's decision. Remember also that information gathered in the field office may never have reached FBI Headquarters, and that many field office files (and parts of files) have been destroyed by the FBI.

FBI documents, like other records, also contain clerical errors, typos, misspellings, and the like. The FBI has traditionally prided itself on accuracy in both form and substance, but its reputation for precision is not entirely deserved. However, typing errors are rather infrequent. Agents do not type their own communications, but do sometimes handwrite documents (especially surveillance logs).

The authors have attempted to protect the privacy of some victims of the FBI by making a few deletions on the documents below. Where we have done this, the material has been replaced by a line of typed number signs — #). The inclusion of identifying data on private individuals would have been gratuitous given our concern here solely with general aspects of FBI practice. Our deletions are therefore excused by the particular and somewhat unusual purpose of publishing these documents.

All other defacings are the work of the FBI. The FBI was required by court order in processing the Rosenberg/Sobell files for release to cite the allegedly applicable FOIA exemption (e.g., "(b) (1)," "(b) (7) (D)") next to each deletion. Since the FBI does not always follow this procedure under normal circumstances, many FBI releases contain deletions but do not indicate the FOIA exemption relied on.

A list of the documents annotated in this section follows. For a listing of other types of material kept in FBI files, See Ch. I, Appendix A, and the entries under "FD" in the Glossary, Ch. V. The Glossary may also be consulted for explanations of many of the terms which appear on the documents below.

List of Annotated Documents

Doc. 1	Security Index Memo
Doc. 2	ADEX Memo
Doc. 3	File Cover Page
Doc. 4	FBI Report
Doc. 5	Administrative Pages of FBI Report
Doc. 6	Letterhead Memo (LHM)
Doc. 7	Teletype
Doc. 8	Secret Service Form
Doc. 9	Request From Navy
Docs. 10 & 11	Covers of Informant Reports
Doc. 12	Intra-Field Office Memo
Doc. 13	Microphone Surveillance (MISUR) Log
Doc. 14	"1A" Envelope
Doc. 15	Request to Resident Agency (RA)
Doc. 16	Destruction Authorization
Doc. 17	Permanent Serial Chargeout
Doc. 18	"JUNE" Material
Doc. 19	Bulky Exhibit Inventory
Doc. 20	Cards from the General Index
Docs. 21 & 22	Search Slips
Doc. 23	Front Page of Correlation Summary
Docs. 24, 25 & 26	Forms Justifying Withholding of Documents
Doc. 27	"Document Justification" Sheet
Doc. 28	Classification Review Memo
Doc. 29	Document Classified Under Carter's Executive Order
Docs. 30 & 31	"National Security" Interview
Doc. 32	"National Security" Informant Report

STANDARD FORM NO. 64

Office Memorandum • UNITED STATES GOVERNMENT

TO   :   Director, FBI (100- ######)   DATE: 4-27-55

FROM :   SAC, New York (100-######)

SUBJECT: Corrected Security Index cards
          ################   attached. Substitute for cards
          SI - C   in file and destroy old cards.
                                          Place photograph and description on
                                          reverse side of geographical card.

_____ It is recommended that a Security Index Card be prepared on the
      above-captioned individual.

      _____ The Security Index Card on the captioned individual should be
      X   changed as follows: (Specify change only)

NAME _____

ALIASES _____

_____

_____

          NATIVE BORN_____ NATURALIZED_____ ALIEN_____

COMMUNIST_____SOCIALIST WORKERS PARTY_____INDEPENDENT SOCIALIST LEAGUE_____

MISCELLANEOUS (Specify) _____

TAB FOR DETCOM_____ TAB FOR COMSAB_____ RACE_____ SEX_____

DATE OF BIRTH _____ PLACE OF BIRTH _____

BUSINESS ADDRESS (Show name of employing concern and address) _____

_____
          ##################################
          ###############Avenue, New York City
KEY FACILITY DATA:
     GEOGRAPHICAL REFERENCE NUMBER _____ RESPONSIBILITY_____
     INTERESTED AGENCIES _____ 100 - ######## -46
RESIDENCE ADDRESS _____
          Apt. ##################### Avenue,
_____
                         New York City
REGISTERED MAIL   MAY 1 7 1955
RGS:RGP

Document 1.

Document 1: Security Index Memo

This is an "FD-122" form, used to recommend that a Security Index (SI) card or, later, an Administrative Index (ADEX) card be prepared or changed. (The Security Index is briefly described in the Glossary, Chapter V.) This particular FD-122 changes the address listed on the "subject's" SI card. Addresses had to be kept up to date so that the FBI could readily find and arrest SI subjects in case of national emergency. Note that while this document recommends the destruction of the "old" SI card and the substitution of a new one, the old FD-122 (recommending preparation of the old SI card) would have been filed in the subject's own file (not in the SI itself) and would not have been destroyed unless the subject's file was destroyed. Thus, despite the destruction of "obsolete" cards, the exact times an individual was on the SI (or Reserve Index, ADEX, Agitator Index, etc.) are normally determinable from the file kept on that individual.

"Key Facility Data" applied to SI subjects working in defense-related industries or strategically important areas. "Responsibility," if applicable, might have been "Army" or "Navy." "Comsab" and "Detcom" are explained in the Glossary, Ch. V.

This document was sent from the New York Field Office to Headquarters, and the file numbers after "SAC, New York" and "Director, FBI" (top left) refer to the files on the *subject* of the document at New York and Headquarters respectively. File numbers in this position on a document always denote the subject of the document, *not* the FBI personnel receiving it.

Document 2: ADEX Memo

This document is an FD-122 as revised on 11/22/71. (FD-122s were revised periodically.) By this time, the SI had been replaced by the ADEX. The abbreviations on this FD-122 formed a checklist of political affiliation. These abbreviations apparently stand for:

AWC: American Workers Communist Party
BNT: Black Nationalist
BPP: Black Panther Party
JFG: Johnson-Forest Group
MIN: Minutemen
NL: New Left
NOI: Nation of Islam
PLP: Progressive Labor Party
PPA: Proletarian Party of America
PRN: Puerto Rican Nationalists
SDS: Students for a Democratic Society
SNC: Student Nonviolent Coordinating Committee
SPL: Sparticist League
SWP: Socialist Workers Party
WWP: Workers World Party

The notation "P*" indicates a "pending inactive case." This means that while the case is technically open, there is no need to report monthly on the progress of the case.

A summary of what is known of the SI and ADEX can be found in *J. Edgar Hoover's Detention Plan: The Politics of Repression in the United States, 1939-1976*, by Caroline Ross and Ken Lawrence. This pamphlet, published by the American Friends Service Committee, includes examples of various revisions of FD-122s and FD-397s.

Note the "block stamp" which appears on the lower right. It

Director, FBI (Bufile-)   JUN 28 1972

100-354897

SAC,

NEW YORK (100- #####) (P*)

###############
SM - C
(OO: NY)

NOTED
ADEX UNIT
DATE 6/28/72

Re: NYlet and LHM, 8/9/71.

Recommend: ☐ ADEX Card   ☐ ADEX Card changed (specify change only)   ☒ Subject removed (succinct summary attached)

Name

Aliases

☐ Native Born   **Tab**
☐ Naturalized   ☐ Category I
☐ Alien   ☐ Category II
   ☐ Category III
   ☐ Category IV

☐ AWC   ☐ COMMUNIST   ☐ NL   ☐ PLP   ☐ PRN   ☐ SNC   ☐ SWP
☐ BNT   ☐ JFG   ☐ NOI   ☐ FPA   ☐ SDS   ☐ SPL   ☐ WWP
☐ BPP   ☐ MIN   ☐ Miscellaneous (Specify) _____

Date of Birth   **Place of Birth**   **Race**   **Sex**
   ☐ Male
   ☐ Female

Business Address, Name of Employing Concern and Address, Nature of Employment, and Union Affiliation, if any.   **Residence Address**

Chief Clerk
Post

Key Facility Data

Geographical Reference Number _____ **Responsibility** _____

2 - Bureau (RM)
1 - New York

JD:dbm
(3)

SEARCHED _____ INDEXED _____
SERIALIZED _____ FILED _____
JUN 28 1972
FBI — NEW YORK

100 - ############ 334

Document 2.

108

indicates that the New York office "serialized" (assigned a serial number to) and "filed" this document on June 28, 1972. The clerk initialed the block stamp on the bottom right.

Note also the distribution of copies on the lower left. Two copies were sent to Headquarters ("Bureau") by registered mail ("RM"). One copy remained in the New York Field Office. "(3)" under the initials indicates the total number of copies made at the time the document was produced. If a document is of particularly wide significance, hundreds of copies, directed to various files in all field offices, may be made.

(OO:NY) in upper left corner indicates that New York is the Office of Origin for this investigation (see Ch. V, Glossary).

Document 3: File Cover Page

Every volume ("section") of every FBI file has a cover page. These pages are normally not released by the FBI, but should be, as they often contain nonexempt information which is encompassed by an FOIA request.

This particular page is the cover of Volume 94 of the New York Field Office file on the National Committee to Secure Justice in the Rosenberg Case. The authors have marked portions of this page with circled roman numerals I through V. At I, the number of the file (100-107111) is listed; at II, the number of the corresponding Headquarters ("Bureau") file. (A corresponding Headquarters file has the same title as the Field Office file, but does not contain all the same documents). The Volume ("Section") number, and the numbers of the serials (documents) which should be in the volume are listed at III. IV calls attention to the various subfiles of this file. Subfiles A-D consist simply of newspaper clippings; Sub E contains Prosecutive Summaries; Sub F concerns New York Field Office informers; and Sub G concerns "Miscellaneous" New York area Rosenberg/Sobell groups. As noted at V, the "Green Sheets" in this case (lists of bulky exhibits) are kept apart from the file, with the exhibits.

Sometimes information listed at IV will include the names and file numbers of relatives of the individual on whom the file is kept. If the subject of the file is on the Security Index, "SI" will be stamped on the file cover. Similarly for those on the Reserve-Communist Index (RCI), those tabbed "Detcom," etc. Since Document 3 concerns an organization, not an individual, this sort of information is, of course, missing.

Document 4: FBI Report

The front pages of FBI reports almost invariably have a format similar to this. (An official FBI investigation report, like Document 4, is quite different from an informant's report. See Documents 10, 11, and

U. S. Department of Justice

(MATERIAL MUST NOT BE REMOVED FROM OR ADDED TO THIS FILE)

FEDERAL BUREAU

of

INVESTIGATION

Bureau file no
100-387835

See also Nos.

Document 3.

110

FEDERAL BUREAU OF INVESTIGATION

Form No. 1				
THIS CASE ORIGINATED AT	NEWARK			FILE NO.

REPORT MADE AT	DATE WHEN MADE	PERIOD FOR WHICH MADE	REPORT MADE BY
NEWARK	6/4/52	5/26/52	BRIAN R. KENNEDY

TITLE	CHARACTER OF CASE
################### *	SECURITY MATTER - C

SYNOPSIS OF FACTS: Subject continues to reside ######### , N.J.

- C -

DETAILS: Newark Confidential Informant T-1, of known reliability, advised that as of 5/26/52 subject I########## (#####) and his wife continue to reside at Apartment #### ################## , ########## .

- C L O S E D -

COPIES

6 - Bureau (100-#####) (REGISTERED MAIL)
3 - Philadelphia (100-####) (INFO.) (REGISTERED MAIL)
  (1 - G2, Phila.) REGISTERED MAIL 16
  (1 - ONI, Phila.) REGISTERED MAIL

65-1664-739

SEARCHED _____ INDEXED ___
SERIALIZED ____ FILED __
JUN 9 1955
FBI - ALBANY

APPROVED AND FORWARDED	SPECIAL AGENT IN CHARGE	DO NOT WRITE IN THESE SPACES

COPIES OF THIS REPORT
1 - G2, Commanding Officer, Army, Governors Island
    (NY 4, NY) (REGISTERED MAIL)
1 - Capt. T.F. DONOHUE, DIO, 3rd ND, NY, NY
    (REGISTERED MAIL)
1 - Albany (65-1664) (REGISTERED MAIL)
2 - Newark (100-####)

Document 4-1.

111

NK 100-34619

ADMINISTRATIVE PAGE

A copy of instant report is being furnished Phila. for information, inasmuch as subject is employed within the jurisdiction of that office. Two additional copies are being furnished Phila. for local ONI and G2, inasmuch as subject is employed by a company handling navy and army contracts.

A copy is furnished Albany for information in view of possible connection subject may have with Sarant investigation.

It is noted that the International Resistence Co. is listed as a vital facility and that security responsibility lies with the Dept. of the Army.

INFORMANTS

T-1, ▬▬▬▬▬▬▬▬▬▬▬▬▬▬▬▬▬▬▬▬▬ b7D
who is designated as a confidential informant at her request,

REFERENCE: Bureau letter to Newark, 1/17/52.
Report of SA ORIAN R. KENNEDY, 3/26/52, Newark.

Document 4-2.

112

32). Since reports are intended for dissemination outside the FBI, they are assigned a national security classification at the time they are written if they contain information considered classifiable. Pre-1975 "internal" documents were not classified.

This particular report had been classified "confidential" in 1952 (presumably under Executive Order 10290) but was not reclassified in 1978 when it was released under FOIA. The Attorney General requires that information withheld under FOIA exemption (b) (1) (the "national security" exemption) be classified under the currently applicable Executive Order (which is now President Carter's E.O. 12065), regardless of the age of the document.

The word "confidential" is crossed out but is still readable. This means that the document, *as released*, contains no classified information. Though this document contains no currently classified information at all, in some cases (such as Document 31) the X-ing of the classification markings means that the classified information *on that copy* of the document has been deleted. (However, the FBI is not completely consistent in crossing out inapplicable classification markings.) FBI reports always carry the legend "Property of FBI, etc." which appears here on the lower right. This is not a classification marking, and is intended for government units receiving official copies of the report, not for FOIA requesters.

The distribution of official copies is shown on the lower left of the document. The report was made in Newark and sent to Headquarters ("Bureau"), to several other field offices, and to some military intelligence offices. Headquarters receives multiple copies of reports (at least 5) in case the need arises to disseminate copies to additional places. If Headquarters does disseminate the extra copies, this fact will be recorded on the first page of the first copy. If extra copies are still in the file after a few years, they are destroyed, and this fact is recorded in a similar manner. (Destruction of multiple copies is part of "stripping" a file). Document 4 is an Albany Field Office copy and so would not show the distribution (if any) of the six Headquarters copies.

On the upper right side of this document there is a place for "File No." If a number appears here, it refers to the file on whomever or whatever is listed under "Title" and it refers to the file of the FBI office making the report, whether or not that office is the "originating" (i.e., controlling) office.

Most reports are longer than this — some run to hundreds of pages. Reports are generally accompanied, as this one is, by "Administrative Pages." See Document 5 for an explanation of "Administrative Pages."

Document 5: Administrative Pages of FBI Report

These "Administrative Pages" identify "T" (temporary) source numbers mentioned in the body of a report. (The report has not been

AL 65-1664

ADMINISTRATIVE PAGE

INFORMANTS

T-1 is ████████████████████ Ithaca Savings and Loan Association, b7d
contacted by the writer on 8-9-51 (deemed advisable).

T-2 is ████████████, rural mail carrier, Ithaca Post Office, contacted
by SA PETER F. MAXSON on 8-13-51.

T-3 is a surveillance of the residence and property of ###########
#########, Ithaca, New York, by SA PETER F. MAXSON on
8-23-51.

T-4 is ████████████████████ Trees, Inc., Miami Beach, Florida (deemed b7d
advisable).

T-5 is an anonymous source.

T-6 is ████████████████ contacted by SAS THOMAS M. CORBETT and b7d
ROBERT W. BROWNELL on 3-8-45 and 6-19-45.

T-7 is ████████████ contacted by SA PETER F. MAXSON on 12-19-51. b7d

T-8 is ████████████ contacted by SA CHARLES F. HEINER on 6-11-47. b7d

T-9 is ████████████████ contacted by SA ROBERT W. BROWNELL on b7d
7-31-45.

T-10 is ████████████, contacted by SA FRED C. ZINCK on 3-1-48;
SA H. P. DUSON on 8-10-49 and 11-25-49, and SA EVERETT K.
DEANE on 3-17-50.

T-11 is ████████████ contacted by SA WALTER E. LEVVIS on 8-8-45. b7d

T-12 is ████████████ contacted by SA WALTER E. LEVVIS on 2-17-46. b7d

T-13 is information made available to SAS ROY ARNOLD and RAY C. COMPTON
at the Secretary of State's Office, Albany, New York.

T-14 is ████████████ contacted by SA CHARLES F. HEINER on 3-3-47. b7d

T-15 is ████████████████████ New York City, contacted b7d
by SA DAMON W. PITCHER on 6-23-49 (deemed advisable).

T-16 is ████████ contacted by SA JEROME M. GARLAND on 5-27-47. b7d

T-17 is New York Confidential Source ████████ contacted by SE WILLIAM b7d
STAPLETON on 8-23-_9 and 7-2_-50; by SA ROBERT F. ROYAL on
9-15-50 and by SE RICHARD D. DODGE on 8-23-51.

- 15 SECRET

104

Document 5-1.

114

ADMINISTRATIVE PAGE

12602

INFORMANTS (Continued)

T-18 is NYT 277-S, mentioned in New York letter to the Bureau entitled "###############", va. ############### dated 5-7-45.

T-19 is a surveillance by agents of the New York Office on 4-28-45.

T-20 is ############ contacted on 7-31-50. b7d

T-21 is ############ mentioned in Charlotte letter to New York dated 4-7-50. b7d

T-22 is a trash cover maintained on ################., Recording Secretary of the ########### Club ###### First and Second AD, 8 Barrow Street, New York City.

T-23 is ################### New York Office. PHA, contacted on 6-5-50 by an agent of the New York Office (deemed advisable). b7d

T-24 is Loyalty Form (LGE) on ##############.

T-25 is ################## contacted by SA PETER J. CATLANDO on 6-1-44. b7d

T-26 is ################## contacted by SA ALBERT RONDBAKER on 6-27-49. b7d

T-27 is ################## contacted by SA EVERETT K. DEANE and SE STEPHEN W. JENNINGS on 2-1-50. b7d

T-28 is United States Federal District Judge HAROLD R. MEDINA.

T-29 is ################## Western Union Office, Ithaca, New York, contacted by SA PETER F. MAXSON in August, 1951 (deemed advisable). b7d

T-30 is Removal Records, Flushing, New York, Post Office.

T-31 is surveillance conducted by SAS JOHN D. MAHONEY and PETER F. MAXSON.

T-32 is ################# contacted by SA ARMAND A. CAMMAROTA on 3-22-51, 4-4-51, 4-27-51 and 12-28-50; by SAS JOHN HARRINGTON and ROBERT F. ROYAL on 7-10-51 and by SAS JOHN HARRINGTON and WILLIAM F. NORTON on 1-18-51. b7d

T-33 is ################# ######### Clerk, Ithaca Post Office, contacted by SA PETER F. MAXSON.

- 105 -

Document 5-2.

printed.) "Administrative Pages" may also contain information on leads to be followed or other action to be taken and often refer to previous FBI communications relating to the report.

Because reports are considered suitable for dissemination to other government agencies, confidential sources in them are protected by "T" numbers, and are only identified on the "Administrative Pages," which are normally not disseminated. This applies of course only to official FBI case reports, not to informant reports, which are never disseminated. Even on the "Administrative Pages," the identities of the most "sensitive" sources are concealed. For example, "T-5" (probably a burglary) is simply called an "anonymous source." "T-18" (probably a "security" TESUR, that is, wiretap) is identified only as "NYT 277-S." Buried under the deletions may be permanent source numbers (such as "NYT 277-S") as well as names. The notation "deemed advisable" (concerning for example, T-1 or T-4) seems to mean that the agent deemed it advisable to conceal the source's identity in the body of the report.

Many of the "informants" listed in "Administrative Pages" are not informants in the strict sense of regular, paid suppliers of information. Some are not persons at all. Most of the "informants" in Document 5 were not contacted in the preparation of this report. FBI reports must be written frequently, whether or not there is anything new to report on. And each report is supposed to be intelligible on its own, so it must include some background. Hence, reports are often little more than rehashes of information previously reported on. The same scrap of information may turn up in scores of reports, over the course of many years.

The FBI often withholds entirely (under FOIA exemption (b) (7) (d)) the "Administrative Pages" of reports. "T" numbers are sometimes deleted from the bodies of reports. Since "Administrative Pages" are often numbered separately from the body of reports (or, rather, are assigned letters while the pages of the report have numbers), interpreters unaccustomed to the format of FBI reports may fail to realize that "Administrative Pages" are missing. As Document 5 illustrates, it is possible for the FBI to segregate and release nonexempt portions of "Administrative Pages," and one should insist that this be done.

Document 6: Letterhead Memo (LHM)

LHMs are meant for dissemination to other government agencies and always carry a warning like the one contained in the last paragraph of Document 6. This particular copy of this LHM does not carry the heading "United States Department of Justice, Federal Bureau of Investigation"; some other copies of this LHM will, however, bear this heading. This document had been classified "confidential" under Eisenhower's Executive Order 10501 (as amended) for nine years. It

New York, New York
January 15, 1969

Committee To Free Morton Sobell
Internal Security-C

The January 15, 1969 issue of the "Daily News"
contains an article on page five, captioned, "Federal
Court Order Frees Atom Spy Sobell." U

Above article reflects that Morton Sobell arrived
at the Port Authority Bus Terminal, New York, New York, at
9:15 p.m., January 14, 1969, after his release from the
Federal penitentiary in Lewisburg, Pennsylvania. He was
sentenced to thirty years imprisonment on April 5, 1951, for
a wartime espionage conspiracy to deliver vital national
secrets to the Soviet Union, and he served more than 18
years imprisonment subsequent to his arrest in Laredo,
Texas, during August, 1950. U

According to above article, Sobell was met at
the bus terminal by his wife and family, and he reaffirmed
his oft-claimed innocence of above charge to interviewing
reporters before retiring to his home at 30 Charlton Street,
New York, New York. Sobell told reporters that he intends
to continue his fight to prove his innocence of the conspiracy
charge, and he plans to resume his studies in the field of
medical electronics. U

This document contains neither recommendations nor
conclusions of the Federal Bureau of Investigation (FBI).
It is the property of the FBI and is loaned to your agency;
it and its contents are not to be distributed outside your
agency.

DECLASSIFIED BY 4913/AP/u
ON 1-21-75

GROUP I
Excluded from automatic
downgrading and
declassification

6-Bureau (100-387835) (RM)
6-New York(100-37158) (MORTON SOBELL) #331
1-New York (100-107111)
1-Supervisor #41
CSM:cbm
(9)

100-37158 232

SEARCHED _____ INDEXED _____
SERIALIZED _____ FILED _____
JAN 22 1969
FBI — NEW YORK

Document 6.

117

was presumably classified when written (1/16/69) and (as indicated at bottom center) was excluded from automatic declassification. It was declassified in 1978 (see bottom left) when Morton Sobell's file was reviewed for partial release in connection with the Rosenberg case.

Six copies of this LHM were sent registered mail ("RM") to headquarters ("Bureau"). Headquarters always receives copies of summary material such as LHMs and reports, but not such raw data as surveillance logs or informants' reports. Three copies remained in New York, where the LHM was prepared. Two of these were filed and one went to a field office supervisor. Numbers following file numbers in distribution of copies often denote the section or squad (of the FBI office) which is handling the case.

If any "T" sources are mentioned in an LHM, they are identified on an accompanying memo or letter, not on "Administrative Pages" as with reports. See Documents 4 and 5.

Document 7: Teletype

Teletypes are the FBI's fastest means of sending written communications. Each field office has a teletype terminal. Teletypes are reserved for urgent messages, apparently in part because teletypes require burdensome encrypting (by the sending office) and decrypting (by the receiving office). This particular teletype was sent from NY to "Director" (that is to FBI HQ in Washington, D.C.). This teletype concerns the Federal Grand Jury testimony of "subj" ("subject") William Perl. The notation "Cleveland advised" (bottom left) does not refer to the telephonic contact with Cleveland mentioned in this teletype, but means rather that Cleveland was sent a copy of this teletype.

On FBI communications other than teletypes, the recipient of the communication is listed *above* the sender. (See, e.g., Document 12.)

Document 8: Secret Service Form

This FD-376 was part of an FBI report sent to the Secret Service. Such forms are frequently drawn up on subjects of "security" investigations, whether or not the subject has demonstrated a propensity for violence. (Such a form was sent to the Secret Service on *every* individual listed in the Security Index.)

The Secret Service is the single most frequent recipient of FBI information, but it claims to retain very little of what it receives. The FBI often invokes FOIA exemption (b) (5) to prevent the release of information sent to the Secret Service.

Document 9: Request From Navy

This is a request from Naval Intelligence ("District Intelligence

TELETYPE

Mr. Tolson
Mr. Ladd
Mr. Clegg
Mr. Glavin
Mr. Nichols
Mr. Rosen
Mr. Tracy
Mr. Harbo
Mr. Belmont
Mr. Mohr
Tele. Room
Mr. Nease
Miss Gandy

WASHINGTON 52 -FROM NEW YORK   18   1057 P

DIRECTOR   URGENT

WILLIAM PERL, WAS., ESP - R. SUBJ TESTIFIED BEFORE FGJ., SDNY, TODAY
FROM ELEVEN THIRTY AM TO ONE THIRTY PM. AUSA, MYLES J. LANE, SDNY,
ADVISED THAT SUBJ CONSISTENTLY MAINTAINED SAME STORY AS PREVIOUSLY
OBTAINED IN RECENT INTERVIEWS. PERL EXCUSED BY GRAND JURY TODAY SUBJ
TO RECALL AFTER SEPTEMBER SECOND NEXT. SUBJ ADVISED HE EXPECTS TO
RETURN CLEVELAND VIA UNITED AIRLINES, FLIGHT FIVE NAUGHT FIVE, LEAVING
LA GUARDIA AIRPORT, NYC, SIX THIRTY PM EDST., ON SATURDAY, AUGUST
NINETEEN NEXT. THIS FLIGHT SCHEDULED TO ARRIVE CLEVELAND NINE NAUGHT
FIVE PM EDST. SURVEILLANCE BEING CONTINUED AT NYC. CLEVELAND WILL
BE ADVISED TELEPHONICALLY OF PERL-S DEPARTATION.

                                              SCHEIDT

CLEVELAND ADVISED   RECORDED - 58 [65 - 59312 - 77
END
WA NY R 52 WA HSU

                          EX-89

Document 7.

119

UNITED STATES DEPARTMENT OF JUSTICE
FEDERAL BUREAU OF INVESTIGATION

WASHINGTON, D.C. 20535

In Reply, Please Refer to
File No. Bureau 100-429445
New York 100-128869

Director
United States Secret Service
Department of the Treasury
Washington, D. C. 20220

Rose Sobell

APPROPRIATE AGENCIES
AND FIELD OFFICES
ADVISED BY ROUTING
SLIP(S) OF *declass*
DATE *2/21/78 agdreng*

Dear Sir:

   The information furnished herewith concerns an individual who is believed to be covered by the agreement between the FBI and Secret Service concerning Presidential protection, and to fall within the category or categories checked.

1. ☐ Has attempted or threatened bodily harm to any government official or employee, including foreign government officials residing in or planning an imminent visit to the U. S., because of his official status.

2. ☐ Has attempted or threatened to redress a grievance against any public official by other than legal means.

3. ☒ Because of background is potentially dangerous; or has been identified as member or participant in communist movement; or has been under active investigation as member of other group or organization inimical to U. S.

4. ☐ U. S. citizens or residents who defect from the U. S. to countries in the Soviet or Chinese Communist blocs and return.

5. ☐ Subversives, ultrarightists, racists and fascists who meet one or more of the following criteria:

   (a) ☐ Evidence of emotional instability (including unstable residence and employment record) or irrational or suicidal behavior;
   (b) ☐ Expressions of strong or violent anti-U. S. sentiment;
   (c) ☐ Prior acts (including arrests or convictions) or conduct or statements indicating a propensity for violence and antipathy toward good order and government.

6. ☐ Individuals involved in illegal bombing or illegal bomb-making.

Photograph ☒ has been furnished   ☐ enclosed   ☐ is not available
☐ may be available through _____
_____.

DECLASSIFIED BY C428
ON 2/21/78

Very truly yours,

John Edgar Hoover
Director

1 - Special Agent in Charge (Enclosure(s) 1
    U. S. Secret Service, NYC (RM)

Enclosure(s) 1   (Upon removal of classified enclosures, if any, this transmittal form
                     becomes UNCLASSIFIED.)

Document 8.

120

SNO. DMO. 23.9

DISTRICT INTELLIGENCE OF
THIRD NAVAL DISTRICT
FEDERAL OFFICE BUILDING
90 CHURCH STREET
NEW YORK 7, N.Y.

DATE: July 22-1952

CASE NO: 11ND-275-3
SARANT

ASSIGNED TO:

CONFIDENTIAL
SECURITY INFORMATION

TO: G-2, 1st ARMY   BCI   STATE POLICE   - CREDIT BUREAU   FBI- New York
                      SSD   Newark
     USAF (OSI)   ORR
                      BI
     OinC ZONE NO. _____

Gentlemen:

In connection with an official investigation it is requested that a search be made of your files concerning the individual described below, and that this office be advised of the results thereof. If derogatory information is found, please furnish date of birth or other positively identifying data.

1. NAMES & ALIASES   SARANT, Alfred   *65-15360*

2. BIRTH: DATE: PLACE:

3. DESCRIPTION SEX: COLOR: HGT.   FT.   IN.   WT.   EYES: HAIR:
   SCARS: SOC. SEC. NO:

4. HOME ADDRESSES: (No. & Street)   - (City & State)   (Date)

   590 Russell Ave.   Long Branch, N.J.
   65 Morton St.   New York, N.Y.   1943 to 1950

5. EMPLOYMENT: (Firm)   (Location)   (Dates)

   Signal Corps Lab.   Ft. Monmouth, N.J.

6. REFERENCES: (For Zone Officers)

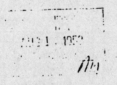

COMMENTS: BACKGROUND   PRIORITY-URGENT-ROUTINE
(Use reverse side if necessary)   DATE DUE:

*Baughman, out states Loesal
will contact SA Royal*

CONFIDENTIAL

65-15360-997   3ND-PBPO-1834

Document 9.

Officer") for information from the FBI. The same request may have gone to other government agencies, the state police, or even a credit bureau. FBI information is frequently shared with military intelligence agencies.

This particular document was received by the FBI NY field office, which filed it as the 997th serial in its file on the individual about whom the Navy requested information. If information is supplied to the Navy or to anyone else, that fact is normally recorded in the file from which the information was taken. However, the FBI sometimes tries to conceal from FOIA requesters the fact that information was disseminated.

Documents containing information originating with agencies other than the FBI will not be released by the FBI until the other agency has been consulted. The FBI "referred" this document to the Naval Investigative Service before releasing it, though one cannot tell from the document itself that this was done.

Documents 10 and 11: Covers of Informant Reports

These are typical FD-306s—"cover sheets" for informant reports. FD-306s, because they indicate where copies of an informant's report are to be sent ("channelized"), are sometimes called "channelizing memos" or "channelization memos." Document 10 and the accompanying informant's report (not printed) were sent to 46 files; 43 files received Document 11. In both cases, all the files receiving copies were in the NY field office; Headquarters did not get the "cover sheets" or the informants' reports. (In both documents, the deleted list of files to which copies are "channelized" is continued on a page we have not printed.) "1-100-(deleted)" means that "1" copy is designated for the "100" (that is, "subversive matter") file on (deleted). The deletions are of particular case numbers, and also of persons or organizations which are the subjects of the cases. Headquarters, and perhaps other interested field offices, may or may not eventually receive summaries of the "pertinent" parts of informants' reports; but they rarely receive the actual informants' reports.

A comparison of the two documents underscores the value of having the FBI cite, on the document released, whatever FOIA exemptions it is claiming. Document 10 accompanies a report by an informant who attended an anti-war rally. His/her identity is concealed under (b) (7) (d), the "confidentiality of informants" exemption. The names and file numbers of those he informed on are covered by claims of (b) (7) (c) and (b) (7) (d) — that is, the FBI is claiming that release of the information would both violate the privacy of these people and tend to identify the person who informed on them. The name of the SA (Special Agent) to whom the informant gave his report is deleted under (b) (7) (c), allegedly to protect the agent's privacy.

| Date received | Received from (name or symbol number) | b7D | Received by | |
| 10/2/72 | ████████████ | | SA ████████████ | b7C |

Method of delivery (check appropriate blocks)

☒ in person   ☐ by telephone   ☐ by mail   ☐ orally   ☐ recording device   ☒ written by Informant

If orally furnished and reduced to writing by Agent:	Date of Report
Date	9/18/72
	Date(s) of activity
Dictated _____ to _____	
Transcribed _____	
Authenticated by Informant	

Brief description of activity or material _____ 9/18/72

Anti-war rally, Kingston, NY, featuring
Jane Fonda and Tom Hayden.

File where original is located if not attached
████████████ b7C

* INDIVIDUALS DESIGNATED BY AN ASTERISK (*) ONLY ATTENDED A MEETING AND DID NOT ACTIVELY PARTICIPATE. VIOLENCE OR REVOLUTIONARY ACTIVITIES WERE NOT DISCUSSED.

☐ Information recorded on a card index by _____ on date _____

Remarks:

All necessary action taken.

46 - New York   b7D
  1 -
  1 - 100-
  1 - 100
  1 - 100
  1 - 100
  1 - 100
  1 - 100
  1 - 100
  1 - 100
  1 - 100
  1 - 100
  1 - 100
  1 - 100
  1 - 100
  1 - 100   b7a+D

GTT:fds
(46)

COPIES TO BE CONTINUED

Block Stamp
65- ########## -803

Document 10.

Cover Sheet for Informant Report or M____ial
FD-301 (Rev. 9-31-6N)

Date prepared
11/14/73

Date received _____ b2   Received from (name or symbol number) ____ b2   Received by _____ b7c

Method of delivery (check appropriate blocks)

☐ in person   ☐ by telephone   ☐ by mail   ☐ orally   ☐ recording device   ☐ written by Inform..

If orally furnished and reduced to writing by Agent:
                              Date

Dictated _____ to _____

Transcribed _____

Authenticated
by Informant _____

Brief description of activity or material

_____ b1

Date of Report _____ b2

Date(s) of activity _____ b1

File where original is located if not attached _____ b2

* INDIVIDUALS DESIGNATED BY AN ASTERISK (*) ONLY ATTENDED A MEETING AND DID NOT ACTIVELY PARTICIPAT_
VIOLENCE OR REVOLUTIONARY ACTIVITIES WERE NOT DISCUSSED.

☐ Information recorded on a card index by _____ on date _____

Remarks:

                    All necessary action taken.

1-   b2
1- 100-
1- 100-   12/26/7_
1- 100-
1- 100-
1- 100-
1- 100-
1- 100-
·1- 100-
¹1- 100-
1- 100-
1- 100-
1- 100-
1- 100-
1- 100-
1- 100-   Block Stamp
1- 100-
1- 100-   65- ########-811
1- 100
1- 100
1- 100-   b7c

WAB:epl   (43)

Document 11.

124

Document 11 invokes exemptions (b) (1) ("national security"), (b) (2) ("internal personnel rules and practices"), and (b) (7) (c), but not (b) (7) (d). This suggests that the "informant" may be an electronic surveillance or burglary, not a human being. (However, a raw electronic surveillance log would not be accompanied by a "cover sheet" such as Document 10 or 11.) There is no indication on this document that it was ever classified. (See Ch. II for a discussion of the marking requirements for classified information.) Thus, strictly on a procedural level, the FBI apparently had no right to invoke (b) (1). (b) (2) also appears to be misused here, since the date of an informant's report and the name or symbol number of an informant involve more than the internal personnel practices of the FBI. (Document 12 is an example of a classified document which was properly marked.)

Document 12: Intra-Field Office Memo

This is a memo from an SA ("Special Agent" — that is, an FBI agent) to his SAC ("Special Agent in Charge"). In general, a memo meant to remain within a field office will be at least nominally an "SA to SAC" memo. Such memos will rarely be sent to Headquarters, and will never be distributed to other government agencies. The distribution of copies is probably hidden by the large deletion on the bottom of the page.

At least if they originated before 1975, memos will not be classified until they fall under an FOIA/PA request. This document was classified on 3/18/78, as shown on the lower left. It is allegedly exempt from the General Declassification Schedule (GDS) of Nixon's Executive Order 11652 because it falls within "category 2," that is, because it is "classified information or material specifically covered by statute, or pertaining to cyptography, or disclosing intelligence sources or methods." (See Ch. II.) Classified sections have been deleted by the FBI, and labeled (b) (1).

For another example of this sort of memo, see Document 32.

Document 13: Microphone Surveillance (MISUR) Log

This is a record ("log") kept by FBI agents listening to a bug ("MISUR") planted in a private apartment. MISUR logs are rarely released, since the FBI attempts to conceal them under the cloak of "national security" (the (b) (1) exemption). The same sorts of log sheets can be used for wiretaps (technical surveillances or "TESURs"), as evidenced by the column (here blank) labeled "IC/OG" ("incoming/ outgoing").

Unlike most FBI documents, electronic surveillance logs are often not serialized. This particular log was kept in the "Sub 1" section of a NY file, and the main sections of this file gave few clues as to the

Office Memorandum • UNITED STATES GOVERNMENT

TO : SAC, NEW YORK (100-   )
CONFIDENTIAL
DATE: 5/13/57

FROM : SA WILLIAM G. LINEHAN

SUBJECT: LOWER EAST SIDE
MORTON SOBELL COMMITTEE
IS-C

Source

Reliability   Who has furnished
reliable information in
the past

Date of Activity

Date Received   5/6/57

Received by   SA WILLIAM G. LINEHAN

Location of original
report

Attached is a verbatim copy of PSI's report concerning the captioned organization. In the event this information is used in a report or otherwise disseminated outside the Bureau, care must be taken to protect the source's identity.

WGL:rmv
(8)

CLASSIFIED BY 4913 AP/egw 3/18/78
EXEMPT FROM GDS, CATEGORY
DATE OF DECLASSIFICATION INDEFINITE

CONFIDENTIAL

SEARCHED _____ INDEXED _____
SERIALIZED _____ FILED _____
MAY 13 1957
FBI — NEW YORK

ALL INFORMATION CONTAINED
HEREIN IS UNCLASSIFIED
EXCEPT WHERE SHOWN
OTHERWISE

Document 12.

126

ime	Initial	IC CG	ACTIVITY RECORDED
⁶⁰⁰ PM			Conversation between ############### and ######### re telephone call from 1 #########
			2041- 40 to 44
⁶⁰⁰ PM	RS		Conversation between ########## + 1##### 2046-37&59 mostly unintelligible
¹⁸ PM	PM		,########_ and ####### in conversation idle chit-chat partially unintelligible 2046-39-43
³⁰ P.M.			,###### and ############# ,##### in background mostly unintelligible 2046-43-40 end 2044 - 44 begin 2042-1 to
¹⁴	RS		Conversation as above 2043-1 To 2

Document 13.

existence of this "Sub" file. This particular microphone had the source number "964-S," and is spoken of in the serialized documents in this file as if it is a human being familiar with the activities of this family. If information in a field office file seems to be coming from an electronic device aimed at the subject of the file, there is a good chance the logs of the surveillance are in numbered "sub" files and are maintained in the "JUNE" area of the FBI, apart from the "Central Records" where most files are kept.

Numbers after entries in "Activity Recorded" sometimes appear to refer to locations on tape recordings where the "activity" can be heard.

Document 14: "1A" Envelope

This "1A" envelope was filed in front of a NY file, and each serial in the envelope has a "1A" number (e.g. "100-109849-1A1"). The lists of contents of "1A" envelopes are most often handwritten rather than typed. The contents of this envelope typify "1A"s: photographs, physical (not electronic) surveillance logs, public source material, and letters (apparently not those illegally obtained) by the subject of the file. If the subject ever signed a statement for the FBI, the statement would be placed in a "1A" envelope. ("1A" envelopes and "bulky exhibits" are explained in Ch. I.)

Document 15: Request to Resident Agency (RA)

This is an FD-203, a form on which an FBI field office requests an FBI Resident Agency (RA) to conduct a "security" investigation on an individual. RAs are small FBI offices, supervised by the usually much larger field offices. This document is from the NY field office file on the "subject" of this investigation. The FBI insists that with very few exceptions RAs keep only those documents they need for current investigations, and maintain no permanent or even long-term files.

Document 16: Destruction Authorization

This document authorizes the destruction of certain "serials" (i.e., documents) in the NY file on the Committee to Secure Justice for Morton Sobell. It illustrates the FBI's willingness to destroy the raw data on which its summary reports are allegedly based. FBI reports, designed for dissemination outside the Bureau, are less candid than internal memos intended for use only by the field office conducting the investigation. The destroyed serials seem to include information obtained directly from informants. For examples of "channelizing memoranda," see Documents 10 and 11.

9/22/55	Card from Helen Sobell to Norma Abrams, N.Y. NEWS.	
11/29/55	Cover letter of Mrs. Morton Sobell.	
11/29/55	Memo to J.E. Benate re: "Conduct of U.S.A.'s Office in case of Mrs. Sobell.	
2/28/56	1 negative and 6 photos of subject Mrs. Helen Sobell. 1 photo sent to New Haven 5/18/56.	
3/22/56	A 4 page leaflet containing 3 poems and a photo of Mrs. Sobell.	
3/22/56	3 photos and one neg. of Mrs. Morton Sobell.	
7/15/57	3 poems by Mrs. Morton Sobell plus her photo received at Sobell Defense.	
7/15/57	Pamphlet entitled "3 Poems by Mrs. Morton Sobell". See serial 266.	
7/16/57	5 neg. 8 prints of Helen Sobell taken from Newspaper photos located in Sub. A Section of 100-37158 and from section 1 of 100-109849 (case file).	
0. 7/25/57	Pamphlet containing 3 poems by and photo of Helen Sobell. See per. 289.	
1. 10/18/57	Announcement of 10/10/57 TV appearance of Helen Sobell.	
2. 12/11/58	Letter dated 1/31/58 from Helen Sobell to Mr. and Mrs. Albert Walter	
3. 12/11/58	Letter dated 7/31/58 from Helen Sobell to Abraham Wells.	
4. 12/11/58	Ltr. dated 7/18/58 from Helen Sobell to Fd. Jacobs, Esqr.	
5. 12/11/58	Letter dated 8/13/58 to Helen Sobell to Fd. Jacobs	
6. 12/11/58	Letter dated 8/17/58 from Helen Sobell to Fd. Jacobs	
7. 7/29/59	1 neg. and 5 photos of subjects passport photo.	
8. 1/30/61	Serv. log for Helen Sobell std 1/19/61.	
9. 3/8/61	Serv. log for 1/12/61.	

NOTE: ABOVE RETIPED FROM OLD EXHIBIT ENVELOPE BLOCKSTAMPED 12/1/61.

NOTE: DO NOT ENTER ANYMORE EXHIBITS IN THIS ENVELOPE. SEE 1A SUPPLEMENT.

Document 14.

FD-203

_7/13/58_, 19_

MEMO, SAC
Attention _MINEOLA_ RA

Re: #################################
was. ###########################
SECURITY MATTER - C

71·5

The captioned subject was reported residing at ##############################
GREAT NECK L.I., N.Y, and employed as a - ################### at the
############################ N.Y.C. , as of _4/55_, 19_.
Subject's spouse is _____.

The subject has been reported involved in the following subversive activity
on the dates shown:
1. _____
2. _____
3. _____

It is requested the following investigation be conducted: (Check where
applicable.)
(✓) A. Verify current employment and residence.
( ) B. Determine current Credit Record, it being noted the subject's credit was
last checked _____, 19_.
(✓) C. Determine current criminal record, it being noted the subject's criminal
file was last reviewed _____, 19_.
{ } D. Obtain background, and dates, from subject's employment record.
{ } E. Check subject's marriage record at Probate Court, it being noted subject
was reported married _____, 19_, at _____
( ) F. Check official birth record at Bureau of Vital Statistics, it being
noted subject reported born on _____, 19_, at _____
{ } G. Determine whether subject has access to classified or restricted material.
{ } H. Conduct neighborhood investigation; the following specific information is
desired: _____
(✓) I. Check Security Informants, it being noted _logical sources_ ,
and _____ have given information in the past.
{ } J. Review INS records.
{ } K. Determine if subject has military service.
{ } L. Obtain photograph of subject ( ), description ( ), handwriting specimen ( ).
{ } M. Determine subject's education; check school or college records, it being
noted subject was reported attending _____ in 19_.
( ) N. Determine subject's status of health.

The agent conducting the investigation will be alert for any evidence of
subversive activity and in addition will _____
Candidate election checks 1950 to 1957
_____ ############### _B'klyn, N.Y._
(use reverse side, if necessary)

Daniel J. Tingley
SA (7-4)(X-452)

Enc. Serial/s 3, 11, 50, 78
100- ; #########

(OVER)

Document 15.

130

UNITED STATES GOVERNMENT

Memorandum

TO : SAC, *New York* (100-107111)   DATE: *JAN 25, 63*

FROM : SA [redacted]   b7c

SUBJECT: *Committee to Secure Justice*
For Morton Sobell
IS-C; ISA of 1950

In connection with the destruction of channelizing memoranda, the information contained on the serials listed below was incorporated in a report dated *1/25/63* . The review for this report was made from serial *4992* through serial *5176* .

In accordance with the above, the following serials are to be destroyed:

Volume	Serials (List by serial or serial scope.)			
111	4996	4997	4999	5000
	5003	5004	5006	5007
	5009	5016	5017	5020
	5021	5022	5023	5024
	5027			
112	5048	5049	5051	5052
	5066	5068	5069	5070
	5071	5072	5073	5074
	5075	5076	5077	5078
	5079	5080	5082	5087
	5089	5090	5091	5092
	5102	5104	5107	5110
	5112	5119	5127	5133
113	5134	5135	5146	5147
	5152	5153	5155	
	5157	5158	5159	5160
	5161	5166	5169	[redacted]
	5171	5173	5174	

No. of copies 1-Vol 111
1-Vol 112   Approved [signature]   6/4/63

Document 16.

Document 17: Permanent Serial Chargeout

Normally, when an agent wants information from a file, he will request an entire "section" or "volume" and then return it when he is finished. Permanent serial chargeouts differ from this norm in that they concern particular documents ("serials") rather than entire volumes, and because the material is never replaced in the file. When a serial is permanently removed, a sheet such as Document 17 is left where the serial had been. Document 17 shows that a serial was removed to the "JUNE" section, an area where material on electronic surveillances and burglaries is kept. However, "JUNE" material often never gets serialized, but is instead kept from the start in "subfiles" so that the file will contain no telltale "permanent serial chargeouts."

Document 18: "JUNE" Material

"JUNE" material concerns electronic surveillances and burglaries performed under FBI auspices. (See Ch. I for a fuller explanation of the "JUNE" system.) Other documents on the individuals mentioned here (especially their NY "JUNE" documents) prove that the "highly confidential source" of Document 18 was in fact a burglary of these individuals' apartments by FBI agents.

The "EXP. PROC." ("expedite processing") stamp means that the document was sent to the appropriate FBI officials before being assigned a serial number. Though this document was eventually assigned a serial number, other "expedite processing" documents may not be.

Document 19: Bulky Exhibit Inventory

This is a so-called "Green Sheet." Copies released to the public always appear white. These sheets are prepared on all "bulky exhibits" housed in the FBI. ("Bulky exhibits" are explained in Ch. I.) Some cases involve hundreds or thousands of "bulkies," each assigned a separate number and listed on a "Green Sheet." (Bulky exhibits are usually assigned "1B" numbers, that is, "1B1," "1B2" etc.) Exhibit (1) in this case was evidently destroyed without the information contained in it ever having been summarized in a report sent to Headquarters.

Document 20: Cards From the General Index

This document, printed exactly as received from the FBI, is a copy of several cards from the "General Index" of the NY field office. Copies of such cards are almost never released, but should be as they may contain relevant nonexempt information. A few were obtained in connection with the release of the Rosenberg files. (On the FBI General Index, see Ch. I.)

DATE OF MAIL _3-1-54_

HAS BEEN REMOVED FOR _Special File Rm. Div 4_

SEE FILE 66-2554-7530 FOR AUTHORITY.

SUBJECT _____ JUNE MAIL _____

REMOVED BY __5 9 MAR 11 1954__

FILE NUMBER _65 - #########-218_

PERMANENT SERIAL CHARGEOUT

Document 17.

133

STANDARD FORM NO. 64

Office Memorandum • UNITED STATES GOVERNMENT

TO   : Director, FBI   DATE: 9/2/54

FROM   SAC, NYC (66-6182-B)

SUBJECT: JUNE   JUNE
                                         PERSONAL & CONFIDENTIAL

    This is to advise the Bureau that symbol NY-1178 S **
has been assigned to a highly confidential source having
access to the personal records of ##############################
############################# ., NYC, on 10/10/53.

JJK:MT

RECORDED-29 65-#######-235
INDEXED-29

EX-128

Document 18.

134

FD-192
(7-17-52)

BULKY EXHIBIT - INVENTORY OF PROPERTY ACQUIRED AS EVIDENCE

Bufile: NEW YORK   Field Division

#/2   7-13-53   Date

Title and Character of Case: ############## was
                                SECURITY MATTER - C
                                N. Y. FILE #100-111786

Date Property Acquired: See below

Source From Which Property Acquired: See below

Location of Property or Bulky Exhibit: Vault

Reason for Retention of Property and Evidence & information
Efforts Made to Dispose of Same: Retain permanently

Description of Property or Exhibit and   See below
Identity of Agent Submitting Same:

(1) Testimony of ########### fro 2-27-53 and 3-2-53. Recd. 5-53 from a highly
    confidential source. Subm. by S^A M. Corcoran, 6-17-53. (NOTE: This info obtained
    on a highly confidential basis & should never be made part of any reprrt)

(2) Letter addressed to Judge Foster Symes from ################.See
    Serial 1 of 121-5642. Subm. by SA J.J.Roth. Transferred from
    1B242 of 121-5642, 8/28/53.

Destroyed per SA Folkins *per per 23 12/8/*

Field File #:

100-111786-1-B-1
SEARCHED..........INDEXED..........
SERIALIZED..........FILED..........
JUL 13 1953
FBI - NEW YORK

Document 19.

135

000061

GREENGLASS, DAVID   65-15299

s. 80 pg. 2   lt. 2-16-51
s. 107 pg. 8, 21   rpt. 3-31-51

GREENGLASS, DAVID (MR)   65-15280-137 p.18

65-15336

.Y. rpt. 2-3-51

GREENGLASS, DAVID   65-15336   JD

AKA DAVE GREENGLASS, DAVID GREEN   Mif,
                                          b1   Apprt 16
                                                           vols
SS #057-12-3377- B.C #10817
ASN #32882473
FBI #439514A
Comm. scientist emp. dev. 7/50100-47343-1416 P 2
Atomic Bomb   6/51   -1451 P 6

GREENGLASS, DAVID   7/61   65-14843-1815 p2

                                            b1

GREENGLASS, DAVID   65-13548-   2231
                              pp 1-4
                            3/19/53

CLASSIFIED BY 4913 AP/jew 5/12/78
EXEMPT FROM CLTL CATEGORY   2
DATE OF DECLASSIFICATION INDEFINITE

TOP SECRET

Document 20.

The top two cards are "see ref." cards — that is, they indicate references to David Greenglass in files which do not carry "David Greenglass" in their titles. In NY file 65-15299, serials ("S."s) 80 (a letter) and 107 (a report) mention Greenglass. Not all references to Greenglass in file 65-15299 need be written on one index card. (Cards are kept in roughly chronological order.)

The third card down indicates that 65-15336 (a NY file, of course) is a main file ("mf") on Greenglass. In general, any card listing only a file number, without a serial number, is a main file on the group or individual which is the subject of the card. The notation "ID" ("identical") and "MF, approx. 16 vols." were not on the original index cards, but were written by an FBI file reviewer attempting to determine how much FBI material was "identical" to David Greenglass (that is, how much pertained to the same David Greenglass who was involved in the Rosenberg case).

The third card is the only one on this page to contain identifying information on Greenglass, including his social security number and his "FBI No." (that is, fingerprint number, not file number). It is believed, however, that both "main" and "see ref." cards commonly include identifying information.

These cards contain information the FBI chose to label "Top Secret" and to delete. Thus, the General Index contains "sensitive" information which, whether or not exempt from release under the FOIA, may be of interest to the public. The cards are also worth seeing simply because they show what references to an individual exist in the files of a given FBI office (though not every name is indexed, and index cards are allegedly destroyed when the file to which they refer is destroyed or when a "correlation summary" is prepared from them; Document 23 illustrates a "correlation summary").

Documents 21 and 22: Search Slips

Slips such as these are filled in by FBI clerks when they are searching the General Index for references to an individual or organization. The index consists of cards like those in Document 20. Document 21 was used in a search of the NY field office General Index; 22 is from Headquarters.

The search can be conducted in various ways. For example, if only "subversive" references need be listed, the clerk will record all references to the subject" in, e.g., "100" ("Security Matters") files, but will omit information contained in, e.g., "144"("Interstate Transportation of Lottery Tickets") files. (Ch. I, Appendix C, explains all FBI file classification numbers.) A search of the General Index is made both when the FBI wants material in connection with an investigation and when an FOIA request is being processed. The searcher is usually required to look for references under several variants of a name

FD-160
(9-20-54)

INDICES SEARCH SLIP

TO CHIEF CLERK: DATE _____

SUBJECT _____########.##########################_._____

ALIASES _____

ADDRESS _____

DATE & PLACE OF BIRTH _____

☐ Exact Spelling   ☐ Criminal and subversive
☐ All references   references only
☐ Subversive references only   ☐ Main files only
☐ Criminal references only   ☐ Restrict search to following locality
                                        _____

FILE & SERIAL NO.   REMARKS   FILE & SERIAL NO.   REMARKS

_######## &##### P##########_   _____ _____

I 100-55806 *   /   _____ _____

_.######### P#############_   _____ _____

I 100-55806 *   c/   _____ _____

_####### H#######_   _____ _____

I 100-55806 *   c/   _____ _____

Mrs. ####### P#############_ _____ _____

I 100-55806 *   c/   _____ _____

_____   _____ _____

_____   _____ _____

_____   _____ _____

_____   _____ _____

Searched by _____ _____ _____
                Clerk   Agent   Squad

References Reviewed by _____

Document 21.

138

☐ Name Check Unit - Room 6523
☐ Service Unit - Room 6524
☒ Forward to File Review
☐ Attention _____
☐ Return to Mr. Lee 1734

    Supervisor Room Ext.

Type of References Requested:
☐ Regular Request (Analytical Search)
☒ All References (Subversive & Nonsubversive)
☐ Subversive References Only
☐ Nonsubversive References Only
☐ Main _____ References Only

Type of Search Requested:
☐ Restricted to Locality of _____
☐ Exact Name Only (On the Nose)
☐ Buildup ☐ Variations
☐ Check for Alphabetical Loyalty Form

all breakdowns, unlimited

Subject Alfred Epaminondas Sarant

Birthdate & Place _____

Address _____

Localities _____

Rs ⑦ Date 7-31 Searcher Initials S9

	FILE NUMBER	SERIAL
I	65-59242	
SI	100-342424-7 p882 Photo	
I	65-59242-365 Photo	
I	65-59242-466 Sum. 10/20/5=	
	I 492 Sum 9/2451	
	I 321 Sum. 11/1/50	
☐37	65-58069-?11 p137	
SE	40-19372-330	
SI	65-25332-8	
SI	65-57449-804,772	
	65-58068-397 p102,510	
SI	65-58236-1153, 1258 p82,	
SI	563 p3,4,5. 7 thru 17, 19, 20, 21,23 Thru 39, 41 thru 45, 47	
I	65-59242-196	
SI	65-59312-415	
SI	65-59324-79	
I	65-59336-192, 3, 21 p13, 5,6,7,8, 9,14,19, 20, 21,22, 28	
SI	65-60203-128	
0!		

Document 22.

("six-way search"). However, when the search is being made in order to fulfill an FOIA request, rather than because the FBI wants information for an investigation, the clerk is expected only to look for the exact name listed as the "subject" of the search ("on the nose search").

In principle, when a number on a search slip has two parts (e.g., "65-59242") it refers to a main case file ("cf"); three part numbers (e.g., "100-342427-7") are "see references." (See material on numbering documents and on General Index in Ch. I.) However, the FBI indices occasionally appear to list people as "see refs" in their own main files. Document 21 lists the main file on this individual four times, as it was found in the General Index under four variants of her name.

After the searcher lists the references from the indices, a file reviewer goes to the actual files to determine whether the references do indeed pertain to the subject on whom information is sought. The file reviewer often writes "I" ("identical") if the information does pertain; "NI" if it does not. ("SI" appears here to mean "same information"; that is, the serial marked "SI" contains no information on the subject that was not contained in a previously listed serial.) A main case file which pertains to the subject is usually starred by the file reviewer.

Document 23: Front Page of Correlation Summary

A "correlation summary" is often prepared when an exceptionally large number of "see refs" has accumulated under an individual's name. This particular "correlation summary" was prepared at Headquarters, but field offices write them as well. Naturally, the "see refs" examined in preparing the summary are only those contained in the FBI office making the summary. After all the "see refs" have been summarized, the "see ref" index cards are supposed to be destroyed.

References to this individual were found under 14 variations of his name. This underscores the need to have the FBI search its indices under all "logical variations" of a name, if the search is to uncover all indexed references to an individual.

Documents 24, 25 and 26: Forms Justifying Withholding of Documents

A court order in the litigation to obtain the Rosenberg case files required that "itemized, detailed, cross-referenced refusal justifications for those documents which defendants (i.e., the FBI) are withholding in their entirety shall accompany the inventory applying to said documents." Instead of complying with the order, the FBI provided thousands of standard forms like Documents 24 and 25, simply filling in the blank spaces left for file number, subject, serial, date, and number of pages. The forms, pitifully inadequate as they are, are more than one usually receives without a court order. Document 26 is an equally uninformative form which the FBI apparently began to use in 1979.

140

CORRELATION SUMMARY

Main File No.: 65-\#####

Date: 5/31/74

Subject: ####################

Date Searched: 3/21/73

All logical variations of subject's name and aliases were searched
and identical references were found as:

######### , ########
######### , ######
######### , #####
######### , #########
######### , #########
######### , #########
######### , #########

######## , #####
######## , #######
######## , ######
######## , #######
######## , ########
######## , ########

7-28-72

This is a summary of information obtained from a review of
all "see" references to the subject in Bureau files under the names
and aliases listed above. All references under these names containing data identical with the subject have been included except any
indicated at the end of this summary under the heading REFERENCES
NOT INCLUDED IN SUMMARY. References indicated in the block as SI
contain the same information as the foregoing serial although the
information may have been received from a different source.

THIS SUMMARY HAS BEEN PREPARED FOR USE AT FBI HEADQUARTERS
AND IS NOT SUITABLE FOR DISSEMINATION. IT IS DESIGNED TO FURNISH A
SYNOPSIS OF THE INFORMATION SET OUT IN EACH REFERENCE AND IN MANY
CASES THE ORIGINAL SERIAL WILL CONTAIN THE INFORMATION IN MORE
DETAIL.

Analyst	Supervisory Clerk	Approved

SIW,CLF:zih

MCI

b7c

65- ########-297

Classified by 4913   3 JUN 5 1974
Exempt from GDS Category 2,3
Date of Declassification Indefinite

Document 23.

FILE #   100-37158

SUBJECT   MORTON SOBELL

SERIAL   *2496*   DATE *5-26-67*

CONSISTING OF   *1*   PAGES

is exempt from disclosure, in its entirety,
under (b)(1) as it has been classified pursuant
to Executive Order 11652 as it contains
information which would disclose an intelligence
source. This serial bears the Classification
Officers number ▨

Document 24.

142

FILE #   100-107111

SUBJECT   ROSENBERG/SOBELL COMMITTEE

SERIAL **3382A** DATE **1-26-59**

CONSISTING OF   **6**   PAGES

is exempt from disclosure, in its entirety,
under (b)(7)(D) as information contained in
this serial would identify an informant to
whom an expressed promise of confidentiality
has been given. This information includes
dates and places of meetings which were
attended by a limited number of people known
to the informant and/or information from these
meetings and situations in which an informant
was in close contact with members of these
organizations, disclosure of which would reveal
his identity.

Document 25.

2 Page(s) withheld entirely at this location in the file. One or more of the following statements, where indicated, explain this deletion.

☑ Deleted under exemption(s) (b)(7)(c) , (b)(7)(D) with no segregable material available for release to you.

☐ Information pertained only to a third party with no reference to you or the subject of your request.

☐ Information pertained only to a third party. Your name is listed in the title only.

☐ Document(s) originating with the following government agency(ies) _____
_____ , was/were forwarded to them for direct response to you.

_____ Page(s) referred for consultation to the following government agency(ies); _____
_____ as the information originated with them. You will be advised of availability upon return of the material to the FBI.

_____ Page(s) withheld for the following reason(s):
_____
_____

☐ For your information: _____
_____

☐ The following number is to be used for reference regarding these pages:
100-23881-13, pages 3+4

XXXXX
XXXXX
XXXXX

```
XXXXXXXXXXXXXXXXXX
X   DELETED PAGE(S)    X
X NO DUPLICATION FEE X
X    FOR THIS PAGE     X
XXXXXXXXXXXXXXXXXX
```

FBI/DOJ

Document 26.

144

The FBI form for (b) (1) withholdings implies, quite incorrectly, that under Nixon's Executive Order 11652, the fact that information would disclose an intelligence source is sufficient grounds for classifying that information. (See the section of Ch. II on the national security information exemption for discussion of the Executive Orders regarding classifications.) The Classification Officer's number is deleted from Document 24. In many cases where this occurs, the document in fact bears no Classification Officer's number and appears not to be actually classified.

Document 27: "Document Justification" Sheet

In a very few volumes in the Rosenberg case files, the FBI prepared sheets such as this. Though more detailed than the forms illustrated by Documents 24-26, they are not much more useful, because they too utilize formulaic language that remains unchanged regardless of its frequent inappropriateness. This particular "Document Justification" sheet is a composite of two pages. Most of the sources protected by (b) (7) (d) were friends or associates of the subject of the investigation. For example, page six of serial 119 contains the passage: "Several (deleted) were contacted. All of them stated that they had known Mrs. Gurewitz casually for several years, and that they regarded her as a loyal citizen. They furnished no derogatory information regarding her." It is improbable that these "informants" could be identified from the missing information. In any case, they were casually contacted more than 30 years ago and there is no reason whatever to think, as the "Document Justification" sheet implies, that the FBI is continuing to make use of these sources even up to the present.

This document is supposed to be the sort of detailed, factual justification required under a "Vaughn Index" (see Glossary). It is obviously not.

Document 28: Classification Review Memo

The FBI normally refuses to release such classification review memoranda, but "mistakenly" provided several of them in the Rosenberg case. The first page is from the "Disclosure Section" of the FBI FOI/PA Branch, to the "Document Classification Review Unit" (CRU). The "Disclosure Section" analyst lists those serials which he feels may require classification. On the second page, the CRU reviewer (a "classification officer") has written his decisions on which currently classified serials should be declassified, and which currently unclassified serials do not warrant classification. Page three lists the precise sections of serials that the classification officer has allegedly classified. The term "Brackets" in the "Paragraph" column means that the classified information on the page has been bracketed. "XGDS Category"

Serial Number	Date of Serial	DELETION (S)
117 with one copy	8/7/50	No exemptions were cited.
118	10/27/49	(b)(7)(D) - This exemption was cited on page 3 to protect the date information was furnished by a source for which an expressed or implied promise of confidentiality has been given. In addition, the designation of informant symbols were withheld on this page to protect the identity of sources who had been assured of complete confidentiality. To release this information would also compromise the further effectiveness of these sources.
119	11/14/44	(b)(7)(D) - This exemption was cited on pages 4, 5, 6, 9 and 10 to protect the identities of sources for which an expressed or implied promise of confidentiality has been given. The release of this information would disclose the identity of these sources. In addition, the designation of informant
		symbol numbers were withheld on page 9 to protect the identity of sources who had been assured of complete confidentiality. To release this information would also compromise the further effectiveness of these sources.
120	4/25/44	(b)(7)(C) - The name of a third party was withheld on page 4 to the extent that the release of this information would constitute an unwarranted invasion of personal privacy.
		(b)(7)(D) - The designation of informant symbol numbers were withheld on pages 1, 2, 3 and 5 to protect the identity of sources who had been assured of complete confidentiality. To release this information would also compromise the further effectiveness of these sources. In addition, this exemption was cited on pages 2 and 5 to protect the identities of and information furnished by sources for which an expressed or implied promise of confidentiality has been given. The release of this information would disclose the identity of these sources.

Document 27.

4-50 (Rev. 9-23-76)

UNITED STATES GOVERNMENT

Memorandum

TO : Chief, Operations Section
     (Attn: Document Classification
     Review Unit)
FROM : Chief, Disclosure Section

DATE:

SUBJECT: FREEDOM OF INFORMATION-PRIVACY ACTS
    REQUEST OF   MEEROPOL V. BELL (CIVIL ACTION # 75-1121)

RE: ROSENBERG; ET AL

Attached records are presently:

☐ Classified   ☐ Both

☐ Unclassified   ☑ Particular attention
                       is directed to serials _____

After reviewing these records to determine if

classification is presently warranted, it is requested

you indicate your determination hereon, and return this

form and the records to the following:

Unit   **F**

Team   **2**

Attention   RICK SABEL

Room   6383

Ext   5776

Volume 30

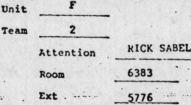

1610, 1611, 1612, 1614, 1615, 1616, 1617, 1618, 1619, 1627, 1631, 1632, 1636, 1647, 1649, 1650, 1655, 1657, 1659, 1660, 1662, 1663, 1665, 1665ᐟ, 1665ᴮ, 1665ᴱ, 1665ᶠ, 1665ᴳ, 1665ᴴ, 1665ᴵ, 1666, 1667, 1668, 1670, 1672, 1673, 1674, 1675, 1676, 1677, 1679, 1680, 1682, 1683, 1684, 1685, 1694, 1699, 1700, 1704, 1704, 1705, 1709, 1711, 1712, 1713, 1720, 1722, 1723, 1726, 1729, 1736, 1737

Document 28-1.

Memorandum to ~~the~~ *Chief Operations Section*
Re: Freedom of Information-Privacy Acts (FOIPA)
Request RE: *MORTON SOBELL set. 30*

ADDENDUM: DOCUMENT CLASSIFICATION REVIEW UNIT : *12/6/77*

Reviewer: *R. HASYCHAR(?)* Ext.: *3726*

The following documents have been declassified:

FILE NUMBER | SERIAL NUMBER
100-37158 | *1737*

The following documents need additional review:
(Additional comments re excisions and impact on ongoing
investigations.) *The following serials are unclassified
and do not warrant classification: 1610, 1611, 1612, 1614,
1615, 1616, 1617, 1618, 1619, 1627, 1631, 1632, 1636, 1647, 1649,
1650, 1655, 1657, 1659, 1660, 1662, 1662(attachment), 1665, 1665A,
1665B, 1665E, 1665F, 16656, 1665H, 1665I, 1666, 1667, 1668,
1670, 1672, 1673, 1674, 1675, 1676, 1679, 1680, 1682, 1683, 1684,
1685, 1694, 1699, 1700, 1701, 1704, 1705, 1709, 1711, 1712, 1713, 1722,*

~~████~~ *, 1729, 1736;*

serial 1726 was not in file.

4 AGENT/CLERICAL TIME EXPENDED FOR THIS REVIEW WAS
HOURS.

Document 28-2.

148

The following records have been reviewed and the following classification determinations made for each serial. All serials not specifically listed remain unclassified.

FILE/SERIAL	PAGE	PARAGRAPH	CLASSIFICATION	XGDS CATEGORY
100-37158/1663	2	2	CONFIDENTIAL	2
100-37158/1677	2	4	CONFIDENTIAL	2
100-37158/1720	1	1	SECRET	2,3
100-37158/1612	1	BRACKETS	CONFIDENTIAL	2
100-37158/1723	1	1	SECRET	1
" "	2	TEXT	SECRET	1

Document 28-3.

149

indicates the exemption from the general declassification schedule (effective under EO 11652) which the reviewer believes is applicable. (See the section of Ch. II on the national security information exemption for discussion of the Executive Orders governing classified information.) It is useful to obtain the FBI classification review memos, in order to verify that information claimed exempt under FOIA exemption (b) (1) has been classified.

Document 29: Document Classified Under Carter's Executive Order

President Carter's Executive Order 12065 is the current basis for classifying information. It is described at some length in Ch. II. Documents classified by the FBI under this order bear a stamp like the one found here centered near the top of the page ("Classified and extended . . . "). (Documents classified under Nixon's E.O. 11652 bear a stamp like the one seen on the bottom left of Document 12.) "FCIM, 11, 1-2.4.2" evidently refers to FBI regulations concerning reasons for extending classification past six years. (See Section 1-502 of Carter's order.) It is not uncommon for the content of an allegedly "released" document to be annihilated as this document's content was.

Documents 30 and 31: "National Security" Interview

These are two copies of the same letter. Document 30 is from the NY file on the subject of this document; Document 31 is from the HQ file. This letter was sent from Headquarters ("Director, FBI") to the New Orleans field office ("SAC, New Orleans"). New York, however, also received 3 copies, as noted on the bottom of the document.

The information deleted under (b) (1) (the "national security" exemption) in Document 30 appears, almost untouched, in Document 31. This is *not* because the information was declassified but simply because the FBI couldn't keep track of whether information was or was not classified. FBI slipups such as this establish how farcical many of its "national security" deletions really are. The information deleted in Document 30 was released in Document 31, but no one can seriously maintain that "national security" was damaged by release of this information. Note that neither 30 nor 31 carries any classification markings, and hence that neither seems to have been classified. (The (b) (1) exemption is applicable only to classified information.)

Document 32: "National Security" Informant Report

This document, like Document 12, is an "SA to SAC" memo. The first page is in effect a "cover page" for an informant's report, and the second page is a copy of the report. (See Documents 10 and 11). This

SAC, NEW YORK

DIRECTOR, FBI

■■■■■■ - S
ESPIONAGE - R
Bufile 65-5,068

February 3, 1950

CLASSIFIED AND
EXTENDED BY 1259 SSP/JAN 12-13-78
REASON FOR EXTENSION 2
FCIM, II, 1-2.4.2
DATE OF REVIEW FOR
DECLASSIFICATION 12-13-88

PERSONAL ATTENTION

(S)

(S)

(S)

CC: Boston
    Los Angeles
    San Francisco
    Washington Field Office

65-3370-26

3 1950

Document 29-1.

151

Document 29-2.

152

SAC, New Orleans   September 29, 194?

Director, FBI

##########################
ESPIONAGE - R
(Bufile 65-50259)
(New Orleans file 100-14800)

########### ################
SECURITY MATTER - C
(Bufile 100-398493)
(New Orleans file 100-14890)

　　　　　Reference is made to New York letter dated
June 30, 1952, Albuquerque letter dated August 8, 1952,
and New Orleans letter dated August 26, 1952, recommending that an interview be conducted with ##############.

　　　　　The New Orleans Office is authorized to
conduct interviews with ############## and her husband,
###########################, concerning all knowledge
they have of ########################'s brother of #####
#######.

b1

CC - 3 - New York   (65-15773; 100-109189)

65-15773-132

100-109189

Document 30.

153

SAC, New Orleans   September 22, 1952

Director, FBI

##########################
ESPIONAGE - F
(Bufile 65-60359)
(New Orleans file 100-14800)

###########, ################
SECURITY MATTER - C
(Bufile 100-388493)   G. I. R. 3
(New Orleans file 100-14870)

65-60359-   47

Reference is made to New York letter dated
June 30, 1952, Albuquerque letter dated August 8, 1952,
and New Orleans letter dated August 26, 1952, recommending that an interview be conducted with ############.

        The New Orleans Office is authorized to
conduct interviews with ############ and her husband,
############################, concerning all knowledge
they have of ###############################, brother .. #####
#######.

        These interviews should be conducted by
two experienced agents, one of whom should be well
acquainted with the facts of both captioned cases,
and extreme care should be exercised to avoid
jeopardizing information furnished by [redacted]
and information furnished by Confidential Informant
        These interviews should be conducted in
accordance with existing Bureau instructions relating
to interviews of subjects of security cases. In
addition, these interviews should be planned carefully
in order to develop as much information as possible
concerning the past and present activities of ###########
########.

CC - 3 - New York (65-15770; 100-109189)

JPL:mem
CC - 100-388493

Document 31.

154

SAC, NEW YORK (100-107111) (411)   3/3/61

SA ▓▓▓▓▓▓▓▓▓▓▓▓▓▓▓▓▓ 422) b7C

NATIONAL COMMITTEE TO SECURE JUSTICE FOR
MORTON SOBELL
IS-C

Identity of Source: ▓▓▓▓▓▓▓▓▓▓▓▓▓▓▓▓▓▓▓ b1

Description of info: SOBELL Luncheon at Brighton
                             Beach Community Center,
                             3200 Coney Island Ave.,
                             B'klyn, NY, on 2/12/61.

Date Received: 2/17/61

Original located: ▓▓▓▓▓▓▓▓▓▓▓▓▓ b1

A copy of informant's report follows:

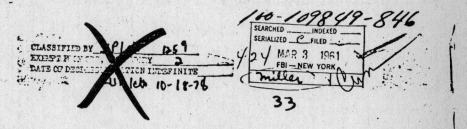

b1

1 - New York (100-26693-C43) (NCCF) (422)
1 - New York (100-119910) (BRIGHTON BEACH COMMUNITY CENTER) (422)
1 - New York (100-109649) (HELEN SOBELL) (424)
1 - New York (100-) (MORTON SOBELL) ( )
1 - New York (100-67344) (################) (42)
1 - New York (100-67348) (.################) (42)
1 - New York (100-107111) (411)

CMH:tmb
(8)

100-109849-846

SEARCHED _____ INDEXED _____
SERIALIZED __C__ FILED _____

4/24   MAR 3 1961
       FBI—NEW YORK

miller

33

CLASSIFIED BY ▓▓▓▓ DS9
EXEMPT ▓▓▓▓▓▓ ▓▓▓▓
DATE OF DECL▓▓▓▓▓▓TION INDEFINITE
▓▓▓▓ 10-18-78

Document 32-1.

155

SOBELL luncheon, Sunday, Feb. 12, 1961

Began at 1 pm. Admittance $1.50

About 60 in attendance, 40 of whom were over 50 years of age and the other 20 were from 35 to 50.

A woman was M/C - whitehaired, about 60. Everyone seemed to know her.

She introduced woman who sangtwo spirituals, then introduced HELEN SOBELL.

Mrs. SOBELL spoke of efforts being made and work being done. Said there was a changed atmosphere in Washington and she had hopes the new administration would listen with some favor SOBELL's plea for freedom. She said that at least she was not meeting a stone wall.

The NYC introduced two more singers (local) and then Mrs SOBELL described MORT SOBELL's life in prison.

b/

b/

During the collection the name of ############### was heard as donating $2.

The name of the man singer was ############.

A circular was distributed, one of which is attached.

-2-

NY 100-107111

3 petitions were circulated

a. against sedition laws.
b. against lifting rent control.
c. For friendship with Cuba.

The luncheon ended at 3:30 pm. Brighton Community Center
3200 Coney Island Ave., Brooklyn, N.Y.

-3-

Document 32-3.

memo (bottom left) carries the stamp used by the FBI in classifying documents under Nixon's Executive Order 11652. This stamp, and the word "confidential" on top and bottom, satisfies the minimal marking requirements of the Nixon order (although the second page should also carry the word "confidential," but does not). We have printed this memo in order to illustrate the FBI's invocation of the (b) (1) "national security" exemption on documents that relate solely to surveillance of legal, domestic political activity. Hundreds of similar examples of political (b) (1)s can be found in the various Rosenberg case files. The FBI's decision, in October of 1978, to classify this document means that the Bureau has not abandoned its position that investigation of such activities as "Sobell luncheons" is lawful and justified in the name of national defense and foreign relations.

Informants' reports tend not to be written in the uniformly stilted style required of agents. Even efforts at humor sometimes creep into informants' reports. The FBI assumes that it would damage national security to tell us where the original of this informant's report is kept. (Note the (b) (1) deletion of the location of the original.) Document 32, including page 2, was typed by the FBI, not by the informant. (Remember that FBI agents do not type; all their communications are dictated for typing by clerical personnel.) Informants' reports are often more detailed than this one, and tend to be replete with names. It is common for larger meetings to be covered by several informants, at least one of whom may tape record the proceedings. It is probably the lack of detail on this informant's report that accounts for our receiving most of it. A more detailed report, or one dealing with a smaller meeting, might be more heavily censored on the grounds that it would reveal information which would lead to the identification of the informant.

CHAPTER V

A GLOSSARY OF TERMS, ABBREVIATIONS AND SYMBOLS

Introduction

FBI documents contain a daunting profusion of code words, symbols, acronyms, catch phrases, names of administrative units, and the like. The entries in this chapter are intended primarily as aids to deciphering these obscure terms. More generally, we have identified expressions wherever we felt it would aid understanding of the FBI and of the FBI's place in the "intelligence community." Thus, many entries are staples of FBI written communications, some appear in documents only rarely, and some — for example, FBI colloquialisms — appear not at all.

The focus is on the FBI's politically motivated operations, but some terms from the "criminal" (as opposed to the "security") side of FBI investigations have also been listed. We have slighted many "intelligence" terms which are primarily used by agencies other than the FBI. This means that few terms concerning cryptology, military intelligence, or the CIA are included. For a glossary that partially fills these gaps, see Book I of the Final Report of the Church Committee.[1]

Another gap in the Glossary is the absence of name of individuals and non-governmental organizations. The inclusion of these items would not have been sufficiently valuable to warrant the enormous space it would have demanded. FBI abbreviations for private groups are rarely esoteric and in any case are frequently explained in FBI documents themselves. Although a few FBI organizational abbreviations are explained in the commentary to Document 2 in Chapter IV, the general rule is that unless a personal name is in some way an FBI code or catch phrase (e.g., "Gregory") it has not been included. We have been most concerned to include terms whose definitions are not readily obtainable from other published sources.

Our sources were varied. The many thousands of pages of FBI documents released from the files bearing on the Rosenberg/Sobell case were our major primary source. We also drew upon the reams of depositions, affidavits, and other proceedings which the suit to obtain the Rosenberg/Sobell files generated. Bonnie Brower, one of the attorneys in the suit to obtain these files, was particularly helpful in our effort to build a glossary.

Most of the published sources cited in the Bibliography also proved helpful. Of particular value were the General Accounting Office reports on the FBI, Books II and III of the Church Committee Final Reports, and Sanford Ungar's book *FBI*. Ungar's excellent book contains a glossary which is much shorter than, and differently focused from, ours. Definitions which we have borrowed from Ungar are identified by an "*."

The reader is cautioned that, despite the authors' efforts to ensure accuracy, the truth about an agency as secretive as the FBI is sometimes all but impossible to uncover.

The main Glossary is followed by a short list of some terms whose meaning and significance are still unknown to us. We hope that our readers will be able to help us shorten this list even more.

GLOSSARY

A-2: Intelligence Staff section of U.S. Army Air Corps. Established 1940.

AAG: Assistant Attorney General.

Abdul Enterprises: Fictitious company invented by FBI for "Operation Abscam," which see.

Abstract System: Summaries of documents, maintained at FBI HQ. See Ch. I.

Action Memo: In connection with FOIA appeals, a DOJ memo recommending action to be taken by a DOJ component such as the FBI.

AD: Assistant Director.

Add. Info.: On a correlation summary, means "additional information" — that is, some information is not being summarized because it can be found in the main file or at another place in the correlation summary.

ADEX: Administrative Index. Initiated 1971 to circumvent repeal of Emergency Detention Act, it originally contained names which had previously been on Security Index and Reserve Index, and FBI assumed it could be used as a basis for detention in an emergency. Maintained at Headquarters and 29 field offices. Field offices reopened all ADEX cases periodically to verify addresses and determine if continued inclusion on ADEX was warranted. Was computerized 1972. Discontinued 1/76. See Ch. IV, Doc. 2.

ADIC: Assistant Director in Charge. The largest field offices (Los Angeles and New York) are headed by ADICs. The SACs in these offices are under the ADICs.

ADM: Administrative. The FBI distinguishes "administrative" from "investigative" matters, but many administrative matters directly concern the procedures to be followed and techniques to be employed in an investigation. All "134" (security informant) files are supposed to have "ADM" and "INV" sections.

Administrative Appeal: Under FOIA, requesters can appeal any agency's refusal to release information. "Office of Privacy and Information Appeals," DOJ, handles appeals related to FBI. Such appeals do not involve suing the government for release of information.

Administrative Closing:
1. Closing of a criminal case on which no suspects were developed and all

logical leads were exhausted.

2. If FOI/PA requester to FBI provides insufficient identifying information, fails to have his/her signature notarized, or fails to remit required fee, FBI asks requester to remedy problem. If requester doesn't respond within 60 days, FBI "administratively closes" case, but reopens it if requester responds.

Administrative Index: See "ADEX."

Administrative Pages: Generally found at the end of FBI reports, they are intended to be kept within the FBI even when the remainder of the report is disseminated to another government agency. They typically contain identifications of "T"-sources, information on investigative leads, and references to previous FBI communications. Most of the information contained in "Administrative Pages" is *not* exempt from release under the FOIA. Information typical of "Administrative Pages" is sometimes placed instead on "Cover Pages" at the beginning of reports. See "Report."

Administrative Report: Not used after 4/20/51. Apparently, FBI reports containing solely information normally placed on "Administrative Pages" of reports. Like Administrative Pages of standard reports, "Administrative Reports" were not meant for dissemination outside FBI. See "Report."

AEA-A; AEA-E: Atomic Energy Act-Applicant; Atomic Energy Act-Employee. FBI cases having classification number "116" are characterized as AEA-A or AEA-E cases, and are considered "applicant" (rather than "subversive" or "criminal") investigations.

AEC: Atomic Energy Commission. Established 1946. Replaced by ERDA and Nuclear Regulatory Commission (NRC), 1/75.

AFSA: Armed Forces Security Agency. Predecessor to "NSA," which see.

AG: Attorney General.

Agent: All FBI agents are called Special Agents (SAs). Most FBI employees are considered either clerks or SAs. Informants, even if paid, are not considered agents or even employees, although SAs are occasionally listed as "informants" in reports. SAs conduct and supervise investigations. In 1978, FBI had 7,924 SAs.

Agent's Handbook: An abridgement of the "Manual of Instructions" and "Manual of Rules and Regulations," it is received by each FBI agent. Includes detailed instructions on initiating, conducting and reporting subversive and extremist investigations.

Agent's Notes: Are often destroyed without being filed. The "substance" of these notes will be reported in typed memos, letters, etc. if considered sufficiently important. However, notes of surveillances seem usually to be retained and filed.

Aggressive Investigation: Term sometimes used by FBI for COINTELPRO-type actions.

Agitator Index: Until March, 1968, called the "Rabble-Rouser Index," which see. Also see "ADEX."

AI: Agitator Index. See "Rabble-Rouser Index."

AIRTEL: An internal FBI communication, urgent enough that it must be typed on the day it is dictated, but routine enough to be sent by airmail rather than teletype.*

AKA: Also known as. Small variations in an individual's name sometimes count as "AKA"s, e.g., "John Doe aka John R. Doe."

AL: Albany Field Office

Alien Act of 1918: Passed "to exclude and expel from the United States aliens who are members of the anarchistic classes." Was the legal excuse used for "Red raids" undertaken by Attorney General Palmer and the GID.

American Legion Contact Program: 11/40-8/54. Used American Legion members as unpaid sources on "domestic security" matters in their communities. FBI contact with American Legion continued after termination of program.

AMSD: Air Mail Special Delivery.

AN: Anchorage Field Office.

Analysts: In FBI FOI/PA Branch, the personnel who make initial decisions as to what information to release to a requester. Analysts are not agents, but work in teams headed by agents.

Analytical Summary: Similar to search slip. At least sometimes, used in preparation of correlation summary.

Anonymous Source: Common FBI euphemism for illegal investigative technique (e.g., black bag).

AO: Auxiliary Office.

APB: All points bulletin.

APL: American Protective League. Formed during WWI as citizen auxiliary to Bureau of Investigation.

Applicant Investigation: Concerns applicants to, or employees of, federal agencies. "Applicant," "criminal," and "security" investigations are the three main types of FBI investigation, and are kept fairly distinct from each other. See "Executive orders 9835, 10450," "Federal Employee Loyalty-Security Program."

Apps: Applicant investigations.

AQ: Albuquerque Field Office.

ARL: Anti-Riot Laws.

ARMS: Automated Records Management System. FBI program to automate mail processing, index searching, and file inventory and control. Not implemented as of 1978.

ASA: Army Security Agency.

ASAC: Assistant Special Agent in Charge — the agent who is second in command of a field office.

Asset: Counterintelligence term for informant.

Assistant Director: Head each Division of FBI Headquarters, and NY and LA field offices. Three additional Assistant Directors were appointed 8/79 to replace Associate Director.

Assistant to the Director: Also called Deputy Associate Director. One of two high-level FBI officials. The Assistant Directors of the investigative divisions report to the "Assistant to the Director (Investigation)."

162

Associate Director: The second in command of FBI. Replaced by three executive "Assistant Directors," 8/79.

Asst. D.: Assistant Director, which see.

AT: Atlanta Field Office.

ATIO: Adjusted Time in Office. Listed on " 'Number 3' Card." Agents are allowed to subtract from "TIO" time spent in conferences or special projects. This becomes "ATIO."

Att. C.F.: Probably means "Attach Case File."

Attorney General's List: List of "subversive" organizations, drawn up pursuant to Executive Orders 9835 and 10450. The FBI justified much of its political surveillance on grounds that the Attorney General (AG) needed the information to draw up his list. However, this attempted justification was used long after 1955, when the AG stopped adding names. Formally abolished 6/74. See "Thumbnail Sketch."

Attorney General's 1976 Guidelines: Established framework for FBI intelligence. Cover "FBI Domestic Security Investigations," "FBI Reporting on Civil Disorders and Demonstrations Involving a Federal Interest," and "FBI Use of Informants in Domestic Security, Organized Crime, and Other Criminal Investigations." The guidelines for foreign intelligence and counterintelligence investigations have not been made public. Guidelines for "FBI White House Personnel Security and Background Investigations" were not formally imposed on FBI but are allegedly substantially followed.

Attorney General's Portfolio Plan: A secret plan, in operation from 1948 until the mid 1960s, which provided for the detention, during a declared national emergency, of U.S. citizens deemed to be threats to the government. Building on an indexing system developed by the FBI during the 1920s Red Scare, a "Custodial Detention List" was established by the FBI in 1939 despite lack of statutory authorization. In 1943, Attorney General Biddle pointed out its illegality and ordered its use terminated. This order was ignored by J. Edgar Hoover, who simply changed the name to "Security Index." In 1948 the system and the Security Index were revived as the "Attorney General's Portfolio." The plan also called for the suspension of the writ of habeas corpus and the use of a master search warrant. This plan was not known to the public, Congress, or the Judiciary. Of the three copies of the plan, two were held by the FBI and one by the Attorney General. See "Security Index."

AUSA: Assistant U.S. Attorney — a member of the prosecutorial staff of a particular federal district.

Auxiliary Office: The field offices that perform only a supporting, not controlling, role in an investigation. Typically, they pursue individual leads at the request of Headquarters or the field office controlling the investigation. See "OO."

AX: Alexandria Field Office.

B.: In informal FBI parlance, "the B." is "the Bureau" (that is, FBI Headquarters).

(b) (1): Section of FOIA which allows agencies to exempt from disclosure any material currently properly classified pursuant to executive order. The so-called "national security exemption," (b) (1), is perhaps the most abused exemption by the FBI. See "Classified Information"; "Executive Order 12065."

(b) (2): FOIA exemption permitting withholding of matters relating solely to internal personnel rules and practices. Prior to 5/77, FBI deleted almost all administrative markings (e.g. file numbers, distortion of copies of documents, etc.) under (b) (2). FBI claims to use (b) (2) less now. See "High 2 Material"; "Low 2 Material."

(b) (5): FOIA exemption applying to inter- or intra-agency communications which would not be available by law to a party other than an agency in litigation with the agency. Used by FBI to withhold Secret Service forms (FD-376) and sometimes agents' opinions and recommendations. (b) (5) is apparently no longer invoked extensively by FBI.

(b) (7) (A): FOIA exemption, permits withholding of law enforcement records where release would interfere with law enforcement proceedings. Generally used by FBI for pending cases; cases where there is possibility of prosecution; and closed cases which affect ongoing investigations. Even on pending cases, FBI is required to release segregable portions of records, but it often fails to do so.

(b) (7) (C): Investigatory records, compiled for law enforcement purposes, disclosure of which would constitute unwarranted invasion of the personal privacy of another person; "(b) (7) (C)" refers to the section of the FOIA that exempts these matters from disclosure.

(b) (7) (D): Investigatory records compiled for law enforcement purposes are exempt from disclosure to the extent that production of such records would disclose the identity of a confidential source, and in the case of a record compiled by a criminal law enforcement authority in the course of a criminal investigation, or by an agency conducting a lawful national security intelligence investigation, disclose confidential information furnished only by the confidential source. "(b) (7) (D)" refers to the section of the FOIA that exempts these matters from disclosure.

(b) (7) (E): FOIA exemption, permits withholding of law enforcement records which would reveal secret techniques and procedures. FBI manual requires release of references to discontinued and/or illegal techniques. Techniques not revealed sometimes include mail covers, pretext phone calls and interviews, trash covers, stop notices, and photo albums.

BA: Baltimore Field Office.

Bag: See "Black Bag Job."

BB: Bank Burglary. FBI "91" case.

Bed to Bed FISUR: Dawn to dusk physical surveillance of a "subject," that is, of a target of investigation.

BEX: Black Extremist.

BH: Birmingham Field Office.

Bicycle: An FBI agent "on the bicycle" is one whom the FBI subjects to frequent transfers from office to office to force a resignation.

Big Manual: The FBI Manual of Instructions and/or the Manual of Rules and Regulations, informally so-called to differentiate it from the "Agent's Handbook."

BL: Bank Larceny. FBI "91" case.

Black Bag Job: Warrantless surreptitious entry by FBI especially for purposes other than microphone installation, e.g., physical search or photographing or seizing documents. Hoover partially banned "black bags" in 1966, but some continued, and ban did not affect surreptitious entries to install microphones.

Black Nationalist-Hate Groups: An FBI COINTELPRO, initiated 8/67 to "expose, disrupt, misdirect, discredit, or otherwise neutralize" the activities of such groups and of members and supporters of such groups. The targets included moderate nonviolent groups and individuals. Allegedly discontinued 1971.

Black Nationalist Photograph Album: List of prominent black leaders who travelled extensively, established 1968. Pictures and biographies were distributed to all field offices. All subjects of "Key Black Extremist Program" were placed in BNPA.

Blind Memo: Memo stripped of identifying markings. The memo will not indicate that it originated with the FBI.

Block Stamp: On the bottom right corner of the front page of most FBI documents, indicates which FBI office document is filed in, and date of handling by clerks. Clerks check off, where appropriate, the words "searched," "serialized," "filed," or "indexed."

Blue Memo: FBI communication on blue paper, destroyed without being filed.

Blue Slip: Voucher for use of confidential FBI funds. See "FD-37."

"Blue Slip" Funds: Funds from which FBI informants are paid.

BNDD: Bureau of Narcotics and Dangerous Drugs, formed in 1968. Was replaced by DEA.

BNPA: Black Nationalist Photograph Album, which see.

Book Agent: FBI slang for exceptionally zealous agent.

BOSSI: Non-FBI abbreviation for Bureau of Special Services and Investigations. See "BSS."

BR Matters: Bank Robbery Matters. FBI file classification "91."

Brick Agent: FBI agent who works "on the bricks" (i.e., conducts investigations) and has not risen in FBI hierarchy (is not supervisor, ASAC, etc.).

Brilab: FBI "Bribery-Labor" undercover operation, begun Spring 1979 and made public 2/80. FBI supposedly set up a dummy business and paid thousands of dollars in bribes in an investigation of organized crime and political corruption in the South and Southwest.

BS: Boston Field Office.

BSS, BSSI: Bureau of Special Services and Investigations, NYC Police Department; has worked closely with FBI on domestic intelligence.

BSU: Black Student Union.

BT: Butte Field Office.

BU: Buffalo Field Office.

Buded: Bureau deadline.

BUFIL: Bureau files; files located and maintained in the Washington D.C. FBI Headquarters.

BUG: Usually called "MISUR" (microphone surveillance) or "ELSUR" (electronic surveillance) by FBI. A concealed listening device or microphone.

Buildups and Variations: Similar to "Six-Way Search," which see.

Bulky Exhibits: Material gathered in the course of an investigation, which does not fit or is too valuable to be kept in a standard-size file, is kept in a "bulky exhibit room" filed by case number. Usually, documents in the main file will explain the exact location of bulky exhibits associated with the file. (See "Green Sheets").

Bureau: An FBI term used primarily to indicate FBI Headquarters in Washington, D.C., but sometimes refers to the FBI in general.

Bureau Bulletin No. : Apparently similar to "SAC Letter No. ," which see.

Bureau of Intelligence and Research (INR): Coordinates intelligence programs for Department of State.

Bureau of Investigation: Established in 1908 as a Justice Department police force. Was later renamed Division of Investigation. In 1935, it became the Federal Bureau of Investigation (FBI).

Bureau Supervisors: FBI agents assigned to HQ are generally called "Supervisors." In principle, field offices must notify HQ any time a full-scale investigation is undertaken, and must report within 90 days on the progress of the investigation. Bureau Supervisors have primary responsibility for reading these reports and deciding whether to approve field office recommendations concerning further action on the cases. However, the Bureau Supervisor's approval is reviewed by his unit chief and section chief before becoming official. See "Unit."

C: 1. As in, "Security Matter—C," means Communist.

2. Found alongside a text, means "confidential," a security classification authorized by Executive Order. See the section of Ch. II on the national security information exemption.

3. Following a source number (e.g., "PH 237-C") means informant on criminal matters. "C*" is often a source unavailable to testify, e.g., a black bag.

4. At end of report, or after file number is listed in document heading, means case is "closed." However, closed files are frequently reopened and documents added.

Capbom: FBI code name for investigation of 3/1/71 bombing of U.S. Capitol.

Caption: The titles of FBI files are often called their "captions." Most FBI documents also have captions, and the original copy of a document will almost always be filed in a file having the same caption as the document.

Case File: Same as "main file."

Case Number: Number after classification number in FBI file number. Sometimes means entire file number.

Cato: FBI code name for microphone surveillance of journalist Joseph Kraft.

CC: 1. Carbon copy.

2. Chief Clerk, which see.

CCH: Computerized Criminal Histories. NCIC files give immediate access to entire criminal record on individuals.

CDG: Civil Disturbance Group, established 7/69 to coordinate Justice Department intelligence on civil disturbances.

CE: Charlotte Field Office.

Central Index: Synonym for "General Index."

Central Intelligence Agency: See "CIA."

Central Intelligence Group: See "CIG."

Central Records System: The principal filing system of FBI Headquarters and of each field office. See Chapter I.

CF: Case File.

CG: Chicago Field Office.

CGR: Crime on Government Reservation. FBI file classification "70."

CH: Appears to mean "channelized," that is, copies of the document have been sent to the appropriate locations.

Chamfering: Surreptitious mail opening.

Change-to Memo: In FBI files, indicates a document has been removed and placed in a more appropriate file. "Change-to memo" is placed where document had been. Is a more routine procedure than the "serial chargeout."

Channelizing Memo: Sometimes called "channelization memo." Directs that copies of a document be placed in ("channelized" to) various files. At least sometimes are "FD-306"s, and summarize activities of an informant as well as "channelizing" copies of informant's report to files of individuals being informed on. These memos are frequently destroyed or denied release by the FBI.

CHAOS: CIA program developed in 1966 to gather intelligence on "radical students and U.S. negro expatriates as well as others traveling abroad." Allegedly designed to uncover foreign connections of U.S. protest organizations. Produced an index of 300,000 individuals, and supplied vast amounts of information to FBI. Ended 1974.

Chargeout Slips: When a volume of a file is removed from an FBI file cabinet, a "chargeout" is supposed to be left explaining where the volume is. Such slips are destroyed when the file is returned. Differs from "Serial Chargeout," which see.

CHICOMS: Chinese Communists.

Chief Clerk: In FBI field offices, responsible for opening files, indexing documents, and routing documents to appropriate FBI employee.

Church Committee: Senate Select Committee to Study Government Operations With Respect to Intelligence Activities. Published series of "Hearings" and "Reports," 1975-76, on U.S. intelligence agencies, including FBI.

CI: 1. Confidential Informant, which see.

   2. Communist Index, which see.

   3. Cincinnati Field Office.

CIA: Central Intelligence Agency, established by National Security Act of 1947 as unit of National Security Council. Accepts FBI requests to surveill Americans traveling abroad, and shares some of its own domestic intelligence with FBI. See "CHAOS," "LP Medley."

CIC: Counter Intelligence Corps of the U.S. Army. Despite "Delimitations Agreement," undertook widespread civilian security investigations.

CIG: Central Intelligence group. Established 1946. Replaced by CIA, 1947.

CINAL: Current Intelligence Analyses. Domestic intelligence information to be disseminated to officials of the executive branch. CINAL files are control files.

CINRAD: Communist infiltration of atomic energy program.

CIP: Counterintelligence Program. See COINTELPRO.

CIRM: Communist Influence in Racial Matters. FBI intensive investigation program, initiated 1964. Used "communist influence" as excuse to intensify investigation of even the most moderate civil rights groups.

Civil Disturbance Reporting Program: By a directive of 8/64, FBI field offices were to submit bimonthly reports to HQ on the "racial situation" within their field divisions.

CL: 1. On file covers, appears to mean "closed."

      2. Civil Litigation.

Classification Number: Also called "file classification." Each FBI file is assigned a classification number (indicating type of case). See Chapter I, Appendix C.

Classification Review: The examination of a document by an individual with authority to classify, to determine whether the document is to be classified, declassified, upgraded, or downgraded.

Classification Review Unit: Within "Operations Section" of FBI FOI/PA Branch, formed 4/76, handles classification and declassification of material requested under FOI/PA. This task was previously handled by the Intelligence Division. See Chapter II.

Classified Information: According to Executive Order 12065, this is information or material "that is owned by, produced for or by, or under the control of, the United States Government, and that has been determined pursuant to this Order or prior Orders to require protection against unauthorized disclosure, and that is so designated." Before 1975, FBI did not classify material not intended to be disseminated to other agencies. However, FBI often classifies pre-1975 information when processing an FOIA request. See "(b) (1)"; "Executive Order 12065."

Classifying Unit: Not to be confused with Classification Review Unit. Determines which of 210 FBI file classification numbers applies to a document, and determines how a document is to be indexed. Except on "expedite" documents, it receives documents directly from "Routing Unit."

Clod Squad: J. Edgar Hoover allegedly once said casually to some high FBI officials: "I have been looking over the [Bureau] supervisors at the Seat of Government. A lot of them are clods. Get rid of them." Without asking Hoover to explain his remarks, the officials formed a panel informally called the "Clod Squad" to expel supervisors having traits which Hoover was known to hate.

Closed Memo Control File: FBI file, contains all memos closing cases in the field office keeping the file.

Clubs: Central FBI plants, located away from regular FBI offices, where electronic surveillances are monitored.

CMC: Communist-Pro-Chinese.

CMS: Communist-Pro-Soviet.

CMT: Communist-Trotskyist.

CNDI: Confidential National Defense Informant.

CO: Columbia Field Office.

COGOG: Communists in Government Groups.

COI: Coordinator of Information. An office established in 1941 for both propaganda and intelligence-gathering purposes. In 1942 was renamed Office of Strategic Services (OSS) and its propaganda functions transferred to the Office of War Information.

COINTELPRO: Counterintelligence Program — overall name for numerous programs of disruption, dirty tricks, and other projects undertaken by the FBI against individuals and organizations targeted by the FBI to be immobilized or destroyed. Though COINTELPRO was not formalized until 1956, and was allegedly discontinued in 1971, COINTELPRO-type tactics were employed both before and after those dates.

COINTELPRO Notification Program: Completed in 1978 by DOJ Office of Professional Responsibility, it sought to notify 527 individuals (61 of whom the program failed to locate) that they could receive information on COINTELPRO actions against them. (Many people besides these 527 were targeted under COINTELPRO.)

Comfugs: Communist fugitives.

COMINFIL: Communist Infiltration. FBI program begun in 1950s which investigated a wide variety of non-Communist and anti-Communist organizations. Any organization which was of a type which the FBI considered susceptible to Communist influence could be a target of a COMINFIL investigation.

COMINT: Supersecret code for NSA reports, stands for "Communications Intelligence."

Comintern: Communist International.

COMM-FBI: FBI Files and Communications Division.

Committee for Expansion of Socialist Thought in America: Fictional organization, purporting to be real, set up by FBI in 1965 to publish newspaper attacking the Communist Party, U.S.A.

Communist: According to 1964 FBI Manual, this term "should be interpreted in its broad sense as including persons not only adhering to the principles of the CP-USA itself, but also to such splinter and offshoot groups as the Socialist Workers Party, Progressive Labor Party, and the like." In practice, FBI treats "communism" not as a doctrine or political party but as an occult force which can secretly enter anywhere. See "COMINFIL," "Front Group."

Communist Control Act: 1954. Denied the Communist Party all "rights, privileges, and immunities attendant upon legal bodies created under the jurisdiction of the laws of the United States."

Communist Index: Established in 1948, and separate from the Security Index, this index listed all individuals who in the FBI's judgment were sympathetic to the Communist Party. In 1956, the list began to include people associated with groups other than the CP. In 1960, its name was changed to "Reserve Index," which see.

Communist Party — U.S.A. Program: See "CP-USA."

COMPIC: Communist Picture Album.

Compromise: To expose secret information (e.g., the identity of confidential sources).

COMPROS: CP, USA, Prosecution.

Comsab: Communist Sabotage. FBI program for identifying subjects on SI with a potential for sabotage "either because of their training or because of their position relative to vital or strategic installations or industry." Apparently abolished 1960. See "Priority Apprehension Program."

Confidential Informant (CI): Though the FBI calls almost all of its informants "confidential," it was not until 1977 that (largely in order to prevent disclosure under the FOIA) FBI policy called for informants to be promised full confidentiality. Prior to this, informants generally assumed that the FBI could choose to expose them whenever it desired (e.g., when it needed public testimony). CI's are characterized in various ways by FBI:

1. has furnished reliable information in the past.
2. of unknown reliability.
3. of known unreliability.
4. of known reliability.
5. has supplied insufficient information to determine reliability.
6. is in a logical position to supply reliable information.
7. reliability cannot be commented on.
8. has furnished reliable information in the past but whose background is questionable.

See "Informant," "Source," "PSI."

Confidential Sources Extremist Informant: Defined by FBI in 3/73 as "an individual who is willing to cooperate with the Bureau by furnishing extremist information brought to his attention by virtue of his position in the community, his employment, or in view of his background in extremist activities."

Consensual Monitoring: Electronic monitoring of a conversation with the consent of one of the participants. Does not require a warrant.

Consolidated:
1. Of files, means that documents from several are combined into one.
2. Of "see references," means that a "correlation summary" or similar document has been made.

Control File: Used for overall supervision of an investigation. Results of investigations are reported in individual case files, and only summaries, evaluations, analyses, and strategic plans are placed in the control file. Control files are usually established only for important cases.

CONUS: Military term for continental United States.

Correlation Summary: Summary of information on a given subject, gathered from various FBI files. See Ch. IV, Documents 2 and 3.

Counterespionage: Aspects of counterintelligence designed to prevent, detect, and neutralize espionage.

Counterintelligence: Executive Order 12036 defines this as: "Information gathered and activities conducted to protect against espionage and other clandestine intelligence activities, sabotage, international terrorist activities or assassinations conducted for or on behalf of foreign powers, organizations, or persons but not including personnel, physical, document, or communications security programs." See "COINTELPRO."

Counterintelligence Branch: Part of the Intelligence Division, FBI Headquarters, it was responsible for matters relating to activities of foreign agents and unfriendly foreign governments within the U.S. Its four sections handled "65," "97," "105," and "117" cases, among others. Was apparently replaced by "Domestic Security-Terrorism Section," which see.

Counterintelligence Program: See "COINTELPRO."

Cover: Guise used to conceal affiliation with FBI or other intelligence agency.

Covert Action: Clandestine activities designed to influence political processes. Term applies primarily to actions taken in foreign countries, but FBI "COINTELPRO" is in effect domestic covert action.

Covert Mail Coverage: Illegal mail opening. Compare "Mail Cover."

CP-DAI: Communist Party-Domestic Administration Issues.

CP-IR: Communist Party-International Relations.

CP-USA: Communist Party-USA. Variations of the expression "CP-USA" reflect subdivisions of the CP-USA, e.g., "CP-NYD" is the Communist Party-New York Division. Allegedly over half FBI's COINTELPRO actions were directed at CP-USA. CP-USA COINTELPRO allegedly existed 1957-71. FBI classes under "CP-USA" many activities which have little or no real connection to CP-USA.

CRC-PO: Clandestine Radio Communications-Potential Operators.

Crime Records Division: At FBI Headquarters, was the chief producer of FBI propaganda. Was renamed "External Affairs Division."

Criminal Division: Division of Department of Justice.

Criminal Investigative Division: At FBI Headquarters supervises investigation in criminal, civil rights, accounting, fraud, and (since 9/76) internal security areas. Until 4/77 was called General Investigative Division. Includes "Domestic Security-Terrorism Section."

CRS: Central Records System. See Chapter I.

CRT: Cathode Ray Tube. To be used in retrieval of information from FBI files in automated FBI Central Records Systems. As of 1979, this automation had not been accomplished.

CRU: Classification Review Unit, which see.

CRV: Conditional Release Violator.

CS: 1. Confidential Source — usually followed by a field office designation and a source number, e.g., "CS NY-903."

   2. Infrequently used abbreviation for "Comsab," which see.

CSC: Civil Service Commission. FBI agents are not hired through Civil Service. FBI, not CSC, conducts "loyalty" investigations of prospective federal employees.

CTNF: Computerized Telephone Number File. Enables FBI to ascertain subscribers to phone numbers. File includes phone numbers of many subjects of "security" investigations.

Cuban Program: FBI COINTELPRO of 1961.

Custodial Detention List: Original (pre-1943) name for Security Index, initiated as a result of the FBI's interpretation of a Presidential directive of 9/8/39. Listed individuals to be considered for custodial detention in the event of a national emergency. See "Attorney General's Portfolio Plan."

CV: Cleveland Field Office.

D: As in "NYD," refers to FBI field division.

DAPLI: Departmental Applicants — Professional Staff. Title of FBI investigations of professional DOJ staff.

Daylet: Daily letter. Are kept in a "Daylet file," a control file. Their significance is not known.

DC: Infrequently used abbreviation for "Detcom," which see.

DCGO: District Coast Guard Office.

DCI: Director of Central Intelligence, the nominal head of the intelligence community. DCI is also Director of CIA, but the two roles are distinct.

DCS: Domestic Contact Service of the CIA, it reported to Operation CHAOS and the FBI on domestic political activity.

DD-553: Defense Department Form, apparently similar to FD-553.

DE: Detroit Field Office.

DEA: Drug Enforcement Administration; branch of Justice Department. Established 7/73.

Dead: A "dead" FBI file is opened when no immediate investigation is to be conducted, but where field supervisor expects soon to receive enough information to conduct an investigation.

Dead Drop: Small inconspicuous cache for hiding and picking up espionage information.

Declassify: To remove security classifications (i.e., "confidential," "secret," "top secret") from information, but not necessarily to release that information to the public.

Deemed Advisable: In listings of "T" sources, appears to indicate that writer of report deemed it advisable to conceal source's identity in body of report. See "T-(number)."

Deep Cover Program: FBI program for infiltrating Weather Underground with FBI agents who adopted elaborate, long-term covers.

Defense Intelligence Agency: Established 8/61 in Department of Defense to coordinate armed forces intelligence activities.

Defense Investigative Service: See "DIS."

Deferred Recording: Apparently means same as "Expedite," which see.

Delimitations Agreement: Adopted by Interdepartmental Intelligence Conference, 6/5/40. Revised 2/43 and 2/49. Assigned most domestic intelligence to FBI, but required FBI to keep military intelligence agencies informed.

Department: Unless the context indicates otherwise, "Department" in any FBI document means "Department of Justice."

Department of Justice (DOJ): FBI is nominally the chief investigative arm of the DOJ, though DOJ has generally exercised little control over FBI.

Department Review Committee: In DOJ, includes FBI representative. Decides, on administrative appeals, whether documents exempted under (b) (1) warrant continued classification.

DESECO: Development of Selected Contacts. FBI program for interviewing Americans returning from trips to "Sino-Soviet-bloc" countries or from foreign meetings where "Sino-Soviet-bloc" personnel might be present. Interviewees were considered potential security informants.

Detcom: Detention of Communists. An FBI program for "tabbing" subjects on SI whose apprehension had high priority. Included "all top functionaries, all key figures, all individuals tabbed under the Comsab program" and anyone else given priority. Was apparently replaced by "Priority Apprehension Program," which went into effect in 1969.

Detention Plan: See "Attorney General's Portfolio Plan."

Deterrent Interview: Conducted by FBI to discourage future actions by letting interviewee know FBI is watching.

DIA: Defense Intelligence Agency, which see.

DID: Domestic Intelligence Division. See "Intelligence Division."

Dies Committee: The informal title during the chairmanship of Martin Dies (Democratic Congressman from Texas), 1938-44, of a Committee of the House of Representatives formally titled "Special Committee on Un-American Activities." Also known as the House Un-American Activities Committee, HUAC, and (in FBI documents) HCUA.

DIO: Duty Intelligence Officer (Air Force); District Intelligence Officer (Naval Districts).

Director: Directors of the FBI have included:
J. Edgar Hoover (5/24-5/72);
L. Patrick Gray III (acting) (5/72-4/73);
William D. Ruckelshaus (acting) (4/73-7/73);
Clarence M. Kelley (7/73-2/78);
William H. Webster (2/78-present).

Director of Central Intelligence: See "DCI."

Directorate for Civil Disturbance Planning and Operations: Established 1969. Coordinated Pentagon's domestic intelligence operations. Now known as Division of Military Services.

DIS: Defense Investigative Service. Established 4/72 within Department of Defense. Directs personnel security investigations for DOD.

Disclosure Section: In FBI FOI/PA Branch, determines what information to release to FOI/PA requester. Established 1/78. See "Operations Section."

Disinformation: FBI disruptive technique of spreading misinformation (e.g., falsely notifying organization members that a meeting has been cancelled).

Disruption Program: Alternate term for "COINTELPRO," which see.

Division: FBI Headquarters is organized into Divisions, each headed by an assistant director. The "Criminal Investigative Division," which see, is responsible for "domestic security" investigations. See also "Intelligence Division," "Special Investigative Division."

Division Five: In FBI HQ, was the Intelligence Division.

DL: Dallas Field Office.

DN: Denver Field Office.

DOB: Date of Birth.

DOD: Department of Defense. Military agencies have voluminous data on political dissent in the U.S., much of it provided by FBI. Political intelligence-gathering by military has been reduced, but not eliminated, since 1971.

DOE: Department of Energy. Established 10/77.

DOJ: Department of Justice, which see.

Domestic Intelligence: Never precisely defined bv the FBI; often used interchangeably with "Internal Security." Allegedly concerns attempts to gather information on persons or organizations within the U.S. which show some possibility of using force, violence, or other illegal means to undermine the government. The GAO considers the following FBI investigations domestic security related: subversion, extremism, sedition, treason, sabotage, certain bombings, violations of anti-riot laws, and protection of foreign officials. Subversive and extremist investigations have been the most common of these.

Domestic Intelligence Division: Former name of Intelligence Division, which see.

Domestic Security-Terrorism Section: Within Criminal Investigative Division of FBI Headquarters. When Internal Security Branch was transferred from Intelligence Division in 7/76 its name was changed to "Domestic Security Section." In 4/77, "foreign terrorism" functions were added and it received its present name. Has 21 agents, 5 concerned primarily with supervising domestic security investigations.

Dom Intell Div: Domestic Intelligence Division. See "Intelligence Division."

"Do Not File": FBI procedure for keeping sensitive material out of Central Records System. See Chapter I.

Dossier: Term used only *outside* FBI to refer to FBI records. FBI personnel speak of "files" or "case files."

Double Sticker File: Appears to be any FBI file to which these rules apply:
  1. "Do not furnish any information from this file to any outside agency without authorization of section   ."
  2. "No information from this file is to be made the subject matter of any report, memo, or correspondence in another investigation without clearance from section   ."
  Notation "double sticker file" appears on file covers.

Downgrade: To lower the classification (e.g., from "top secret" to "secret").

DS: Written next to a reference on a search slip, indicates the document or file has been destroyed.

DST: Direction de la Surveillance du Territoire — the French equivalent of the internal security side of the FBI.* Has cooperated with FBI in surveillance of Americans in France.

Duplicate Yellow: Copy on onionskin paper.

EBF: "This generally refers to an item too bulky to house in the main section but small enough to be placed behind the file in the same cabinet housing the file. The use of enclosures behind file occurs only at FBI HQ, and not in the field offices." (FBI Affidavit, 6/24/79).

Electronic Surveillance: Surveillance conducted by microphone or wiretap. Called "ELSUR" by FBI.

ELSUR: Electronic surveillance; includes "TESUR" and "MISUR."

ELSUR Index: A card file on individuals subject to, overheard on, or mentioned in electronic surveillances. Maintained at Headquarters since 1966 and at each field office conducting ELSURs since 1960. (See Ch. I.)

Emergency Detention Act: Section of Internal Security Act of 1950. Repealed 1971. Authorized detention in national emergency of individuals considered dangerous to internal security. FBI considered the act's standards for apprehension unworkable, and continued with its own detention program. See "Attorney General's Portfolio Plan," "Master Search Warrant," "Master Warrant of Arrest."

Emergency Detention Program: See "Attorney General's Portfolio Plan."

EP: El Paso Field Office.

ERDA: Energy Research and Development Administration, established 1/75. Took over military and production activities and nuclear research and development of AEC. Consolidated into DOE, 10/77.

Esp-R: Espionage-Russian.

Esp. Sec.: Espionage Section.

Established Sources: Sources or informants who are already providing information to FBI.

EW: Wanted Person Entry. Concerns entering of case in NCIC. (EW probably stands for "Entry Wanted.")

Executive Order 9835: 3/21/47. Sometimes called the "Loyalty Order." Dealt with employee loyalty programs. Established authority for "Attorney General's List" to be made. Was revoked in part by Executive Order 10450.

Executive Order 10450: 4/27/53. Ordered that "the appointment of each civilian or employee in any department or agency of the Government shall be made subject to investigation." Also provided authority for Attorney General to draw up his list of subversive organizations. See "Applicant Investigation"; "Federal Employee Loyalty-Security Program."

Executive Order 10501: Effective 12/15/53 — provided procedures and criteria for classifying government documents as Confidential, Secret, and Top Secret. Superseded by Executive Order 11652.

Executive Order 11605: 7/2/71. Amended Executive Order 10450. Authorized SACB to hold hearings to determine whether an organization is subversive. Broadened definition of "subversive."

Executive Order 11652: Effective 6/1/72. Provided procedures and criteria for classifying government documents as Confidential, Secret, and Top Secret. Superseded by Executive Order 12065.

Executive Order 11905: 2/18/76. On "United States Foreign Intelligence Activities." Presented as a "reform," it in effect legitimated FBI abuses. Superseded in part by Executive Order 12036.

Executive Order 12036: Effective 1/24/78. Concerns organization and control of intelligence activities. Provides some restrictions on FBI investigative techniques.

Executive Order 12065: Effective 12/1/78. Specifies substantive and procedural requirements for classifying documents confidential, secret, and top secret; hence, provides criteria for (b) (1) FOIA exemptions. Is only basis, other than Atomic Energy Act, for classifying information. Revoked Executive Order 11652. Unlike previous orders, 12065 permits properly classified information to be released if public interest outweighs expected damage to national security. See "(b) (1)"; "Classified Information"; and Ch. II.

Executives Conference: Top FBI officials, including Director, who meet regularly to decide policy.

Exemption: In connection with the Freedom of Information Act, refers to sections of the Act which permit agencies to withhold certain records, and hence "exempt" those records from the Act. See Ch. II on exemptions.

Expedite; Expedite Processing: Communications so marked are sent by messenger to appropriate persons in FBI, before going to Classifying Unit. After action has been taken, communication is supposed to be sent to Classifying Unit. If an "expedite" document is not sent to Classifying Unit, it is not filed; it is unknown whether this occurs often.

Exp. Proc.: Expedite Processing. See "Expedite."

External Affairs Division: At FBI Headquarters, maintains contact with press and public and conducts research on law enforcement. Until 5/75, contained a unit for processing FOIA requests. Formerly called "Crime Records Division."

Extremist Activities: The FBI Manual of Instruction defines these as "activities aimed at overthrowing, destroying, or undermining the Government of the United States or any of its political subdivisions by illegal means or denying the rights of individuals under the Constitution or prohibited by statutes. "Extremists" are generally Black or Native American radicals or members of "white hate" groups. "Extremist" groups include the Black Panther Party, Nation of Islam, American Indian Movement, and the Ku Klux Klan. Though the FBI considers "extremist" groups less centralized and structured than "subversive" groups, it sometimes nevertheless chooses to investigate all members of an extremist group. See "Subversive Activities"; "Terrorism."

Extremist, Revolutionary, Terrorist, and Subversive Activities in Penal Institutions Program: Initiated July 1974 in order to increase cooperation between the FBI and prison officials in investigating subversive activities inside prisons. Field offices are required to submit quarterly reports on contacts with prison officials.

Extremist Section: Originally called "Racial Intelligence Section," established 9/67 within Intelligence Division at FBI Headquarters. Handled investigation of black militants, white hate groups, and ethnic "extremists." As of 1975, had "Civil Disorders Reporting Unit" and four units responsible for different parts of the country. Its functions were apparently taken over in 1976 by "Domestic Security Section." See "Domestic Security-Terrorism Section."

FAG: Fraud Against the Government.

False Identities Program: Established 1973 to investigate use of false identities. Required reports from field offices; information was disseminated to other government agencies. Attempts were made to link use of false identities to subversives and extremists. See "Thumbprint Program."

FBI: Federal Bureau of Investigation, the principal investigative arm of the Department of Justice (DOJ). In addition to Headquarters (FBIHQ), it maintains 59 field offices, 477 resident agencies (RAs), and 12 foreign liaison posts (legats). In 1978, it had 7,924 agents ("special agents" or "SAs") and 11,397 clerical, stenographic, and technical personnel, in addition to its informants.

FBI Academy: FBI training school, Quantico, Va.

FBI HDQ or FBI HQ: FBI Headquarters, Washington, D.C.

FBI Number: An identification or fingerprint number. Within the FBI, file numbers are *not* referred to as FBI numbers. However, other agencies communicating with FBI sometimes confuse FBI file numbers with FBI numbers.

FBW: Fraud by wire.

FCI: Foreign Counterintelligence.

FD-1C: Agent assignment card, indicates which SA is assigned to a particular case.

FD-4: "Routing Slip," which see.

FD-5: FBI form indicating that a document (serial) has been removed ("charged") from a file. See "Serial Chargeout."

FD-9: Form on which FBI HQ Identification Division is requested to furnish the identification or criminal record on an individual to a field office.

FD-26: Form on which an individual authorizes FBI agents to search his/her residence and to take whatever they desire.

FD-28: "Daily Report" form.

FD-37: A "blue slip." Attached to FD-221, it certifies that money received by SA was paid to a specified source, for information on a specified investigation.

FD-65: FBI form recording information on a fugitive.

FD-67: Acknowledgment of Transfer Orders. To be destroyed when it has served its purpose.

FD-71: Misleadingly called a "Complaint Form." Generally used by an FBI agent when taking notes on a telephone call to FBI. Also used to recommend opening a case file.

FD-73: Automobile Record Form.

FD-76: Field Stenographer's and Typist's Daily Report.

FD-115: FBI form, sent to a postmaster, requesting a mail cover.

FD-122: FBI form used in preparing a Security Index or Reserve Index card on an individual. FD-122a is used for recommending inclusion in Section A of the Reserve Index. See Ch. IV, Docs. 1 and 2.

FD-128: FBI form authorizing a change in "Office of Origin" for a case.

FD-141: A "Green Sheet," which see. Similar to FD-192.

FD-142: FBI form on which is written a "recommendation for installation of technical or microphone surveillance."

FD-143: FBI form for supplying justification for continuation of technical or microphone surveillance.

FD-153: "Interview Log" form on which FBI agents record time and place someone is interviewed.

FD-154: FBI form used in verifying information on a person's Security Index or ADEX card.

FD-160: FBI form used in writing down reference found in the general indices. Also known as a "search slip" or "indices search slip." See Ch. IV, Docs. 21 and 22.

FD-165: Form used by FBI field office to request information or action from FBI HQ Identification Division.

FD-169: Form used to record fact that information from an FBI file was furnished orally to another government agency.

FD-177: FBI form sent to registrant in many Selective Service investigations.

FD-178: FBI form, sent to person listed as always knowing address of registrant, in many Selective Service investigations.

FD-179: FBI form, sent to employer, in many Selective Service investigations.

FD-180: FBI form, sent to an acquaintance of registrant, in many Selective Service investigations.

FD-181: FBI form, sent to Post Office in many Selective Service Investigations.

FD-186: Form on which an SA records results of personal observation of a Security Index (SI) subject. The FBI Manual of Instructions required that a photograph of each SI subject be placed on the back of his/her SI card, and that each SI subject be observed personally by an SA.

FD-192: FBI form recording an inventory of property held by the FBI. See Ch. IV, Doc. 19, a "Green Sheet."

FD-203: FBI form on which a request is made to a resident agency to conduct an investigation. See Ch. IV, Doc. 15.

FD-205: Form used by FBI field office to inform HQ that, and why, it cannot meet the deadline for completing a case or a report on a case.

FD-209: FBI form cover sheet recording results of contact with an FBI informant.

FD-216: FBI form on which is summarized information received from a source. Is sometimes used for Administrative Pages of reports.

FD-221: Receipt for money received by SA from SAC to pay for source or informant. See "FD-37."

FD-221b: Receipt for money, paid by FBI, for "services rendered." Apparently, agents frequently break regulations and fail to have informants sign receipts.

FD-227: FBI Field Office request to Headquarters to authorize mail cover. Mail covers are often placed without any FD-227s being made.

FD-245: "File Cover," which see.

FD-249: Arrest and institution fingerprint card.

FD-256: " 'Number 3' Card," which see.

FD-258: Applicant fingerprint card.

FD-263: Form used for front page of FBI report. See. Ch. IV, Doc. 4.

FD-266: FBI form for requesting information on a person; sent from one field office to another.

FD-302: Interview report form. Often records interviews of sources such as bank employees. Agents are often cross-examined in court about them.

FD-305: FBI form summarizing background information and subversive activity of a person. Reflects "current data concerning subject's continued status as a Security Index subject."

FD-306: FBI form, a cover sheet for an Informant Report. See Ch. IV, Docs. 10 and 11.

FD-315: FBI form used to request Immigration and Naturalization Services to place or remove a Lookout Notice on a person whose location the FBI wishes to know about.

FD-330: Itinerary.

FD-332: FBI form used in recommending that an individual be placed on the list of Potential Clandestine Radio Operators.

FD-338: FBI form used for authorizing destruction of individual documents (serials). See Ch. IV, Doc. 16.

FD-340a: A "1A Envelope," which see.

FD-341: "Radio Equipment Maintenance Log" form.

FD-345: "Photographic-Photocopy Log" form.

FD-353: Personal identification fingerprint card.

FD-356: Form used by an FBI office in requesting information on an individual (particularly passport information) from another FBI office or from CIA, INS, or the military.

FD-366: FBI form, sets forth change in address of a subject of investigation.

FD-376: FBI form for recording information concerning a person allegedly potentially dangerous to the President; sent to the Secret Service. Often denied release under (b) (5). Commonly concern nonviolent political activists. See Ch. IV, Doc. 8.

FD-397: Form used in preparation of "Rabble-Rouser Index" or "Agitator Index" card. Form places subject on or removes him/her from Index, or else changes an already existing card on the subject.

FD-411: FBI form submitted to Selective Service Headquarters in lieu of a report closing a case.

FD-503: Inventory Worksheet. When ordered by court to provide inventory of documents, FBI uses these forms.

FD-553: Form used by the Army to tell FBI to watch out for AWOLs (i.e., GIs who are absent without leave or authorization).

Federal Employee Loyalty-Security Program: Established under Executive Order 9835, 1947. Continued under E.O. 10450, 1953. Required loyalty investigation of all federal civilian employees. FBI checks names of applicants for federal jobs and conducts investigation when initial check reveals "subversive" connections. Program has changed since 1947, but remains in effect today.

FGJ: Federal Grand Jury. FBI often uses threat of grand jury subpoenas against people it finds uncooperative.

FHD: Federal House of Detention.

Field: Any place except FBI Headquarters.

Field Division: The territory for which a given field office has responsibility. Generally corresponds to Federal District Court jurisdiction. Boundaries between them are usually strictly observed by field offices.

Field Office: These 59 FBI offices have primary responsibility for conducting investigations. They report the "substance" of their findings to HQ, and supervise the RAs within their field divisions.

Field Supervisor: See "Squad."

Field-wide: Concerning all field offices.

File Classification: See "Classification Number."

File Cover: The front of each volume or section of a file. It lists the file number, section number, and serial numbers contained in the section. Often, it lists other files relevant to the case, such as files on other members of the individual's family, other files on the individual or (in a field office) the corresponding Headquarters file. It sometimes indicates whether the file has any subfiles, and whether the subject is on the Security Index. See Ch. IV, Doc. 3.

File Number: Each FBI file has a two-part number, e.g., "65-14873." See Ch. I on numbering documents.

File Review: FBI clerical unit, also called "Reference Review", checks files and documents referred to on "search slips" to determine if references are "identical" (that is, if they in fact refer to the individual or organization listed at the top of the search slip). See "Name Searching Unit."

Files and Communications Division: At FBI Headquarters, maintained FBI files and indices. Is apparently now called "Records Management Division."

FINCASE: Case involving Reino Hayhanen, self-professed Soviet espionage agent.

FINDER: FBI Headquarters automated fingerprint scanner machine.

First-Party Request: Request under FOI/PA where requester desires information about himself/herself. Attorney General's regulations state that first-party requests for FBI records deniable under PA should be processed under FOIA.

FISUR: Physical Surveillance; e.g. observing and photographing a picket line, an audience at a meeting, or trailing an individual. Results of physical surveillances are maintained by SAs in log (diary) form. See "Logs."

Five: In FBI HQ, often meant Division Five (Intelligence Division).

FNU: First Name Unknown (to FBI).

FO: Field Office, which see.

FOIA: Freedom of Information Act. Effective 7/67. Amendments effective 2/75. See Ch. II.

FOIA Exemption: The FOIA permits agencies to withhold ("exempt" from release) certain records. See "(b) (1)," "(b) (2)," "(b) (5)," "(b) (7) (A)," "(b) (7) (C)," "(b) (7) (D)," "(b) (7) (E)"; and Ch. II.

FOI/PA Section: Unit of any agency that handles Freedom of Information and Privacy Act requests from the public.

FOOCASE: FBI designation for matters relating to Klaus Fuchs, British scientist accused of espionage.

Foreign Agents Registration Act of 1938: Amended several times. Requires registration of some agents of foreign governments, particularly propagandists.

Foreign Counterintelligence: Defined by FBI as "information gathered and activities conducted to protect against espionage and other clandestine intelligence activities, sabotage, international terrorist activities or assassinations conducted for or on behalf of foreign powers, organizations or persons." However, domestic counterintelligence is often rationalized by calling it foreign counterintelligence.

Foreign Counterintelligence Informant: Often, a domestic intelligence informant. The FBI claims that between 1976 and 1978 the number of domestic intelligence informants it used dropped from 535 to 42. However, it acknowledges that part of the difference resulted simply from administratively transferring the same informants, engaged in the same activities, into "foreign counterintelligence."

Foreign Intelligence: Defined by FBI as "information relating to the capabilities, intentions and activities of foreign powers, organizations or persons." See "Foreign Counterintelligence," "Domestic Intelligence."

Foreign Intelligence Surveillance Act of 1978. Provides procedure under which AG can obtain judicial warrant for use of electronic surveillance in U.S. for foreign intelligence.

Form 0-1: Form on which HQ requests field office to submit report, explain why a report was not submitted, or advise of status of a case.

Form 0-9: FBI form, on green paper, criticizes field office for its handling of a case.

Form 0-17: Used by FBI Headquarters to inform a field office that some communication contained an error. They are evidently not retained in investigative files except by mistake. See "Substantive Error."

Form 0-25: Routing Slip, on which FBI explains whether accompanying document is "for information" or "for appropriate action."

Form 1-12: "Wanted Notice" form.

Form 1-221: Form on which Identification Division at FBI HQ responds to a request for information or for placement of a wanted notice.

Form 4-413: Form used for "Serial Chargeout," which see.

Four-bagger: FBI document on which all margins have been filled by handwritten notes.

F.P.C.: Fingerprint classification.

FRC: Federal Records Centers. Serve as repositories for some FBI payroll and voucher material, but not for investigative files. Some documents from FBI personnel files are kept under seal in a National Personnel Records Center.

Freedom of Information Act: See "FOIA."

FRN: Foreign Affiliation. A suffix indicates which country.

Front Group: A subversive or extremist "front" is a group substantially directed, dominated, or controlled by a subversive or extremist group. The FBI distinguishes primary subversive groups from "fronts," and from targets of subversive "infiltration."

FTL: Federal Telecommunications Laboratory. See "Semontel."

FUDE: Fugitive/Deserter. FBI file classification "42."

Fug: Fugitive.

Full Investigation: Also called full-field investigation. Under AG's 4/76 guidelines, they must be authorized by FBI Headquarters, and only on basis of specific facts. Full investigations can use informers (subject to some guidelines), mail covers, and legal electronic surveillance. Are not to continue longer than one year without DOJ approval. See "Preliminary Investigations," "Limited Investigation," "Preliminary Inquiries."

G-2: Intelligence section of General Staff, U.S. Army. Established 1903.

GAO: General Accounting Office. The investigative arm of Congress, it has issued studies of FBI. Despite its authority to investigate the administration and operation of FBI, FBI has denied it access to certain files.

GDS: General Declassification Schedule (as defined in Executive Order 11652, which see).

General Files: "0" ("Zero") and "00" ("Double Zero") files. See Ch. I.

General Index: An alphabetized set of cards, referring to FBI files. FBI Headquarters and each field office has its own "General Index." See Ch. I; Ch. IV, Document 20.

General Intelligence: Intelligence collected on "trends" or "developments," when the targets of investigation are not narrowly specified. For example, in 1970 the FBI conducted "general intelligence" investigations of all black student unions and similar campus groups. See "Targeted Intelligence."

General Intelligence Division of the Justice Department: See "GID."

General Intelligence Index: FBI term for custodial detention list, which later became the Security Index (SI).

General Investigative Division: See "Criminal Investigative Division."

Ghetto Informant Program: Initiated 10/67 to monitor militant blacks intensively. Officially terminated 7/73, but some informants developed under the program were retained. At its height in 1972, it involved 7,500 ghetto informants around the country.

GID: General Intelligence Division — established as part of the Justice Department in 1919 by Attorney General A. Mitchell Palmer. Run by J. Edgar Hoover, then a twenty-four-year-old special assistant to the Attorney General, it compiled files on "subversives" and was later incorporated into the Bureau of Investigation.*

GIIF: General Investigative Intelligence File. Catchall file for all references to organized crime. Apparently replaced by Top Hoodlum Program, 1957.

GILROB: FBI code for bank robbery/police murder case, Boston 1970.

GJ: Grand Jury.

Glove: As in "covered like a glove," can mean electronic surveillance.

G-Men: Nickname for FBI agents.

Goon: In unofficial FBI jargon, an FBI inspector.

Graymail: Ploy in which an accused lawbreaker (e.g., an FBI or CIA official or former official) threatens to disclose classified information at trial in the event he is prosecuted.

Great Freak In-Service: Informal designation of Specialized Weatherman In-Service, attended by FBI agents in hippie guise. See "In-Service."

Green Sheet: List of exhibits in possession of FBI (copies released to the public always appear white). Often they are filed in a main file and indicate the disposition of bulky exhibits. (They will probably show if the exhibit was, e.g., returned to owner, destroyed or placed in an FBI vault.) See "FD-141," "FD-192." See also Ch. IV, Doc. 19.

"Green Weenie": "Form 0-9," which see. Also known as "greenie."

Gregory Case: Case of FBI informant Elizabeth T. Bentley, called "informant Gregory" by FBI.

Group I: With reference to classification, indicates document excluded from automatic declassification under Executive Order prior to E.O. 11652 (1972).

HA: Havana Legat.

Handbook: See "Agent's Handbook."

Handling Agent: Each FBI informant is in regular contact with an FBI agent, who receives information and gives pay (usually monthly). Handling agent tries to direct informant and is supposed to maintain a close relationship.

Hard Copy: Information on paper (that is, not on microfilm or computer tape).

Hatch Act: 1939. Prohibited federal employees from membership in organizations advocating overthrow of U.S. form of government.

HCUA: FBI abbreviation for House Committee on Un-American Activities, aka House Un-American Activities Committee (HUAC).

HDQ: Headquarters. Usually written "HQ."

Headquarters: For FBI Field Offices, "Headquarters" is FBI HQ in Washington, D.C. However, an FBI Resident Agency tends to regard the Field Office supervising it as "headquarters" or "headquarters city."

High 2 Material: Documents such as investigative manuals whose release allegedly could disrupt investigations, and which are allegedly exempt from disclosure under (b) (2) of the FOIA. See "Low 2 Material."

HILEV: Code name for the Bureau's intensified intelligence collection program overseas, after the legats were expanded in 1970 at Hoover's insistence. Material tagged "HILEV" sometimes went directly to the President or the Secretary of State.

HISC: "House Internal Security Committee," which see.

Hit: A positive response when NCIC records are checked for information on some matter.

HN: Honolulu Field Office.

HO: Houston Field Office.

Hoodwink Program: See "Operation Hoodwink."

House Internal Security Committee (HISC): The successor to HUAC. Abolished in 1975.

HQ: FBI Headquarters, Washington, D.C.

HTLINGUAL: CIA mail opening program, 1953-1973.

HUAC: Non-FBI abbreviation for House Un-American Activities Committee. (See "HCUA").

Huston Plan: Plan proposed in 1970 to coordinate and expand domestic intelligence activity. Plan openly included use of illegal techniques. Though Nixon revoked official approval shortly after giving it, aspects of the plan were implemented. See also "IEC."

I: On search slips, means "Identical," which see.

IA: Informative Asset.

IACP: International Association of Chiefs of Police.

IC: 1. On TESUR logs, means "incoming" (that is, an incoming phone call).
2. Investigative clerk.

ICIS: Interdepartmental Committee on Internal Security. Established by NSC 1949 at same time as IIC. Had responsibility to coordinate noninvestigatory internal security activities. Included DOJ representative. Supervised by AG after 1962.

ICRC: "Interagency Classification Review Committee," which see.

IDA: Probably Institute for Defense Analyses.

Identical: Of files, means that the file or reference pertains to the person (or organization) about whom information is being sought.

Identification Division: In FBI Headquarters, the repository of 170 million fingerprints. Posts "Wanted Notices" and "Missing Persons Notices."

IDIU: Interdivisional Information Unit. Name was changed to Interdivisional Intelligence Unit, and then to Civil Disturbance Unit. Established 1967 in DOJ. Coordinated vast amounts of "domestic security" intelligence for DOJ, most of it from FBI. Computer system, added 1968 but later dismantled, could generate reports listing all persons affiliated with a given organization, as well as their location and travel.

IEC: Intelligence Evaluation Committee, created within the Justice Department in 1970 to consider expansion and coordination of CIA and NSA involvement in domestic intelligence — an attempt to carry out elements of the Huston Plan after it was disapproved by the President. The group focused on the anti-war movement, in part under the guise of looking for "foreign influence." Terminated 7/73.

IES: Intelligence Evaluation Staff, established 1/71, prepared the studies and evaluations issued by the Intelligence Evaluation Committee (IEC). Terminated 7/73.

IGRS: IRS Intelligence Gathering and Retrieval System, operated 5/73-1/75. Had 465,442 individuals and companies in its indices. Gathered some political intelligence which was available to FBI.

IIC: See "Interdepartmental Intelligence Conference."

Illegals: Foreign nationals who enter U.S. either fraudulently or legally, and who spy for foreign governments without maintaining any open contact with foreign establishments in the U.S.

184

Index: FBI maintains numerous indices. "To index" a document is to prepare "see ref" cards on persons or things mentioned in it. Unless context indicates otherwise, "Indices" are FBI General Indices. See Ch. I.

Info: Information. When written next to the number of a file to which a copy of a document is being sent, indicates that the copy is for information only and no specific action is required.

Informant: Person who supplies information on a regular basis, generally for pay. The FBI distinguishes between criminal informants (who provide information on possible violations of federal crimes) and security informants (who engage chiefly in surveillance of political activities). An informant, unlike a source, usually enters into some agreement with the FBI and in some instances obtains information at the direction of the FBI. FBI sometimes disguises identity of electronic sources and burglaries by calling them "informants." Informants are allegedly used in about 85% of domestic intelligence cases.

Informant Cards: Cards filed in the Informant Index. See Ch. I.

Information and Privacy Section, DOJ: Defends government in suits brought under FOI/PA.

Information Security Oversight Office: Established by Executive Order 12065. Oversees compliance of agencies with this Order and considers appeals from decisions on declassification requests. Replaces Interagency Classification Review Committee.

Informer: Because of its unsavory connotations, this term is avoided in FBI communications. See "Informant," "Source."

INFT: Informant.

Initial Processing Unit (IPU): After an FOI/PA request is "perfected," the IPU takes 15-20 days to prepare records for processing by analysts.

Inlet: "FBI Intelligence letter for the President." Instituted November 1969; discontinued December 1972. A letter which consolidated intelligence information to be shown to the President, Vice President and Attorney General. Field offices marked documents "INLET" when they contained information to be placed in such a letter. Often concerned derogatory information on prominent people.

INR: See "Bureau of Intelligence and Research."

INS: Immigration and Naturalization Service.

In-Service: Two-week training sessions, required of FBI agents every two years.

Inspection Division: Conducted internal inspections of FBI offices. In 1976, became "Office of Inspections" within Planning and Inspection Division of FBI Headquarters. See "Inspector."

Inspector: High FBI official in FBI Headquarters Inspection Division who usually travels to various field offices to conduct annual inspections. Documents kept in special safes under the "Do Not File" procedure were supposed to be destroyed after annual inspection. "Special" inspections are conducted when special problems arise. Inspectors were required to find some "substantive errors" ("subs") on every inspection. If a "contract" were out at Headquarters for a particular SAC, an inspector could easily find enough wrong to have the SAC demoted and/or transferred.

Instant: Present, current. "Instant investigation" means "the investigation being discussed in this document."

INTC: Intelligence Corps.

Intelligence: Information, usually gathered clandestinely, supposedly used for purposes of advising or policy-making. Intelligence gathering rarely leads to criminal prosecution. The FBI was formed as a law-enforcement agency and its authority to gather intelligence is questionable.

Intelligence Advisory Committee: Created in 1950 as interdepartmental panel for government agencies engaged in intelligence gathering. Absorbed by U.S. Intelligence Board (USIB), 1960.

Intelligence Community: Executive Order 12036 defines this as: CIA; NSA; DIA; offices within DOD for collection of intelligence through reconnaissance; the Bureau of Intelligence and Research of the Department of State; intelligence elements in military; FBI; Department of Treasury; DOE; DEA; and "staff elements of the Office of the Director of Central Intelligence."

Intelligence Division: An "investigative" division of FBI Headquarters, it contained "Counterintelligence Branch" and the "Internal Security Branch." Formerly called "Domestic Intelligence Division." Until 1978 it handled classification and declassification of material requested under FOI/PA. See "Internal Security Branch."

Intelligence Oversight Board: See "IOB."

Intensive Investigation: Sometimes, an FBI euphemism for COINTELPRO-type activities.

Interagency Classification Review Committee (ICRC): Established by NSC, 6/72. Authorized to ensure compliance with executive orders dealing with classification and declassification. Considers appeals from an agency's denial of a declassification request. Is to be replaced by Information Security Oversight Office.

Interagency Committee on Intelligence (Ad Hoc): Prepared the "Huston Plan," which see.

Interdepartmental Committee on Employee Investigations: Created 1942 to assist agencies in evaluating FBI federal employee-loyalty reports.

Interdepartmental Committee on Internal Security: See "ICIS."

Interdepartmental Intelligence Conference (IIC): Established 1939 to coordinate security investigations of FBI and military intelligence agencies. Transferred to supervision of Attorney General, 1962. See "Delimitations Agreement."

Internal Security Act of 1950 (ISA): Effective 9/23/50. Also known as the McCarran Act. Established the SACB, with which all communists were required to register. Persons and organizations registering were denied certain rights. The "Emergency Detention Act" (which see) was included in the ISA.

Internal Security Branch: Within Intelligence Division at FBI Headquarters, had 3 sections as of 1975: "Extremist," "Subversive," and "Research." Transferred to General (Criminal) Investigative Division of FBI Headquarters, 9/76. See "Domestic Security-Terrorism Section."

Internal Security Division: See "ISD."

Internal Security Section:
1. In FBI Headquarters Domestic Intelligence Division, Internal Security Branch, supervised domestic security programs other than espionage and counterespionage. While Subversives Control Section existed, Internal Security Section focused on organizations and Subversives Control Section on individuals. Was apparently replaced by "Subversive Section," which see.
2. In Criminal Division of DOJ, responsible for laws affecting national security. See "ISD."

Interpol: International Criminal Police Organization. Began 1923; reorganized, with Paris headquarters, 1946. Is essentially a communications network between 126 countries. FBI withdrew in 1950 and U.S. Bureau of Interpol has been a Treasury Department Unit. However, FBI has cooperated with Interpol, including sharing NCIC data.

Intertel: Private intelligence and security agency, formed 1970.

Int. Sec. C: Internal Security Communist.

INV: Investigative. Often follows file number of an informant file in the distribution of copies, on lower left of FBI documents. See "ADM."

Investigations Review Unit (IRU): Established 1976 within DOJ, responsible for providing policy guidance on FBI's domestic intelligence operations.

Investigative Insert: An FD-302 (interview report form) or a memo containing the same information as an FD-302, which also specifies the files that are to receive copies of the FD-302 or the memo. Similar to a "Channelizing Memo," which see. See "FD-302."

Investigative Matter: FBI administrative term to measure workload. One case or investigation may entail many "investigative matters."

I.O.: Identification Orders; that is, "wanted" notices such as appear in post offices.

IOB: Intelligence Oversight Board. Established by Executive Order 12036. Reviews intelligence activities and reports to President and Attorney General.

IOC: Interception of communications.

IP: Indianapolis Field Office.

IPAL: Information and Privacy Acts Litigation.

IPU: "Initial Processing Unit," which see

IRS: Internal Revenue Service, has acted in conjunction with FBI and other agencies to harass political activists through selective enforcement of tax laws. IRS illegally supplied considerable tax information to FBI. See "SSS," "IGRS."

IRU: See "Investigations Review Unit."

IS: Internal Security. Often followed after a dash by abbreviation for country which allegedly is potential threat to U.S. internal security, or by "C" (for Communist).

IS-1, 2, 3: The Internal Security Branch of the FBI Headquarters Intelligence Division had 3 sections (as of 1975): IS-1 (the "extremist" section); IS-2 (the "subversive" section); and IS-3 (the "research" section). See "Internal Security Branch."

ISA of 1950, ISA-1950: "Internal Security Act of 1950," which see.

IS-C: Internal Security-Communist.

ISD: Internal Security Division of DOJ, made separate division in 1954. Received numerous FBI communications, and partially reviewed Security Index, but exercised little control over FBI. On 3/22/73, its functions were transferred to DOJ Criminal Division. See "Internal Security Section."

ISINT: Israeli Intelligence Service.

ISIS: Investigation Support Information System. FBI proposed this name for its increasingly automated Central Records System, but abandoned ISIS in 1979.

ISS: Indices Search Slip. See "Search Slip."

ITAR: Interstate transportation in aid of racketeering.

ITOM: Interstate transportation of obscene matter.

ITSMV: Interstate transportation of stolen motor vehicles.

ITSP: Interstate transportation of stolen property.

J-2: Joint Staff Director for Intelligence, DOD.

JAHAM: FBI code for case involving Jay David Whittaker Chambers and Alger Hiss.

JCS: Joint Chiefs of Staff.

JEH: J. Edgar Hoover. When preceded by a number, refers to a room in J. Edgar Hoover Building (FBI HQ), so named in 1972.

JK: Jacksonville Field Office.

JN: Jackson Field Office.

"JUNE" or "JUNE Mail": Code name for files maintained apart from main files of person or organization they relate to, which contain information obtained from a variety of techniques (e.g., burglaries, electronic surveillance, telephone taps, microphone surveillance, surreptitious photography, etc.). These files sometimes also contain the authorization forms for the illegal activities that are undertaken to obtain the information that FBI wants. Ch. IV, Doc. 18.

Justice Department: See "Department of Justice."

K-(number): Laboratory specimen identification number.

KBE: Key Black Extremist. See "Key Black Extremist Program."

KC: Kansas City Field Office.

Key Activist Album: Identified subjects in Key Activist Program. Used in same way as BNPA was used for Key Black Extremist Program.

Key Activist Program: Begun 1/68; allegedly discontinued 2/75. The program called for intensive investigation of every facet of the lives of a small number of political activists. These activists were prime targets of COINTELPRO actions.

Key Black Extremist Program: Initiated 12/70. This FBI program, similar to the Key Activist Program, called for concentrated investigation of and COINTELPRO actions against black leaders. In January, 1973, it became the "Key Extremist Program," and began to include "white-hate" and American Indian leaders. Allegedly discontinued 2/75.

Key Figure Program: Operated by FBI separately from Security Index, Communist Index, etc., "to select for special attention those individuals in a subversive movement who are of outstanding importance to the effectiveness of the movement." Field office obtained photographs and handwriting samples, and maintained informant coverage.

KGB: Komitet Gosudarstvennoy Bezopasnosti — (Committee for State Security), the Soviet agency that combines the functions of the FBI, CIA, National Security Agency, and other American government intelligence institutions into one.*

KX: Knoxville Field Office.

LA: Los Angeles Field Office.

LCN: La Cosa Nostra. FBI abbreviation for organized crime.

LD card: Lead card. Made for agents in following leads. Seem to be destroyed without being filed. Not to be confused with lead sheet or page, which is among the "administrative pages" of some reports, and which sets out leads to be followed by offices receiving report.

LEAA: Law Enforcement Assistance Administration, established 1968. A bureaucratic rival of FBI. Its funding of urban intelligence units contributed to growing surveillance by local police.

Leak: Unauthorized disclosure of classified or otherwise restricted information.

Leased line letter: An official letter from the FBI to a telephone company ordering the setting up of a separate line to enable the FBI to monitor a telephone tap that the FBI is having installed on a subject's phone.

Legal Attache: Cover title given most FBI agents working overseas, based in a U.S. embassy or consulate; also denotes any FBI overseas office.

Legals: Foreign nationals who spy for foreign governments and who maintain open contact with foreign commercial or diplomatic establishments in U.S.

Legat: Shorthand term for "Legal Attache," which see.

LEIU: Law Enforcement Intelligence Unit. Composed of intelligence officers from 225 state and local police departments, it collects and disseminates information to many organizations — public and private — including the FBI. It claims that it has ceased to collect political intelligence and has destroyed its files on political figures.

Letterhead Memo: See "LHM."

Letters of Censure: Agents were often censured for trivial infractions of FBI rules. One letter would delay promotion 6 months, 2 or 3 a year would put an agent on probation.

LGE: Loyalty of Government Employees, a type of investigation now considered obsolete by the FBI.

LHM: Letterhead Memo. FBI summary report intended for dissemination to other agencies. Conceals confidential sources. See Ch. IV, Doc. 6.

Liaison Program: Each field office kept lists of airlines, banks, defense and military agencies, schools, hotels, companies, police departments, state and local agencies, stockbrokers, trucking companies, federal agencies, and news media. Every institution on this list had to be contacted by liaison agent at least once every six months, to create "good will" and ensure that FBI would receive information from institutions on list.

Liaison Section: FBI section for dealing with other government agencies. "Foreign liaison offices" are "legats," and are unrelated to Liaison Section.

Limited Investigation: Type of domestic security investigation established by AG, 4/76. Undertaken when techniques authorized for preliminary investigations are insufficient to determine whether full investigation is warranted. It can use physical surveillance (for purposes other than identifying the subject of investigation) and interviews (with approval of SAC). Is to be closed within 90 days of opening of preliminary investigation, except when extended by Headquarters.

Listening Post: An informant who reports on the situation in the area where he lives or works. Though not supposed to receive specific assignments from FBI, he often does.

LMRA: Labor Management Relations Act, 1947.

LNU: Last Name Unknown (to FBI).

Locator Card: See " 'Number 3' Card."

Logs: Written versions of raw data gathered from surveillance. FISUR logs, ELSUR logs, TESUR logs, and MISUR logs are generally maintained in the field, physically separate from the rest of the files concerning an investigation. However, information derived from them (often with the source of the information thinly disguised) is sent to Headquarters in reports, letters, etc. (The FBI rarely releases under FOIA any but the FISUR logs.) The FBI maintains a separate index to electronic surveillance logs (ELSUR).

Low 2 Material: Routine administrative markings which, until 1977, were denied release by FBI under (b) (2) of the FOIA. See "High 2 Material."

Loyalty Form: Personnel Security Questionnaire (PSQ).

Loyalty Investigation: Same as "Applicant Investigation," which see.

Loyalty Program: See "Federal Employee Loyalty-Security Program."

Loyalty Review Board: Under Executive Orders 10450 and 9835, the Department of Justice was to supply this board with names of subversive organizations. The Loyalty Review Board was to disseminate this information to all departments and agencies.

LP Medley: CIA code name for program of opening mail to and from Russia. Results of this program were sometimes shared with the FBI.

LR: Little Rock Field Office.

LRC: Last Relevant Communication.

LS: Louisville Field Office.

LV: Las Vegas Field Office.

M-8: Squad at FBI NY field office, conducts investigations into political corruption.

Mail Cover: Procedure whereby post office records names and addresses of people who correspond with subject of an investigation, and passes that information on to FBI. The routine use of this procedure was ruled in court in 1978 to be illegal. (Term is also sometimes used for the illegal opening of mail and the reading and/or copying of the contents thereof.)

Mail Intercept: Mail opening.

Mail Survey: Any FBI mail opening program.

Main File: A file, in which is placed material considered relevant to the investigation of the matter designated by the title. See Ch. I.

Major Case Indices: Established by FBI, apart from General Indices, to keep track of information on large cases.

Mann Act: See "White Slave Traffic Act."

Manual of Instructions: Explains FBI investigative policies and techniques. See "MIOG" and "Agent's Handbook."

Manual of Rules and Regulations: FBI administrative manual, includes rules on dissemination, communication, indexing, and filing of documents. See "MAOP" and "Agent's Handbook."

MAOP: FBI Manual of Administrative Operations and Procedures. 646 pages, contains FBI administrative rules, including rules on reporting requirements of field offices to Headquarters. Apparently was formerly called "Manual of Rules and Regulations." See "MIOG."

Mark IV: Large aerosol tear-gas dispenser, issued to FBI agents as needed.

Mass Media Program: FBI program for leaking derogatory information on radicals to the news media.

Master File: Same as "Main File," which see.

Master Search Warrant: Warrant required only date and AG's signature to be activated. Authorized confiscation of any "subversive" propaganda, records of "subversive" organizations, printing presses, money, and much else. Though this warrant was drawn up after the passage of ISA-1950, the ISA had no provision for search or confiscations. See "Master Warrant of Arrest."

Master Warrant of Arrest: Under the Internal Security Act of 1950, individual arrest warrants were to be written for each person detained in time of national emergency. Finding this too "time-consuming," the FBI and Attorney General set up a "Master Warrant" to which a list of names would be attached. See "Security Index," "Attorney General's Portfolio Plan."

MC: Mexico City Legat.

McCarran Act: See "Internal Security Act of 1950."

ME: Memphis Field Office.

Medburg: FBI code name for its investigation of the burglary of its resident agency in Media, Pennsylvania in 1971.*

Media Papers: Non-FBI term for FBI documents stolen from Media, Pennsylvania resident agency and published in WIN magazine, 1971. Gave general public its first indication of the extent of the FBI's surveillance and disruption of political activities. See "Medburg."

Merrimac: CIA project, 4/67-9/70, involved infiltration by CIA of 10 Washington-based domestic activist organizations.

Message Switching Capacity: Capacity to transmit data to any number of terminals in a telecommunication system. The use of NCIC as a message switching center for state and local police was approved 1977.

Mexican border program: FBI COINTELPRO in 1960s, attempted to interfere with relations between American and Mexican Communist parties.

MF: 1. On a search slip, indicates Main File. Normally not written, since any file reference without a serial number is assumed to be to a main file.

2. Rarely, means microfilm.

MI: 1. Written next to a reference on a search slip, indicates that the name on the search slip was misindexed (that is, the name is not mentioned in the document to which the search refers).

2. On an SI card, an individual is "tabbed MI" if he/she is missing.

3. Military Intelligence.

4. Milwaukee Field Office.

MI-5: British counterpart to FBI, called British Security Service; primarily concerned with counterintelligence.

MI-6: British counterpart to CIA; called British Intelligence Service.

MIBURN: FBI code name for its investigation of the killing of three civil-rights workers in Philadelphia, Mississippi, in 1964. (The case was captioned under an earlier probe into the burning of a church.)*

Micro File: Appears to be any file maintained on microfilm.

MID: Military Intelligence Division, established 1885 within Army. Also called G-2, abbreviated "MI" by the FBI.

MIDEM: FBI code for its coverage of demonstrators at 1972 Democratic National Convention in Miami.

Miketel: Telephone which has been turned into an open microphone, capable of intercepting all conversations within hearing range.

Minaret: NSA program, checked all electronic messages (including phone calls) having terminal outside U.S. for names on watch lists provided by FBI and other agencies. Officially ended 1973, but similar activities continue.

Minimization: Under Foreign Intelligence Surveillance Act of 1978, concerns procedures designed to limit the acquisition, retention, and dissemination of information (derived from electronic surveillances) that concerns United States persons and that is unrelated to foreign intelligence.

MIOG: FBI Manual of Investigative Operations and Guidelines. 1,943 pages, in three volumes, explains FBI investigative responsibilities and procedures. Apparently was formerly called "Manual of Instructions." See "MAOP."

Miporn: "Miami pornography." Vast FBI undercover operation, disclosed 2/80, involved the pornography industry and film piracy.

MIREP: FBI code for its coverage of demonstrators at 1972 Republican National Convention in Miami.

MISUR: Microphone surveillance, frequently resulting from an illegal break-in or burglary of the place in which the "bug" (microphone) is to be hidden.

MKULTRA: CIA drug-testing program, used unsuspecting subjects.

MM: Miami Field Office.

MO: Mobile Field Office.

MOI: "Manual of Instructions," which see.

Moocase: FBI code for case involving Boris M. Morros, an alleged double agent who is supposed to have helped FBI crack a Soviet spy ring.

MOSNAT: Movement of Soviet Nationals.

MP: Minneapolis Field Office.

MPD: Metropolitan Police Department.

MS: Written next to a reference on a search slip, indicates the document or file is missing.

MSC: Miscellaneous.

MURKIN: FBI code name for its files on "Assassination of Martin Luther King, Jr., Civil Rights."

NA: FBI National Academy. A training program for state and local policemen.

NAC: New Agents' Class.

Name Check Forms: Sent by other agencies to FBI in connection with loyalty investigations under Executive Order 10450. See "Federal Employee Loyalty-Security Program." More generally, any search of FBI indices for references to an individual is a "name check."

Name Searching Unit: Searches the FBI general indices for references to a particular individual or organization and writes its findings on "search slips." See "File Review."

NARS: National Archives and Records Service. Is responsible for overseeing the records management practices of Federal agencies and has approved FBI timetables for destruction of files. FBI records which NARS considers permanently valuable are to be retained by NARS after FBI no longer needs them.

National Defense Division: At FBI Headquarters, predecessor of Intelligence Division.

National Intelligence Authority (NIA): Created in 1946 to coordinate intelligence activities and advise the President about them. Its staff arm was the Central Intelligence Group. Was a predecessor to the NSC.

Nationalistic Tendency: Country whose interests a suspected security risk allegedly represents.

National Security: According to Executive Order 12065, this means "the national defense and foreign relations of the United States."

National Security Act of 1947: Title I of this act ("Coordination for National Security") established the National Security Council (NSC), the National Security Resources Board (abolished in 1953) and the Central Intelligence Agency (CIA). Title II dealt with "The National Military Establishment" and the Secretary of Defense.

National Security Agency: See "NSA."

National Security Classification: See "Classified Information."

National Security Council: See "NSC."

Nature of Source: Written under identification of "T" numbers in administrative pages of reports, means that the source is one which, by its nature, should be kept confidential. Source may be live or nonlive. See "T-(number)."

NCIC: National Crime Information Center. FBI computerized file of law enforcement data supplied from around the country. Provides over 6,000 criminal justice agencies access to over 7 million records, but not to FBI Central Records System.

NCIC Cleared: Indicates fugitive has been apprehended.

ND: Naval District.

Need-to-Know: Particularly sensitive information is handled on a "need-to-know" basis, that is, only those who must know it are told.

Neutralize: To render harmless or inactive.

New Left: Target of one of FBI's major COINTELPROs, 1968-71. Referred principally to student activists and to opponents of the Vietnam War, but also functioned as a catchall term for political dissidents.

New Left Movement Reporting Program: Initiated 10/68; terminated 2/74. Required comprehensive reporting on "new left" by FBI field offices to FBI HQ. Reports were disseminated to other government agencies.

NF: Norfolk Field Office.

NFIB: National Foreign Intelligence Board. Established by Executive Order 12036 to advise DCI. Includes FBI officers.

NH: New Haven Field Office.

NI: Not Identical; used on search slips to indicate that the person or organization referred to on a particular card in the indices is not the same as the person or organization on whom the FBI researcher is seeking information.

NIA: See "National Intelligence Authority."

NIS or NISO: Naval Investigative Service, or Naval Investigative Service Office.

Nitel: A Bureau communication that is important enough to go by teletype, but routine enough to wait for transmittal overnight at cheaper rates.*

NK: Newark Field Office.

NKVD: A forerunner of the Soviet KGB.

NO: New Orleans Field Office.

No Contact List: Established by J. Edgar Hoover, it named individuals who criticized him or the FBI. In effect, an "enemies list."

Non-record Material: Extra copies, duplicates, shorthand notes, preliminary drafts, used carbon paper, and similar temporary material. Not considered an agency's "records," it can be destroyed without NARS approval, though it sometimes includes information not incorporated into records.

No-Record Main-File: When the FBI finds no information in its central indices on the subject of an FOI/PA request it tells the requester it has "no record." When it finds "see refs," but no "main file," it considers the request a "no-record main-file" and asks the requester for further information. The further information is allegedly so that the "see refs" can be positively identified as pertaining to the subject of the request.

Notional: Organization or other entity covertly run by FBI. See "Proprietary"; "Notional Records."

Notional Records: Intentionally inaccurate documents, contrived to mislead the reader. It is not known whether the FBI ever prepares notional records for release under the FOIA.

November Committee: FBI front, established 1972 in Los Angeles. Consisted entirely of undercover agents, who arranged housing and transportation for numerous protestors and thereby kept close watch on them.

NP: Not Pertinent. On search slips, means that the reference is not relevant to the search. Sometimes used by FBI as if it were an FOIA exemption, in which case it is synonymous with "OS." See Ch. II.

NPC: Newspaper clippings.

NR: Written next to a reference in a search slip, means "no record." Indicates that the reference does not pertain to the individual listed on the search slip. This usually occurs when the reference is to another individual who has the same name as the individual listed on the search slip.

NRO: National Reconnaissance Office.

NSA: National Security Agency. Was originally AFSA. Reorganized as NSA, 1952. Is exempt by statute from FOIA. Its files on Americans in its "Office of Security" were destroyed, 1974. FBI has burglarized foreign embassies at request of NSA. NSA has monitored international communications of Americans, in part because of FBI requests. See "SHAMROCK," "MINARET."

NSC: National Security Council. Established by National Security Act of 1947 to study security matters and make recommendations to President. Issued secret 1949 directive authorizing FBI and military counterespionage and "subversive" investigations. See "CIA."

Number One Man: Second in command; fills in when the FBI official over him (e.g., his section chief) is not available.

"Number 1" Register: Signed each morning by each employee of an FBI office.

"Number 2" Register: Register in which FBI personnel sign out.

"Number 3" Card: Filed daily by each FBI agent, details the agent's projected activities for the day, including exact times and places. Extremely inaccurate, the cards (also called "FD-256s") are often altered at later times. Are apparently never released under FOIA. See "VOT," "TIO," "ATIO," "TOPCI."

NY: New York Field Office.

Φ: Written next to a name, appears to mean that the name has been indexed (as a "see reference") in FBI general indices. However, absence of this symbol doesn't show name has not been indexed.

O: As in "NYO" or "WFO," means "office."

O: FBI Headquarters and each field office keeps "0" ("Zero") files for miscellaneous information. See "00." Also see Ch. I.

O & C: Official and Confidential. Some files kept in J. Edgar Hoover's office were "O & C," and allegedly contained incriminating information on many prominent people. "O & C" is not a national security classification authorized by Executive Order. See Ch. I.

OC: 1. As in "tab OC," means "Out of the Country." An "Out of the Country" Section of SI was maintained for subjects not in U.S.
   2. Oklahoma City Field Office.

3. Organized Crime.

4. "O & C," which see.

ODALE: Office of Drug Abuse Law Enforcement. Merged into DEA.

ODI: Office of Defense Intelligence.

Office of Information Law and Policy: Established 1978 in DOJ to coordinate FOIA policies of federal agencies, including DOJ components such as FBI.

Office of Intelligence Policy and Review: Justice Department Office, created 1979 to provide intelligence community with legal advice and legislative assistance.

Office of Origin: See "OO."

Office of Planning and Evaluation: Established 1972. Studies FBI operations and advises Director. Now part of Planning and Inspection Division, FBI/HQ.

Office of Privacy and Information Appeals (OPIA): Established 3/75 within office of Deputy Attorney General. Originally called Freedom of Information Appeals Unit. Handles administrative appeals regarding the withholding of information.

Office of Professional Responsibility: Two offices: one in DOJ, established 1975, oversees investigations of alleged misconduct by DOJ employees; one in FBI, established 1976, performs same function for FBI employees, and allegedly works closely with its DOJ counterpart.

Official and Confidential: See "O & C."

OG: On TESUR logs, means "outgoing" (that is, an outgoing phone call).

OK, H: Notation of J. Edgar Hoover, indicating his approval of recommendations made in an FBI document.

Old Dog: Soldier AWOL for over two years. Unofficial FBI slang.

OM: Omaha Field Office.

OMB: Office of Management and Budget. Responsible for (among other things) developing guidelines for agencies' implementation of PA. OMB has exercised little influence over FBI, especially during J. Edgar Hoover's reign.

Omnibus Crime Control and Safe Streets Act of 1968: Established procedures for obtaining judicial warrants for wiretaps, but left open the issue of warrantless "national security" taps.

1A Envelope: Envelopes, placed in front of or behind files in field offices, which usually contain "physical evidence" (e.g., signed statements, photographs, FISUR logs) that might be used in trials. See Ch. IV, Doc. 14.

ONI: Office of Naval Intelligence, established 1882, currently known as the Naval Intelligence Command.

"On-The-Nose" Search: Procedure approved by Attorney General in 1975, whereby FBI searches general indices only for exact names provided by FOI/PA requester. Differs from standard FBI "Six-Way Search," which see.

OO: 1. Office of Origin, the FBI field office that has primary responsibility for an investigation. The "OO" is aided by other field offices (see "auxiliary offices"). The "OO" can change during the course of investigation. If a person is the target (subject) of several different FBI investigations simultaneously, he/she *may* have several "OO"s at the same time.

2. FBI Headquarters and each field office keeps "OO" ("Double Zero") files concerning policy and procedure. See Chapter I.

OOJ: Obstruction of Justice.

OP: Office of Preference, i.e., the FBI office to which an agent wants assignment. It is difficult to get one's "OP," and FBI has often used transfers to undesirable offices to punish agents.

OPE: "Office of Planning and Evaulation," which see.

Operation Abscam: FBI "Arab scam" operation. Began 2/78; publicly revealed 2/80. American officials, including a U.S. Senator, allegedly accepted supposed bribes from undercover FBI agents pretending to be or to represent Arab sheiks.

Operation Big Squeeze: Drive, initiated 1961 by AG Robert Kennedy, to deal with organized crime.

Operation Border Coverage: FBI COINTELPRO of 1961.

Operation Dragnet: FBI Emergency Detention Program. See "Attorney General's Portfolio Plan"; "Security Index."

Operation Frontload: FBI plan for penetrating organized crime in construction industry. It ended in fall 1978 with no indictments, and the FBI's informer was accused of cheating construction companies of hundreds of thousands of dollars.

Operation Hoodwink: FBI COINTELPRO, in 1960s, attempted to disrupt Mafia and CP-USA by making them angry at each other. FBI forged signatures of CP-USA personnel on letters to Mafia leaders.

Operation Leprechaun: IRS program in Florida, initiated 4/72, used illegal methods to gather personal information on prominent individuals. Was part of "IGRS," which see.

Operations Section: In FBI FOI/PA Branch, supports "Disclosure Section." Its units are: training and research; field coordination; appeals and corrections; classification review; and initial processing.

OPO: Old Post Office, where FBI Washington Field Office (WFO) was located.

OPR: "Office of Professional Responsibility," which see.

Organized Crime: Has been defined by FBI as "criminal activity by two or more persons who are engaged in a continuing enterprise for the purpose of obtaining monetary or commercial gains or profits wholly or in part through racketeering activity."

ORI: Originating Agency. NCIC code for office entering information.

Origin: Synonymous with "office of origin." See "OO."

OS: Outside Scope. Written next to deletions to indicate material allegedly outside scope of FOIA request. "OS" is not an exemption provided for by the FOIA.

OSI: Office of Special Investigations, U.S. Air Force.

OSS: Office of Strategic Services, established 1942 for intelligence and counter-intelligence operations everywhere but Western Hemisphere. Terminated 1945, but was succeeded by CIG-CIA. Had jurisdictional disputes with FBI's "SIS."

P: Pending; a matter still under investigation.

P*: Pending Inactive. Pending case in which no further investigation is to be conducted for the time being, except for such investigation (e.g., checking of records) as can be handled by clerks.

PA: Privacy Act of 1974. Effective 9/75. FBI considers most of its files exempt from disclosure under PA. PA, unlike FOIA, prohibits certain investigations and gives individuals the right to have certain changes made in files on them. See "First-Party Request." See Ch. II.

P&C: Personal and Confidential. Can refer either to one document, a series of documents or to whole files deemed by the FBI to be particularly sensitive. Not a classification authorized by executive order; hence, not grounds for invoking exemption (b) (1). See Ch. I.

P & P: Pamphlets and Publications.

Pair Number: Identifying number for a telephone. Helps FBI install wiretaps.

Panel Sources: Individuals, not involved in groups under investigation, who attend public gatherings for intelligence purposes or as potential witnesses. First developed in 1950s to obtain witnesses in Smith Act trials without exposing regular informants.

Passport Office: Was furnished quarterly list of SI Priority I subjects so FBI could be advised of foreign travel by these subjects.

PC: Same as "P & C," which see.

PCI: Potential criminal informant. Category abolished by 1977. Were rarely promoted to CIs (Criminal Informants).

Pct: Precinct.

PD: 1. Police Department.
2. Portland Field Office.

PEAD: Presidential Emergency Action Documents, prepared under the Emergency Detention Program.

Pending Inactive: See "P*."

Pending Kept in Closed: Apparently, same as "Pending Inactive." See "P*."

Pendorf: Chicago-based FBI investigation publicly revealed in 2/80, allegedly involved a Teamsters' Union pension fund and businessman Allen F. Dorfman, and other figures including a U.S. Senator.

Perfected FOI/PA Request: Request to FBI under FOI/PA which has a notarized signature and, in the FBI's judgment, has enough information positively to verify the requester's identity. FBI estimates only about 55% of requests are "perfected" when first received. See Ch. II.

Permanent Serial Chargeout: See "Serial Chargeout."

Permissive Search: Search of premises made with permission of resident.

Personal and Confidential: See "P & C."

Personal Folder: Operational details of "surreptitious entries" were filed in SACs' Personal Folder. Authorizations for such entries were filed under the "Do Not File" procedure.

PF: Personal file. See Ch. I.

PG: Pittsburgh Field Office.

Ph: Phonetic spelling of word or name.

PH: Philadelphia Field Office.

PHS: Personal History Statement.

Pike Committee: House Select Committee on Intelligence. Published some findings

(1975-76). Congress suppressed its final report, but portions appeared in the *Village Voice* of Sept. 20, 1979.

PINAP: FBI code name for its investigation of the kidnapping of Virginia Piper of Minneapolis in 1972.*

Pink Memo: FBI communication on pink paper, destroyed without being filed.

Plain Text: Information not written in code.

Planning and Inspections Division: Formed 1976 out of "Inspection Division" and "Office of Planning and Evaluation," in FBI Headquarters.

Plant Informant Program: Begun 9/40 to develop FBI sources in defense plants. By 9/42 had 23,746 confidential sources in 3,879 plants. Terminated 3/69.

POB: Place of Birth.

Portfolio Plan: See "Attorney General's Portfolio Plan."

Potential Confidential Informant: Even if an individual has supplied much information to the FBI, the FBI may consider him merely a "potential" informant if his reliability has not been established. See "PCI," "PRI," "PSI."

Potential Extremist Informant: Category adopted by FBI, 3/73. Could be promoted to "extremist informant" after 6 months if he produced sufficient information. Would be eliminated if not promoted within 1 year. See "PSI," "PRI."

PR: Prosecutive Report. Forwarded from field offices to FBI HQ at the end of a criminal investigation, but prior to rendering prosecutive opinion.

Predication: The basis on which an investigation is undertaken. This can be either information about alleged criminal or subversive activity, or the statutory justification for conducting an investigation of such activity.

Preliminary Inquiries: Undertaken to determine whether a full investigation should be started, they are supposed to be made only through established sources and to last at most 90 days. Their use was initiated 9/73. About 90% of investigations are opened as preliminary inquiries. There is no requirement to notify Headquarters about a preliminary inquiry, provided its results are negative and it is completed in 90 days. However, the GAO found in 1976 that *most* preliminary inquiries continue longer than 90 days and that even those extending past the 90 day limit are usually *not* reported to Headquarters. In 4/76, AG established new criteria for "Preliminary Investigations," which see.

Preliminary Investigations: Formerly called preliminary inquiries. AG's 4/76 guidelines established 3 levels of domestic security investigations: preliminary, limited, and full (or full-field). Preliminary investigations can be started based on any information that a person or group may be engaged in activities which involve or will involve force or violence, in violation of federal law, to impair the government or deprive persons of civil rights. Field offices can examine FBI records, public information, other government records; can contact previously established informants; and can conduct physical surveillance and interviews to identify the subject of the preliminary investigation. Is to be closed within 90 days, but Headquarters can authorize extension.

Preprocessed Documents: Documents available for public review at FBI reading room at FBI Headquarters. See list of these documents under "For Further Information" section of this book.

Presumptive Duplicate: In processing the Rosenberg 'case files, FBI refused to release a document from one file if another copy of the same document had "presumably" already been processed from another file on the case. The document refused was called a "presumptive duplicate," but often no copy of the document had in fact been previously processed. It is possible that FBI uses this procedure in other large FOIA requests.

Pretext Telephone Call: FBI, without identifying itself, invents an excuse for calling and determining, e.g., if an individual is at home, if he/she still lives at a certain address, where he/she can be reached, etc. FBI frequently uses (b) (7) (E) to hide pretext calls.

Preventive Intelligence: Information relating to "potential" espionage or sabotage. In practice it does not differ from "pure" intelligence concerned with alleged "subversive activities."

PRI: Potential Racial Informant. Term probably used before "Potential Extremist Informant."

Priority: As a routing notation, indicates the manner in which a communication is to be sent, e.g., air mail, registered, by courier.

Priority Apprehension Program: Effective 1969. Replaced "Detcom" tabbing. Subjects on Security Index were assigned to apprehension priorities; "I" for top-level leaders; "II" for second-level leaders; 'III" for rank and file. FBI verified home and business addresses every three months for Priority I subjects; every year for others. Was replaced by the four categories of the ADEX.

Privacy Act: See "PA."

PRN: Puerto Rican Nationalist.

PRNC: Potomac River Naval Command.

Pro-Active Enforcement: Operation in which FBI is in on the planning of a crime which has not yet been committed. Opposite of "reactive" law enforcement in which FBI responds to an already committed crime.

Processing: Procedure FBI follows in preparing a file for release under FOIA. A case is considered "processed" whether the request is granted in full, denied in part, or denied in full, but not if request is "administratively closed" or if no file relevant to request is found.

Project Hunter: FBI code for information received under CIA's New York mail intercept program, 1958-73.

Project Onslaught: 5/77. Five-month "crash program" to eliminate backlog of un-processed FOIA and PA requests to FBI. It reduced, but did not eliminate, backlog.

Project Request: FOIA request to FBI which involves 15 or more "volumes" ("sections"). Project requests are handled by different units of the FOI/PA branch from nonproject requests, in order to keep small requests from being held up by the processing of large ones.

Proprietary: Ostensibly private commercial entity surreptitiously established and controlled by a government intelligence agency. FBI has developed many proprietaries, mostly since the mid 1970s. See "Abdul Enterprises," "Brilab," "Operation Abscam."

PROSAB: Protection of Strategic Air Command Bases of U.S.A. Air Force.

Prosecutive Summary: Reports prepared by FBI field offices, summarize evidence and availability of witnesses in a case under investigation. Are usually not prepared in subversive-type investigations, and, even when they are, FBI may have little expectation that criminal prosecution will be initiated.

Pros-memo: Prosecution memo. DOJ summary of evidence compiled by FBI. Copies are sent to appropriate FBI officials.

Protect: Often, means "protect identity," that is, keep the individual's name confidential.

PSI: Potential Security Informant. It may take a year of supplying information before a PSI is promoted to Security Informant. A "potential" informant *is* paid. See "Potential Extremist Informant."

PSQ: Personnel Security Questionnaire.

Public Affairs Office: Adjunct to FBI Director's Office, handles news media requests and other public information matters.

Puerto Rican Bomber Program: FBI COINTELPRO, initiated 1966, sought to disrupt Puerto Rican independence groups.

Pure Intelligence: Supplies information believed useful in making policy decisions. Is entirely unrelated to enforcement of federal law. See "Preventive Intelligence."

PV: Parole Violator.

PX: Phoenix Field Office.

Q (number): Specimens for examination by FBI laboratory generally are assigned numbers preceded by "Q."

R: At the end of a source number, e.g., "WFO 305-R," indicates a source of "racial" intelligence. "R*" is a source unavailable to testify, e.g. a black bag or ELSUR. See "S."

RA: Resident Agency or an agent assigned to such an agency (Resident Agent). See "Resident Agency."

Rabbi: FBI vernacular for a friend or unofficial sponsor at FBI Headquarters who provides informal help to an agent.

Rabble-Rouser Index: Created 8/67; renamed Agitator Index, 3/68. Established by Hoover to intensify investigation of individuals supposedly having a propensity to foment violence or racial discord. Overlapped with SI, but provided list of primary targets for COINTELPROs. List grew from 100 names (1967) to 1,131 (1970). Abolished 4/71. See "ADEX."

RAC: Apparently means "racial matters."

Racial Calendar: FBI list, established 1968, to advise all field offices of "the dates of black nationalist-type conferences and . . . racial events and anniversaries." Expanded 1969 to include "antifascist, antidraft and anti-Vietnam" demonstrations and conferences.

Racial Intelligence Section: Original name of "Extremist Section," which see.

Racial Matter: FBI investigation, usually of an organization of a racial minority, sometimes of a white hate group.

RAIPE: Revolutionary Activities Informants Program-Extremist.

Rap Sheet: Criminal record.

RCI: On cover sheets of file, probably means that subject of file is on Reserve or Communist Index.

RCMP: Royal Canadian Mounted Police — The Canadian counterpart of the FBI and CIA.

Rebuairtel (date): In reference to previous airtel from Bureau (HQ) of (date).

Rebulet (date): In reference to previous letter from Bureau (HQ) of (date).

Rebutel (date): In reference to a teletype from Bureau (HQ) of (date).

Rec: Recorded. Indicates that a document has been placed in the appropriate file, and has been given a case and serial number.

Records Branch: In FBI Headquarters Records Management Division, is responsible for searching General Index.

Records Management Division: At FBI Headquarters, maintains files and indices. Contains FBI FOI/PA Section.

Redaction: Deletion.

Red Squad: Popular term for "antisubversive" units of local police forces, which sometimes work closely with FBI.

Ref: Same as "See Ref," which see.

Refer 5 IS: Indicates that the document should be routed to the 5th squad, an "internal security" squad.

References Review: Same as "File Review," which see.

Referral: When the FBI sends a document to another government agency in order to ask that agency whether the document should be released under FOI/PA, the document is known as a "referral." "Referrals" occur because information in FBI files is sometimes obtained from other agencies.

Reg.: After file number (in distribution of copies) on lower left of FBI documents, probably means "send by registered mail."

Registration Act: See "Internal Security Act of 1950"; "Foreign Registration Act of 1938."

Relet (date): Referring to letter of (date).

Relief Supervisor: Heads FBI squad in absence of regular field supervisor. The first step up from "brick agent." See "Squad."

Remytel (date): Referring to my (i.e., this office's) teletype of (date).

Report: FBI communication, often quite long, from a field office to Headquarters, with copies to other interested field offices. Except for "Administrative Pages," (which see) reports are intended for dissemination to other government agencies. Normally, five copies of each report are sent to Headquarters. Dissemination and destruction of copies are supposed to be noted on front page of report at Headquarters. Sources in reports are often referred to by the "T-(number,)" which see. Until 1/75, a report was required on each pending investigative matter at least once every 45 days. See Ch. IV, Docs. 4 and 5.

Req. Rec'd.: Request received.

Research Section: Within "Internal Security Branch" at FBI Headquarters. In addition to research, it was responsible for preparing requests for electronic surveillance and for monitoring electronic surveillance records.

Reserve Index (RI): Prior to 1960, known as the Communist Index. Abolished in September, 1971. Listed persons considered dangerous to national security and who would receive "priority consideration" after the allegedly more dangerous Security Index subjects had been apprehended. Persons meeting the criteria for inclusion in the RI were divided into two groups. Section A consisted of teachers, journalists, lawyers, physicians, and others whom the FBI considered well placed to work against the national interest. Section B contained all other RI subjects. The Communist-Reserve Index, consisting of 5"x8" cards, was, during most of its existence, maintained only by the field offices, not HQ.

Resident Agency: A small FBI office (1-35 agents) within the field division of a field office. Set up to cover geographical areas far from the field offices, and also to cover areas which allegedly have some special need for FBI offices, e.g., airports, university towns, and state capitals.

RESISTANCE: CIA project, 12/67-6/73, allegedly established to protect CIA recruiters on college campuses, collected political intelligence on students and others. CIA Targets Analysis Branch, established to process RESISTANCE information, also received FBI reports.

Responsibilities Program: Short for "Responsibilities of the FBI in the Security Matter Field."

Restricted: "Security Information-Restricted" was a classification lower than "confidential," used principally for information which was to be limited to official use. Executive Order 10501 (effective 12/15/53) eliminated this classification. It is doubtful that the FBI made use of this classification.

Restricted Data: Data concerning atomic weapons and/or fissionable material which the Atomic Energy Commission (or its successors) has not determined may be published. Not to be confused with the term "Restricted."

Reurtel (date): Referring to your (i.e., your office's) teletype of (date).

REV: Revolutionary.

Reverse FOIA Suit: Brought to prevent disclosure to FOIA requester of information held by government. It is unclear what rights the FOIA provides to bring such a suit.

RFMT: Radio Frequency Microphone Telephone Surveillance.

RH: Richmond Field Office.

RI: "Reserve Index," which see.

RICO: Racketeer Influenced and Corrupt Organizations. 1970 law aimed at organized crime, but so broadly worded that it covers much else.

RM: 1. Registered Mail, usually appears after distribution of copies is indicated on lower left corner of FBI document.

2. Racial Matter.

ROCIC: Regional Organized Crime Information Center. National police information network, founded 1976. It is not subject to FOIA and little is known about it.

Routing Block: Stamp, often found on upper right of FBI documents, lists high officials, units, squads, etc. The names of whoever is supposed to see the document are checked off. After seeing it, the official initials the document.

Routing Slip: Printed form directing internal distribution of attached papers to specific persons or sections within the FBI. Can also contain an explanation or notation about action taken on a case.

Routing Unit: In FBI Headquarters, opens mail addressed to FBI, stamps date of receipt, and determines who within FBI should receive the mail. Unless mail is considered "expedite," it is sent to Classifying Unit.

R/S: "Routing Slip," which see.

RUC: Referred Upon Completion. Used by an auxiliary office to indicate that, until further notice, it has completed its role in an investigation and is referring the matter back to the office of origin.

RWBS: Report Will Be Submitted.

S: 1. Secret (found alongside text); security classification used for information the disclosure of which could reasonably be expected to cause serious damage to national security.
2. As in a source number, e.g., "PH-27-S," indicates "security" source. "S*" is a source unavailable to testify, e.g., an ELSUR or black bag.

S-2: Intelligence branch, Army Special Staff.

SA: 1. Special Agent, the title of any FBI agent. See "Agent."
2. San Antonio Field Office.

SAB: Security Advisory Board. Established 5/43, composed of armed services officers, it handled matters relating to classification of sensitive information. Eliminated in 1947.

SAC: Special Agent in Charge. All FBI field offices except L.A. and N.Y. are headed by SACs. N.Y. and L.A. are headed by Assistant Directors, and have several SACs each.

SACB: Subversive Activities Control Board. Established by the Internal Security Act of 1950 to ferret out "communist action" and "communist front" organizations, but eventually denied funds by Congress and abolished in the 1970s after the federal courts had curbed its powers.

SAC Letter No. : Numbered SAC letters are directives from the FBI Director, and are usually concerned with general policies or with cases of interest to all field offices. "SAC Letter No. 55-30" is the 30th SAC Letter of 1955.

Sanitize: To paraphrase so as to eliminate sensitive source information while retaining the gist of the intelligence.

SAS: Special Agents. See "Agent."

S-B: Soviet-Bloc.

SC: 1. Special Clerk.
2. Sacramento Field Office.

Scam: A swindle. Used of FBI "sting" operations, e.g., "Operation Abscam," which see.

SCC: Special Coordination Committee of NSC, established by Executive Order 12036. When developing counterintelligence policy, it includes FBI Director.

SD: San Diego Field Office.

SE: 1. Special Employee of FBI, not an agent (SA) or clerk. SEs are often used to check records of credit bureaus, other government agencies, etc. Translators and photographers are sometimes SEs.

2. Seattle Field Office.

"Search as: ": An FBI general indices searcher will generally search for references to an individual under several variants of that individual's name; the searcher will look up in the indices whatever variants are listed after "search as." See "Six-Way Search."

Search for File Number: After a document has been classified and marked for indexing, FBI determines if it already has a file in which document should be placed. If not, document becomes first serial of a new file. See "Block Stamp."

Search Slip (or Indices Search Slip): Lists the references found on Index Cards for any given subject of investigation. Includes only file reference of FBI office being searched. See Ch. IV, Docs. 21 and 22.

Seat of Government (SOG): FBI HQ.

Sec: Followed by number, means "Section."

Secret Service: Within Treasury Department, protects the President, his family and some other political figures; and investigates counterfeiting. FBI sends information to Secret Service more often than to any other single government agency, but the Secret Service claims to retain very little. See "FD-376."

"Section": Large fil s are usually divided into "sections" or "volumes" consisting of *roughly* 200 pages of documents. Generally, FBI HQ uses the term "sections" whereas field o' ices use the term "volumes." The term "section" is also used to refer to units f FBI HQ Divisions and Branches. Which of the two meanings is intended is erally clear from the context.

Section 87 D- . of the Manual f Instructions: Section of the FBI manual detailing matters s ch as the criteria to. inclusion in the SI or RI, or the criteria for initiatir an investigation of a group.

Secure a esidence: To illegally break into a re idence.

Securi : One of the three main types of FBI investigation, the others being cri inal and applicant. Up to one-third of FBI s investigative force has been ir volved in Security cases. See "National Security," "Domestic Intelligence," Security Matter."

Security Division: Forerunner of FBI Domestic Intelligence Division; established 1940 as a reactivated version of GID.

Security Flash: Notice sent by field office to Headquarters Identification Division (ID), asks if fingerprints of Security Index subject have been received since last check. If ID has subject's fingerprints, it adds a notice in the fingerprint record to advise field office of subsequent fingerprint submissions.

Security Index (SI): A list of persons whom the FBI thinks are potentially dangerous to the public safety or internal security of the U.S.; until 1943, called the Custodial Detention List. It was replaced by the ADEX in 1971. Every SI subject was placed in one of three categories, depending on the priority the FBI gave to his/her apprehension. Though the SI declined from its height of over 26,000 names in 1955, this was primarily because subjects removed from the SI were placed on the Communist Index-Reserve Index. Cards, 5" x 8", were maintained in both HQ and the appropriate offices of origin. See Ch. IV, Doc. 1.

Security Matter: Starting 1943, investigations of individuals (other than alien enemies) considered potentially dangerous to internal security were characterized as "Security Matters," rather than the earlier characterization, "Custodial Detention."

Security Squad: FBI field office squad specializing in "security" cases.

See Ref.: Short for "See Reference." See ref. cards in FBI general indices show where references to an individual are found in files other than those captioned in the individual's name. See Ch. I.

Semontel: Suspected Espionage-Fort Monmouth, N.J., and Federal Telecommunications Laboratory, Nutley, N.J. A widespread investigation for "spy" suspects in the 1950s.

Sensitive:

1. Of information, likely to produce embarrassment if disclosed. Is *not* a national security classification authorized by executive order.

2. Government employment position related to national security.

Serial: An individual document within a file. Each serial in a file has a different number. See Ch. I.

Serial Chargeout: Authorizes the removal of a document from an FBI file, and placement of document in, e.g., confidential file room or a supervisor's office. Document is replaced by the "serial chargeout." Normally, an agent wanting to see a document will call for an entire "section" of a file and the section will later be returned. "Serial chargeout" is thus a fairly unusual procedure. See Ch. I; Ch. IV, Doc. 17.

Serialize: To assign a serial number to a document.

Service Unit: Prepares FBI correlation summaries; and, in cases requiring experienced clerks, searches the general indices. See "Name Searching Unit."

SF: San Francisco Field Office.

SF 64: Standard Form, used by FBI agent to report observations.

SF 115: Standard Form, used by FBI to request authorization from NARS to destroy records.

SGE: Security of Government Employees.

SHAMROCK: NSA program, involved interception of all private cables leaving U.S. Begun 1945. Officially ended 5/75, but interception of telegrams continues. See "MINARET," "LP Medley."

SI: 1. "Security Index," which see. (See also "ADEX" and "Attorney General's Portfolio Plan.")

2. On correlation summaries or search slips next to a file and serial number, means "Same Information."

3. Security Informant.

4. Springfield Field Office.

SIS: Special Intelligence Service of FBI, established 6/40 by Roosevelt for intelligence gathering in Western Hemisphere. Abolished 1946; functions taken over by CIG.

SIS Section: Special Intelligence Service, Intelligence Division, New York City Police Department.

Six-Way Search: FBI researchers, searching in the indices for references to an individual, are normally supposed to check six variants of the individual's name, e.g., "John Paul Jones," "John P. Jones," "John Jones," J.P. Jones," "J. Jones," and "P. Jones" or "Paul Jones." Six-way searches are conducted for FBI investigative purposes, but not in connection with FOIA requests. See "On-The-Nose Search."

SJ: San Juan Field Office.

Skim: Practice of FBI agent's pocketing a portion of pay supposedly going to his informants.

SL: St. Louis Field Office.

Sleeper: Individual with past record of "subversive" activity, whom FBI suspects will become active again.

SM: 1. As in "SM-C," is "Security Matter-Communist." See "Security Matter."

      2. Summary. Used for summaries of ELSUR logs.

Smith Act: Passed as a rider to the federal Alien Registration Act of 1940, it prohibited advocating the overthrow of any government in the U.S. by force or violence. Also banned publication or distribution of material advocating this. Often cited by FBI as basis for investigation of suspected subversives.

SMUN: Soviet Mission to the United Nations.

Snitch Jackets: False documents, planted by FBI, purporting to show that a member of some organization is an FBI informer. Used primarily, but not exclusively, in COINTELPRO actions.

Socialist Workers Party (SWP) Program: FBI COINTELPRO, initiated 1961, subsumed under New Left COINTELPRO 1969.

Society of Former Special Agents of the FBI: Private organization of 6,600 former SAs, many of whom hold high-level positions in the public and private sector. SAs must retire fairly young; hence many have second careers. The secretive society, New York City based, helps the FBI maintain a network of powerful ex-agents who will supply information FBI cannot otherwise obtain.

SODAC: Soviet diplomatic activities.

SOE: Special Operations Executive; established 1940, British World War II counterpart to OSS. Coordinated and initiated sabotage against enemy.

Soft Files: Temporary files housing sensitive or embarrassing information, maintained apart from an agency's normal files and not searched in response to FOIA requests.

SOG: Seat of Government, i.e., FBI Headquarters, in Washington, D.C.

Sound Man: Expert in electronic surveillance techniques.

Sound School: Training in electronic surveillance. Agents in "sound school" also received "specialized lock-training" and other bank robber's techniques to help them in performing surreptitious entries.

Source: Any supplier of information to FBI, human or otherwise. Sources, unlike informants, tend not to be paid and are likely to be persons whose position gives them access to information — e.g., bankers, employers, landlords. Allegedly, confidential sources are used in about 50% of domestic intelligence cases. See "Informant," "Confidential Informant."

Special Agent (SA): Any FBI agent. See "Agent."

Special Correspondence List: List of individuals friendly toward FBI who regularly received FBI publications.

Special Desk: Supervises a special group of investigations, e.g., a group being intensified. See "Substantive Desk."

Special File: Apparently, same as "Double Sticker File," which see.

Special File Room: Location outside Central Records for particularly sensitive FBI files. See Ch. I.

Special Indices: FBI indices apart from General Indices. See Ch. I.

Special Inquiry Section: At FBI Headquarters, handles mostly "name checks" for White House.

Special Investigative Division: In 1975 contained three sections: Criminal Intelligence-Organized Crime; Fugitive; and Employees' Security and Special Inquiry. The "employee" (or "applicant") investigations frequently concentrate on "subversive" matters. See "Criminal Investigative Division."

Special Operations: Supersecret COINTELPRO operation, allegedly concerned with the intelligence service of a hostile foreign power, but also targeted the Black Panther Party.

Special Projects: Can be a euphemism for COINTELPRO activities.

Special Section of the Security Index: Listed those in SI whose apprehension by FBI in case of national emergency would be difficult or somehow undesirable. These individuals would not be arrested immediately in a national emergency, unlike other SI subjects. In 9/50 the Special Section of the SI had over 200 names.

Special War Policies Unit: W.W. II DOJ unit, originally called Neutrality Laws Unit, responsible for reviewing FBI Custodial Detention List and for analyzing FBI intelligence reports. Abolished 7/43, functions transferred to Internal Security Division of DOJ.

SPECTAR: Special Target Informant Development Program, under which informers on the Weather Underground would be paid up to $1,000 per month for their efforts regardless of how much information they supplied.

Spl. Msgr.: Special Messenger.

Squad: The average field office has 126 agents organized into eight squads, though some field offices are considerably larger. The larger a field office, the more numerous and specialized its squads. The squad or "field" supervisor is responsible for the day-to-day control of his squad and has considerable authority, especially in cases which the Bureau Supervisors consider relatively minor.

Squad 47: In the New York Field Office, a squad of over 60 agents which specialized in the use of illegal techniques against suspected subversives and extremists.

S/R Card: Card on which is listed an individual considered to be an atomic energy security risk.

SRA: Senior Resident Agent; coordinates the work of a Resident Agency, but often has little authority because of the control exercised from the field office.

SS: "Search Slip," which see.

SSA: Selective Service Act.

SSN: Selective Service Number.

SSS: Special Services Staff of IRS. Harassed dissidents through selective enforcement of tax laws. Many of its targets were provided by FBI. Established 7/69; abolished 8/73.

SSS 301: Selective Service form, sometimes used to refer Selective Service case to FBI for investigation.

STAG: Student Agitation. An FBI new left intelligence gathering program on antigovernment demonstrations and protest rallies.

Stats: FBI vernacular for "statistics." J. Edgar Hoover impressed Congressional appropriations committees each year with highly distorted "stats" on such matters as convictions, fines, savings, and recoveries. Any SAC whose "stats" did not go up every year was in trouble.

Status: An FBI case's "status" can be pending (P), pending inactive (P*), referred upon completion (RUC), or closed (C).

Sting: Expression used since 1976 for undercover operations using fictitious businesses to gather information. FBI uses "stings" despite some questions about their legaltiy.

Stop Index: Initiated 4/71. Intended to follow activities of "extremists" not carried in NCIC wanted persons files. Law enforcement records supplied to NCIC were compared daily with Stop Index in hopes records would involve Index subjects. When discontinued in 2/74, had 4,300 names.

Stop Notice: When FBI wants to keep track of an individual, it may notify a government agent (e.g., INS, local police) to alert FBI if contact is made with the individual.

Street Agent: "Brick Agent," which see.

Stripped: When a file is "stripped," documents are removed and destroyed. Allegedly, most such destructions are of "non-record" material.

SU: Salt Lake City Field Office.

SUB: "Subject," which see.

Subfile: Subdivision of a main file. Subfiles are lettered or numbered. Lettered subfiles (Sub. A, Sub. B, etc.) are likely to contain, e.g., newspaper clippings or prosecution summaries. Numbered subfiles tend to concern electronic surveillances and black bags. See Ch. I.

Subj.: "Subject," which see.

Subject: A person or thing investigated by the FBI is a "subject" of that investigation. A "subject" is, in the vast majority of cases, a person or organization. Any person on the SI is an "SI subject," and similarly for the other FBI lists of names.

"Submarine": See "Torpedo."

Substantive Desk: The agent (in a field office or headquarters) responsible for the

209

supervision of matters falling under a particular classification number.

Substantive Error ("sub"): A failure to follow required or even suggested FBI procedures. FBI agents live in dread that they will be found guilty of committing "subs" and will be severely disciplined. The profuse and unrealistic FBI rules ensure that almost all agents will always be guilty of "subs."

Subv. Contr. Sec.: "Subversives Control Section," which see.

Subversive Activities: According to the FBI Manual of Instructions, these are "activities which are aimed at overthrowing, destroying, or undermining the Government of the United States or any of its political subdivisions by illegal means prohibited by statutes." The FBI has tended to investigate *all* members of "subversive" groups, on the theory that such groups exercise rigid control over their rank and file. "Subversive" groups include the Communist Party, U.S.A., Socialist Workers Party, Venceremos Brigade and Vietnam Veterans Against the War. In practice, any activities intended to promote social change can be investigated as alleged "subversive fronts" or targets of subversive "infiltration." See "Extremist Activities," "Front Group," "Terrorism."

Subversives Control Section: Established 1955 in Internal Security Branch of Domestic Intelligence Division, FBI Headquarters. Supervised Security Index and related programs. Functions transferred to Internal Security Section 1967, and later to "Subversive Section," which see.

Subversive Section: Within Intelligence Division at FBI Headquarters, supervised investigations of "subversives," formulated policy on "subversive matters," disseminated information to other government agencies, and maintained "ADEX." As of 1975, had 2 units concerned with "Communist" groups, 2 with "urban guerrilla" groups, and an informant control unit. Its functions were apparently taken over in 1976 by "Domestic Security Section." See "Domestic Security-Terrorism Section."

Suicide Wiretap or Bug: Same as "Wildcat Wiretap or Bug," which see.

Sulet: Submit letter; a direction to an SA or a field office to submit a letter on the particular matter in question.

SUM: In a search slip, indicates that the document referred to contains a summary which would be particularly helpful to anyone seeking basic information on the person named on the search slip.

Summary of File References: Same as "Correlation Summary," which see.

SUPV: Supervisor. See "Squad" and "Bureau Supervisor."

Surep: Submit Report. See "Sulet."

Surface: To publicly expose the identity of an informant.

Surveillance: Unless otherwise noted, a "surveillance" is usually a physical surveillance (FISUR) rather than an ELSUR (electronic) surveillance.

Survey: Sometimes means illegal entry. See also "Mail Survey."

Survey No. : Series of 7 FBI mail opening programs in various U.S. cities, 1959-1966. See "Z-Coverage."

Sutec: FBI "technical surveillance" workshop and monitoring area. Devices for electronic surveillances are put together in Sutec. (Also called "Sutech.")

SV: Savannah Field Office.

SWAT Team: Special Weapons and Tactics Team. Group of agents, at least one group per field office, that has been trained in the use of "special weapons and tactics," especially on confrontations with suspected urban guerrillas and other terrorists.*

T-(number): Indicates confidential informant or source; a "T" number is temporary, and applies only to the document in which it appears; for example, the same source may be T-1 in one document and T-5 in another. The identity of the "T" sources used in a report is usually provided on an "Administrative" page attached to the report; however, these identifications are generally deleted by the FBI when the reports are released. See "Report."

Tab: To place in a special category in an FBI list such as Security Index, e.g., to tab an SI subject "Detcom."

Targeted Intelligence: Intelligence designed to determine whether a particular group or individual is "subversive" or "extremist." See "General Intelligence."

Tech: "Technical" (that is, telephone) surveillance.

Technical Surveillance: Telephone Surveillance (wiretap).

Teletype: The secure, encrypted communications network maintained by the Bureau, with a terminal in every field office. Also used to refer to an urgent FBI communication sent over that network.* See Ch. IV, Doc. 7.

TEPCI: Top Echelon Potential Criminal Informant.

Terrorism: Since 1976, FBI has preferred to use the word "terrorist" rather than "subversive" or "extremist," as an excuse for conducting domestic security investigations. Officially defined as any activity that involves violence, or risks serious bodily harm, or involves aggravated property damage, for the purpose of intimidating or coercing any segment of the civil population, influencing or retaliating against the government or influencing or retaliating against any entity engaged in foreign commerce.

Terrorism Program: Initiated under Attorney General's Guidelines of 1976. Under this program, the FBI is not supposed to conduct an internal security-type investigation of any organization unless it has information that the organization is engaging in, or plans to engage in, acts of force or violence against the U.S.

TESUR: "Technical" (that is, telephone) surveillance.

TFIS: Theft From Interstate Shipment. FBI file classification "15."

TGP: Theft of Government Property. FBI file classification "52."

Thumbnail Sketch: Brief summary, revised periodically, of an organization's "subversive" tendencies. Frequently appended to FBI reports mentioning organizations. After 1955, served to supplement "Attorney General's List."

Thumbprint Program: 3/73-9/75. Sacramento FBI field office investigated many persons refusing to provide "optional" thumbprints on application for California driver's license. Program was allegedly initiated to locate Weatherman fugitives.

TIC: Tickler copy of documents made.

Tiger: FBI code name for wiretap on Judith Coplon, accused Russian spy.

TIO: Time in Office. Listed on "Number 3 Card." Case agents were permitted to spend at most fifteen percent of their time in the office, but many agents avoided this problem by doing paperwork in libraries, etc. See "ATIO."

TOPCI, TOPSI, TOPRI: Time on Potential Criminal/Security/Racial Informants. On agents' "Number 3 Cards," indicates time spent developing informants in criminal, security, or "racial" areas.

Top Functionary Program: FBI program similar to "Key Figure Program," which see.

Top Hoodlum Program: FBI intelligence program, initiated 1957. Each field office designated five "top hoodlums" for intensive investigation.

TOPLEV: Top Level.

Top Ten: Informal term for the Ten Most Wanted Fugitives.

Torpedo: FBI agent who spies and informs on other FBI agents, normally for minor infractions of FBI rules. Sometimes called "submarines."

TP: Tampa Field Office.

Transfer-call #: Seems to be notation used on file covers when transferring files to new location (e.g., to J Edgar Hoover Building from old FBI Headquarters).

Trash Cover: Investigative technique consisting of going through a person's thrown out garbage in a search for information — letters, leaflets, notes, bills, reading material — about subject of an investigation or persons in communication with subject.

TRIBOMB case: FBI code for case involving three bombs planted at Israeli offices in New York.

TS: Top Secret. Security classification supposedly used for information the disclosure of which reasonably could be expected to cause exceptionally grave damage to the national security.

T symbol: See "T-(number)."

Turn: Informal expression for having a member of an organization become an FBI informant. FBI finds it easier to plant informants in political groups than to turn people who are already members.

U: 1. On a search slip, means "unavailable reference." There are several reasons why a reference may be "unavailable" to a file reviewer; for example, it may be lost, or in use by an agent, or filed in a special file room.

    2. Unclassified. Material is usually not marked "unclassified" or "U" unless the classifying officer wants to indicate that a decision has been made not to classify it.

UACB: Unless advised to contrary by the Bureau (i.e., by FBI Headquarters).

UCR: Uniform Crime Reports. National statistical compilation, administered by FBI.

UFAC: Unlawful flight to avoid confinement.

UFAP: Unlawful flight to avoid prosecution.

Unassigned Detcom Apprehension Status: Status of Security Index subject who has not been assigned a particular FBI agent with responsibility for apprehending him/her in event of national emergency.

Unclassified: Bearing no national security classification. See "Classified Information."

(Underlining): Typographical errors on FBI documents are sometimes underlined.

Unit: Sections of FBI Divisions consist of "units." "Units" have primary responsibility for monitoring field investigations and for coordinating investigations of a certain type within a geographic area. Each unit has several "Bureau Supervisors."

United States Intelligence Board: See "USIB."

Unrecorded Serial: Document to which no serial number has been assigned, but which is placed in an FBI file.

UNSUB: Unknown Subject. For example, if the FBI receives information on an alleged spy who uses the alias "John," it may open a file entitled, "Unsub., wa. (with alias) John; Richard Roe, informant."

Upgrade: To raise the classification (e.g., from "secret" to "top secret").

U.P.S.: Uncontested physical search. A euphemism for "Black Bag Job," which see.

Urfile: Your file; that is, the file your office keeps on the subject of the document.

USA: United States Attorney.

USAINTA: U.S. Army Intelligence Agency.

USC: 1. United States Court.

2. United States Code.

USDS: United States Department of State.

USIB: United States Intelligence Board. Established in 1960 as successor to Intelligence Advisory Committee. Was coordinating and advising forum, chaired by the CIA, and including representatives of FBI and other agencies concerned with intelligence. Abolished 1976.

UTL: Unable to locate.

Vacuum Cleaner: Informant who reports *everything* he can find out. FBI has admitted its informants are, most often, "vacuum cleaners."

Vaughn Index: Prepared by a government agency when so ordered by a court, it itemizes all records withheld from an FOIA requester and justifies in detail each exemption claimed. So-called after case of *Vaughn* v. *Rosen* (1973).

VIDEM: Vietnam Demonstrations. An FBI New-Left intelligence program. Each field office was required to submit weekly memos to HQ reporting on demonstrations during the previous week.

Volume: See "Section."

Voorhis Act: 1941. Required the registration of all subversive organizations having foreign links and advocating the violent overthrow of the government.

VOT: Voluntary Overtime. FBI agents were *required* to put in considerable "voluntary" overtime. "VOT" is listed on the "Number 3 Card."

WA: With alias.

Walk-In: 1. Individual overheard on an electronic surveillance who is not the subject of that surveillance.

2. Case requiring no investigative effort.

3. Individual who volunteers information to FBI, usually on a one-time basis.

WAS: With aliases.

Watch Lists: Lists of Americans whose international mail was to be opened by CIA and whose international electronic communications were to be monitored by NSA. FBI supplied many of the names for lists.

Weight Program: FBI campaign initiated by Hoover in 1950s to ensure that no male employee was overweight. Employees failing to meet arbitrary weight standards could suffer severe administrative penalties. Program officially called "Physical Examination Matters-Weight Standards."

WFO: Washington Field Office. It covers the Washington, D.C. area just as the New York field office covers the New York area. It is distinct from FBI Headquarters.

White Hate Group Program: FBI COINTELPRO, 1964-71. The targets of this COINTELPRO were more precisely defined, and the risks to the targets smaller, than with other COINTELPROs.

White Slave Traffic Act: 1910. Also known as Mann Act. Prohibited transportation of women across state lines for immoral purposes. Provided FBI's earliest excuse for invasive investigations of private matters.

Wildcat Wiretap or Bug: Placed by FBI agent without FBI authorization.

Wiretap: Usually called "TESUR" (technical surveillance) or "ELSUR" (electronic surveillance) by FBI.

WLM: Women's Liberation Movement.

WLMBE: When letter may be expected.

WRMBE: When report may be expected.

WSTA: "White Slave Traffic Act," which see.

XGDS Category: Exemption from general declassification schedule category. These categories are listed in Executive Order 11652.

Yugoslav Program: FBI COINTELPRO of 1969.

Z-Coverage: FBI mail-opening program. Initiated 1940; suspended after W.W. II; reinstituted in Washington, D.C. early or mid 1950s; extended to New York, 1959; terminated 1966. Targeted primarily at foreign diplomatic establishments.

"0" Files: Headquarters and each field office keeps "0" ("Zero") files for miscellaneous items. See Ch. I.

"00" Files: FBI Headquarters and each field office keeps "00" ("Double Zero") files concerning policy and procedure. See Ch. I.

0-1: See "Form 0-1."

ZW: Inquiry on a Wanted Person, NCIC code.

?: On search slips, means "not identifiable"; that is, the file reviewer cannot determine whether or not the reference pertains to the individual listed on the search slip. A file captioned in the same name as that listed on the search slip may be marked "?" if there are insufficient identifying data to rule out the possibility that the file pertains to another individual who has the same name. The alleged lack of identifying data in a file, or in a FOIA request, can thus be used to deny you a file to which you are entitled.

The following is a list of codes and abbreviations the meaning and significance of which are not yet known with certainty.

BCI:

Blue Sheet:

COMRAP Case:

Corker:

Daylet: Stands for "Daily letter," but the significance of this term is not yet known.

Ex (number):

FCIM:

Five-Point Documentation:

GIR- (number):

MCT- (number):

OCA:

RAB:

RACAG:

R/D:

Running Memo:

SIRP:

SOVME, Sovme Case:

TROPUS:

2 + 4 Operations:

U.T.D.:

NOTES

Note: Publishing data for the sources cited in the footnotes can be found in the Bibliography.

Chapter I

1. U.S. Department of Justice, FBI, Records Management Division, *The Central Records System*, pp. 9-10.

2. *Meeropol et al.* v. *Bell et al.* (D.C., D.C., Civ. No. 75-1121), Second Affidavit of Laurence E. Fann, Feb. 9, 1978, pp. 19-20

3. U.S., Department of Justice, FBI Records Management Division, *The Central Records System*, p. 11.

4. FBI, N.Y. File (caption deleted by FBI), 65-14843-1, Memo, Hoover to SAC, Washington Field Office, June 4, 1948, pp. 54-55.

5. Memo, FBI Director to SAC, Albany, August 25, 1971, printed in National Lawyers' Guild, *Counterintelligence: A Documentary Look at America's Secret Police*, Vol. One, p. 14. Also printed in Nelson Blackstock, *COINTELPRO: The FBI's Secret War on Political Freedom*, p. 30.

6. Athan Theoharis, *Spying on Americans*, p. 131.

7. Memo from J. Edgar Hoover, Oct. 1, 1941, reproduced as Exhibit C in U.S., Congress, House, Committee on Government Operations, *Hearings on Inquiry into the Destruction of Former FBI Director J. Edgar Hoover's Files and FBI Recordkeeping*, pp. 154-5.

8. U.S. Congress, Senate, Select Committee to Study Government Operations with Respect to Intelligence Activities, *Hearings*, Vol. 6, Exhibit 5.

9. U.S., Congress, House, Committee on Government Operations, *op. cit.*, p. 173.

10. U.S. Congress, Senate, Select Committee, *op. cit.*, Exhibits 23, 24, 25, 26-1, 26-2.

11. *Ibid.*, Exhibits 34, 35 (1-10), 36.

12. U.S., Congress, House, Committee on Government Operations, *op. cit.*, p. 173.

13. FBI Headquarters File, 65-60203-205 (Nov. 23, 1953).

14. William R. Sullivan, *The Bureau: My Thirty Years in Hoover's FBI*, pp. 222-3; David Wise, *The American Police State*, pp. 41, 77.

15. U.S., Congress, Senate, Select Committee to Study Government Operations with Respect to Intelligence Activities, *Final Report*, Book III, pp. 326-7, 343; Theoharis, *op. cit.*, p. 194.

16. Sullivan, *op. cit.*, p. 78.

17. Jeff Gerth, "U.S. Aides Disclose A Wide Inquiry Into Alleged Southwest Corruption," *New York Times*, Feb. 9, 1980, p. 10.

18. William W. Turner, *Hoover's FBI: The Men and the Myth*, pp. 315-16.

19. U.S., Congress, Senate, Select Committee, *Final Report*, Book II, *op. cit.*, p. 148.

20. U.S., Congress, House, Committee on Government Operations, *op. cit.*, pp. 160-1.

21. U.S., Comptroller General, General Accounting Office, *FBI Taking Actions to Comply Fully with the Privacy Act*, p. 49.

22. *Ibid.*, p. 11.

23. For a description of these indices, see *ibid.*, pp. 102-3.

Chapter II

1. U.S., Department of Justice, FBI, *The Central Records System*, p. 16.

2. *Ibid.*

3. *Ibid.*

4. The information in this section is based on the plaintiffs' legal papers and on depositions and other testimony in the case of *American Friends Service Committee et al.* v. *William H. Webster, et al.*, Civil No. 79-1655, 485 F. Supp. 222 (D.C., D.C. 1980). Complaint filed June 26, 1979. Hearing on preliminary injunction Oct. 22-26, 1979. Order and Opinion January 10, 1980. Copies of the complaint, affidavits by historians, journalists, and others, an index to 12 days of depositions with NARS and FBI officials and copies of the Order and Opinion are available from FOIA, Inc., 36 W. 44th St., N.Y.C. 10036. Papers pertaining to the case have been deposited at the Meiklejohn Civil Liberties Institute (Box 673, Berkeley, CA 94701).

5. See U.S., General Services Administration, National Archives and Records Service, Office of Federal Records Centers. *Disposition of Federal Bureau of Investigation Field Office Investigative Files.*

6. FBI, Headquarters File, 66-3286-1266, Memo, Decker to Jenkins, Aug. 2, 1976. Plaintiffs Exhibit No. 8, *AFSC* v. *Webster*. See footnote 4 above.

7. SF-115, Request for Records Disposition Authority, FBI. Job No. NC1-65-78-5. Submitted by FBI 11/10/77; approved by NARS 1/13/78. Reported by Prof. Harold Fruchtbaum, American Historical Association Annual Meeting, Session on FOIA, Freedom of Instruction and the Federal Government: Sources for the Classroom, Dec. 28, 1979, New York, N.Y.

8. SF-115, Request for Records Disposition Authority, FBI (extension of NC1-65-77-2) Job No. NC1-65-78-36. Submitted by FBI 6/7/78; approved by NARS 6/30/78. Reported by Prof. Harold Fruchtbaum. See footnote 4.

9. All quotations in this section are from FBI, *Proposed Amendments to the FOI/PA.* Introduction by Director William H. Webster. Unpublished typescript, June 19, 1979.

10. *Socialist Workers Party* v. *Attorney General of the U.S.* 458 F. Supp. 895 (S.D.N.Y. 1978) (Attorney General Bell held in contempt of court); *In Re Attorney General of the U.S.* 596 F. 2d 58 (2d Cir. 1979) (reversed contempt order).

11. U.S., General Accounting Office, Comptroller General, *Impact of the Freedom of Information and Privacy Acts on Law Enforcement Agencies*, title page.

12. *Statement of William H. Webster*, Director FBI, Before the Subcommittee on Government Operations and Individual Rights of the Committee on Government Operations, House of Representatives, Feb. 28, 1979.

13. U.S., General Accounting Office, Comptroller General, *Impact, op. cit.*, p. 14.

14. *Ibid.*

15. U.S., Department of Justice, *Annual Report of the Attorney General of the U.S.*, 1978, p. 45.

16. See Jonathan Kwitny, "FBI Agents Rap Policy of Burning Files, Link it to Public-Access Acts," *Wall Street Journal*, Sept. 27, 1978, pp. 1 and 21.

17. This section relies principally on U.S., General Accounting Office, Comptroller General, *Timeliness and Completeness of FBI Responses to Requests Under Freedom of Information and Privacy Acts Have Improved.*

18. *Ibid.*, p. 10.

19. See *ibid.*, p. 46. The Attorney General's May 1977 letter is printed in full in Christine M. Marwick (ed.), *Litigation Under the Amended Federal Freedom of Information Act*, Appendix pp. 94-5.

20. U.S., Congress, House, Subcommittee on Government Information and Individual Rights of the Committee on Government Operations; Senate, Subcommittee on Administrative Practice and Procedure of the Committee on the Judiciary. *Freedom of Information Act and Amendments of 1974 (P.L. 93-502). Source Book: Legislative History, Texts, and Other Documents*, pp. 524-25. The Attorney General's memo is also printed in *Access Reports*, Access Reference File, Section 14.02. The Access Reference File prints many documents bearing on the FOIA.

21. U.S., General Accounting Office, Comptroller General, *Timeliness, op. cit.*, p. 32.

22. *Ibid.*

23. On "Vaughn" motions, see Marwick (ed.), *op. cit.*, text pp. 83-86 and Appendix pp. 43-61.

24. The present chapter does not pretend to treat the various relevant court cases. It is not meant as a substitute for Marwick (ed.), *op. cit.*, which lists and discusses many FOIA cases. Two looseleaf services provide up-to-date information on FOIA litigation: *Access Reports* (published by Plus Publications, Washington, D.C.) and *Government Disclosure* (published by Prentice-Hall, Englewood Cliffs, N.J.).

25. "37 FR 5209" denotes the 37th volume of the Federal Register, p. 5209.

26. See Harold C. Relyea, "The Evolution of Government Information Security Classification Policy: A Brief Overview (1775-1973)," U.S., Congress, Senate, Subcommittee on Intergovernmental Relations of the Committee on Government Operations, p. 14. Another survey of the growth of executive secrecy is Arthur Macy Cox, *The Myths of National Security: The Peril of Secret Government*, Chapter 2.

27. U.S., Congress, House, Subcommittee on Government Information and Individual Rights of the Committee on Government Operations; Senate, Subcommittee on Administrative Practice and Procedure of the Committee on the Judiciary. *Source Book, op. cit.*, pp. 511-12.

28. See also David Wise, "The New Secrecy," *Inquiry*, 1, Oct. 16, 1978, pp. 20-23.

29. For discussions of possible reforms of the classification system, see Cox, *op. cit.*, Chapters 6 and 7; and Morton H. Halperin and Daniel N. Hoffman, *Top Secret: National Security and the Right to Know*, Chapters 4 and 5.

30. *Access Reports*, Access Reference File, Section 14.03.

31. *Ibid.*, Section 14.04.

32. One such instance was the effort of Prof. Harold Fruchtbaum of Columbia University to secure release of material necessary to write a history of the secrecy surrounding the development of the atomic bomb. His FOIA request for the FBI's files on Niels Bohr, one of the giants of 20th century physics, was denied on grounds of privacy and lack of significant public interest. An administrative appeal to the Justice Department was required to force the FBI to agree to release its Bohr files.

33. U.S., Congress, House, Subcommittee on Government Information and Individual Rights of the Committee on Government Operations; Senate, Subcommittee on Administrative Practice and Procedure of the Committee on the Judiciary. *Source Book, op. cit.*, p. 230. Also printed in Harold C. Relyea, *Evolution of the Freedom of Information Act Amendments of 1974 (P.L. 93-502)*, Congressional Research Service, p. 215.

34. *Ibid.*

35. Chapter I above briefly discusses the nature of FBI "security" operations. For a more detailed look, see, for example, U.S. Congress, Senate, Select Committee to Study Government Operations With Respect to Intelligence Activities, *Final Report*, Book III.

36. "Former Agent Challenges FBI Claims on Withholding Files in SWP Case," *Access Reports* 5, Jan. 23, 1979, pp. 8-9.

37. Cited in *ACLU* Plaintiffs' Memorandum in Opposition to Federal Defendants' Motion to Reconsider June 7, 1977 Order Relating to Informer's Privilege, *American Civil Liberties Union* v. *City of Chicago* (N.D. Ill. No. 75 C 3295, 1978), p. 14.

38. See *T.V. Tower, Inc.* v. *Marshall*, 444 F. Supp. 1233, 1236-37 (D.C., D.C. 1978). The court in this case rejected the "potential witness" rule but cited a number of cases accepting it. For a decision critical of the court in the *T.V. Tower* case, see *Nemacolin Mines Corp.* v. *N.L.R.B.*, 467 F. Supp. 521, 525 (W.D. Penn. 1979).

39. The apparatus of "T" symbols is briefly described in William W. Turner, *Hoover's FBI: The Men and the Myth*, p. 199.

40. U.S., Congress, Senate, Select Committee to Study Government Operations With Respect to Intelligence Activities, *Final Report*, Book III, p. 262.

41. *Ibid.*, p. 441.

42. U.S., Congress, House, Committee on Government Operations, *A Citizen's Guide on How to Use the Freedom of Information Act and the Privacy Act in Requesting Government Documents*, p. 24.

43. U.S., General Accounting Office, Comptroller General, *Timeliness, op. cit.*, pp. 62-3.

44. See, for example, John M. Crewdson, "Former FBI Agent Tells Investigators of Widespread Abuse and Corruption," *New York Times*, Jan. 20, 1979, p. 8.

45. U.S., General Accounting Office, Comptroller General, *Timeliness, op. cit.*, p. 62.

46. *Ibid.*, p. 64.

47. See Marwick (ed.), *op. cit.*, p. 15.

48. *Access Reports*, Access Reference File, Section 14.05.

49. *Dept. of the Air Force* v. *Rose*, 425 U.S. 352, 369-70 (1976).

50. For a summary of the statutes most often cited by various agencies when invoking (b) (3), see Harold C. Relyea, *The Administration of the Freedom of Information Act: A Brief Overview of Executive Branch Annual Reports for 1977*, Congressional Research Service, pp. 15-21.

51. U.S., General Accounting Office, Comptroller General, *Timeliness, op. cit.*, pp. 54-5.

52. See "FBI Withholding Too Much Information, Senator Charges at Hearing on FOIA," *Access Reports* 3, Nov. 15, 1977, pp. 4-5.

Chapter III

1. Gary Wills, "The FBI Files Tell a Story," *Philadelphia Inquirer*, Dec. 4, 1978.

Chapter IV

1. Anthony Villano, *Brick Agent*, p. 200.

2. See, for example, David Burnham, "Ex-Agent Alleges Fraud in F.B.I.; Says Many Informers Are Bogus," *New York Times*, Dec. 6, 1978, p. 13.

Chapter V

1. U.S., Congress, Senate, Select Committee to Study Government Operations With Respect to Intelligence Activities, *Final Report, Book I*, pp. 617-629. Reprinted in Tyrus G. Fain (ed.), *The Intelligence Community*, pp. 967-979.

FOR FURTHER INFORMATION

Selected Bibliography

The bibliography is divided into two sections: Government Publications and Nongovernment Publications.

The starred items contain substantial collections of documents. For additional material see "Sources of Intelligence Documents Released Under FOIA" following Bibliography.

Government Publications

Relyea, Harold C. *The Administration of the Freedom of Information Act: A Brief Overview of Executive Branch Annual Reports for 1977.* Congressional Research Service, Library of Congress, Report No. 78-195 GOV. Nov. 15, 1978.

Relyea, Harold C. *Evolution of the Freedom of Information Act Amendments of 1974 (P.L. 93-502).* Congressional Research Service, Library of Congress, Sept. 16, 1976.

Relyea, Harold C. "The Evolution of Government Information Security Classification Policy: A Brief Overview (1775-1973)." U.S., Congress, Senate, *Government Secrecy, Hearings Before the Subcommittee on Intergovernmental Relations of the Committee on Government Operations,* May 22-June 10, 1974, 93rd Congress, 2nd Session, 1974.

U.S., Congress, House, Before a Subcommittee of the Committee on Government Operations. *FBI Compliance With the Freedom of Information Act. Hearings.* (April 10, 1978.) 95th Congress, 2nd Session, 1978.

U.S., Congress, House, Committee on Government Operations. *A Citizen's Guide on How to Use the Freedom of Information Act and the Privacy Act in Requesting Government Documents.* House Report No. 95-793, 95th Congress, 1st Session, 1977.

* U.S., Congress, House, Committee on Government Operations, *Hearings on Inquiry into the Destruction of Former FBI Director J. Edgar Hoover's Files and FBI Recordkeeping,* before the Subcommittee on Government Information and Individual Rights, 94th Congress, 1st Session, 1975.

U.S., Congress, House, Committee on Government Operations, *Hearings on Justice Department Internal Investigation Policies,* before the Subcommittee on Government Information and Individual Rights, 95th Congress, 1st Session 1977.

U.S., Congress, House, Subcommittee on Government Information and Individual Rights of the Committee on Government Operations, Senate Subcommittee on Administrative Practices and Procedures of the Committee on the Judiciary. *Freedom of Information Act and Amendments of 1974 (P.L. 93-502). Source Book: Legislative History, Texts, and other Documents.* Joint Committee Print, 94th Congress, 1st Session, 1975.

U.S., Congress, House, Select Committee on Intelligence (Pike Committee). *U.S. Intelligence Agencies and Activities. Hearings and Report.* 94th Congress, 1st and 2nd Sessions, 1975-76. [The report, suppressed by the House, was acquired by Daniel Schorr and published by the *Village Voice* Sept. 20, 1976.]

U.S., Congress, Senate, Select Committee to Study Government Operations with Respect to Intelligence Activities. *Final Report,* (Books I-VI.) 94th Congress 1st Session, April 26, 1976.

* U.S., Congress, Senate, Select Committee to Study Government Operations With Respect to Intelligence Activities. *Hearings,* Vol. 1-7. (Sept. 16, 1975-Dec. 5, 1975.) 94th Congress, 1st Session, 1975. [Vol. 6 of these "Church Committee" hearings is on the FBI.]

U.S., Department of Justice, *Annual Report of Attorney General of the United States* (Washington, D.C.: Government Printing Office, 1978).

U.S., Department of Justice, Federal Bureau of Investigation, Records Management Division, *The Central Records System.* (Feb., 1978), (Washington, D.C.: Government Printing Office, 1978).

U.S., Department of Justice, Office of Information Law and Policy, *Freedom of Information Case List.* (March 1979 Edition). (Washington, D.C.: Government Printing Office, 1979).

U.S., General Accounting Office, Comptroller General, *An Informed Public Assures that Federal Agencies Will Better Comply With Freedom of Information/ Privacy Laws.* (October 24, 1979), (Washington, D.C.: General Accounting Office, 1979).

U.S., General Accounting Office, Comptroller General, *FBI Domestic Intelligence Operations: An Uncertain Future.* (Nov. 9, 1977), (Washington, D.C.: General Accounting Office, 1977).

U.S., General Accounting Office, Comptroller General, *FBI Domestic Intelligence Operations — Their Purpose and Scope: Issues that Need to be Resolved.* (Feb. 24, 1976), (Washington, D.C.: General Accounting Office, 1976).

U.S., General Accounting Office, Comptroller General, *FBI Taking Actions to Comply Fully with the Privacy Act.* (Dec. 26, 1977), (Washington D.C.: General Accounting Office, 1977).

U.S., General Accounting Office, Comptroller General, *Impact of the Freedom of Information and Privacy Acts on Law Enforcement Agencies.* (Nov. 15, 1978), (Washington, D.C.: General Accounting Office, 1978).

U.S., General Accounting Office, Comptroller General, *Timeliness and Completeness of FBI Responses to Requests Under Freedom of Information and Privacy Acts Have Improved.* (April 10, 1978), (Washington, D.C.: General Accounting Office, 1978).

U.S., General Services Administration, National Archives and Records Service, Office of Federal Records Centers. *Disposition of Federal Bureau of Investigation Field Office Investigative Files.* (Dec., 1978), (Washington, D.C.: General Services Administration, 1978).

Nongovernment Publications

American Friends Service Committee. *The Police Threat to Political Liberty.* Philadelphia: American Friends Service Committee, 1979.

* Blackstock, Nelson. *COINTELPRO: The FBI's Secret War on Political Freedom.* Introduction by Noam Chomsky. New York: Random House, 1975.

The Center for National Security Studies. *Using the Freedom of Information Act: A Step by Step Guide.* Washington, D.C.: The Center for National Security Studies, 1979.

* "The Complete Collection of Political Documents Ripped-Off From the FBI Office in Media, PA., March 8, 1971." *Win Magazine,* March 1972. Volume VIII, Numbers 4 & 5.

Cook, Fred J. *The FBI Nobody Knows.* New York: Pyramid Books, 1964.

* Cowan, Paul, Nick Egleson, and Nat Hentoff. *State Secrets.* New York: Holt, Rinehart and Winston, 1974.

Cox, Arthur Macy. *The Myths of National Security: The Peril of Secret Government.* Boston: Beacon Press, 1975.

Donner, Frank. *The Age of Surveillance.* New York: Alfred A. Knopf, 1980.

Dorsen, Norman, and Stephen Gillers (eds.). *None of Your Business: Government Secrecy in America.* Introduction by Anthony Lewis. New York: Penguin Books, 1975.

Elliff, John T. *The Reform of FBI Intelligence Operations.* Princeton: Princeton University Press, 1979.

Fain, Tyrus G. (ed.). *The Intelligence Community: History, Organization, and Issues.* Introduction by Senator Frank Church. New York: R.R. Bowker Company, 1977.

Goldstein, Robert. *Political Repression in Modern America: 1870 to Present.* Cambridge: Schenkman Publishing Co., Inc., 1978.

Halperin, Morton H., and Daniel N. Hoffman. *Top Secret: National Security and the Right to Know.* Washington, D.C.: New Republic Books, 1977.

Halperin, Morton H., Jerry J. Berman, Robert L. Borosage and Christine M. Marwick. *The Lawless State: The Crimes of the U.S. Intelligence Agencies.* New York: Penguin Books, 1976.

Hoover, J. Edgar. *Masters of Deceit: The Story of Communism in America and How to Fight It.* New York: Henry Holt, 1958.

Lowenthal, Max. *The Federal Bureau of Investigation.* New York: William Sloane Associates, Inc., 1950.

* Macy, Christy, and Susan Kaplan. *Documents: A Shocking Collection of Memoranda, Letters, and Telexes from the Secret Files of the American Intelligence Community.* New York: Penguin Books, 1980.

Marwick, Christine M. (ed.). *Litigation Under the Amended Federal Freedom of Information Act.* Washington, D.C.: The Center for National Security Studies, Fourth Edition, 1978.

Mitford, Jessica. *A Fine Old Conflict.* New York: Alfred A. Knopf, 1977.

Morgan, Richard E. *Domestic Intelligence: Monitoring Dissent in America.* New York: Twentieth Century Fund, forthcoming.

* National Committee to Reopen the Rosenberg Case. *The Kaufman Papers.* New York: The National Committee to Reopen the Rosenberg Case, n.d.

* National Lawyers' Guild. *Counterintelligence: A Documentary Look at America's Secret Police.* Vol. One, revised edition. Chicago, Ill.: Counterintelligence Documentation Center: A project of the National Lawyers' Guild Task Force on Counterintelligence and the Secret Police, 1978.

Ollestad, Norman. *Inside the FBI.* New York: Lancer Books, 1967.

O'Reilly, James T. *Federal Information Disclosure: Procedures, Forms and the Law.* Colorado Springs, Colorado: Shepard's, 1977.

Payne, Cril. *Deep Cover: An FBI Agent Infiltrates the Radical Underground.* New York: Newsweek Books, 1979.

Preston, William, Jr. *Aliens and Dissenters: Federal Suppression of Radicals, 1903-1933.* New York: Harper and Row, 1966.

* Ross, Caroline, and Ken Lawrence. *J. Edgar Hoover's Detention Plan: The Politics of Repression in the United States, 1939-1976.* Jackson, Miss.: American Friends Service Committee, 1978.

Schneir, Walter and Miriam. *Invitation to an Inquest: Reopening the Rosenberg "Atom Spy" Case.* New York: Doubleday and Co., 1965.

Schott, Joseph L. *No Left Turns.* New York: Ballantine Books, 1975.

Sherick, L.G. *How To Use the Freedom of Information Act (FOIA).* New York: Arco Publishing Company, Inc., 1978.

Sullivan, William C., with Bill Brown. *The Bureau: My Thirty Years in Hoover's FBI.* New York: W.W. Norton & Co., 1979.

"Symposium: The Freedom of Information Act a Decade Later," Harold C. Relyea (ed.), *Public Administration Review,* 1979, pp. 310-332.

Theoharis, Athan. *Spying on Americans: Political Surveillance from Hoover to the Huston Plan.* Philadelphia: Temple University Press, 1978.

* Tiger, Edith (ed.). *In re Alger Hiss: Petition for a Writ of Error Coram Nobis.* Introduction by Thomas I. Emerson. New York: Hill and Wang, 1979.

Turner, William W. *Hoover's FBI: The Men and the Myth.* Los Angeles: Sherborne Press, Inc., 1970.

Ungar, Sanford J. *FBI.* Boston: Little, Brown and Company, 1976.

Villano, Anthony, with Gerald Astor. *Brick Agent: Inside the Mafia for the FBI.* New York: Quadrangle, 1977.

Watters, Pat, and Gillers, Stephen (eds.). *Investigating the FBI: A Tough, Fair Look at the Powerful Bureau, Its Present and Its Future.* New York: Doubleday, 1973.

Wexley, John. *The Judgment of Julius and Ethel Rosenberg.* New York: Ballantine Books, Inc., 1977.

Whitehead, Don. *The FBI Story: A Report to the People.* New York: Random House, 1956.

Wilson, James Q. *The Investigators: Managing FBI and Narcotics Agents.* New York: Basic Books, Inc., 1978.

Wise, David. *The American Police State: The Government Against the People.* New York: Random House, 1976.

Sources of Intelligence Documents Released Under FOIA

Carrollton Press, Inc., 1911 N. Ft. Myer Dr., Arlington, VA 22209

Declassified Documents References System is principally a subscription service for libraries. Publishes selected de-classified documents (primarily from FBI, CIA, NSC, State Dept. and Dept. of Defense) on microfiche; annual collections; and a retrospective collection (the FBI documents are mainly in the retrospective and the 1976, 1971 collections). Abstracts and Index can be purchased with the microfiche or separately. Individual documents can be ordered after consulting Index and Abstracts in a library.

Center for National Security Studies. 122 Maryland Ave., N.E. Washington, D.C. 20002

The Center publishes an Abstract of documents on Foreign Policy, National Defense and Civil Liberties. Documents described in the Abstract can be ordered from the Center or from the issuing governmental agency.

Counterintelligence Documentation Center (a National Lawyers' Guild project), 343 South Dearborn (Rm. 918), Chicago, Ill. 60604.

Publishes *Counterintelligence: A Documentary Look at America's Secret Police.* (90 pp.) (FBI documents on Black, Puerto Rican, Native American, and Chicano/Mexicano movements.) (See Bibliography.)

Provides (at 10¢ per page) sets of COINTELPRO files covering the New Left, "Black Extremist" groups, and "Special Operations." Divided by city and year. Write for index and price list.

Scholarly Resources, Inc., 104 Greenhill Ave., Wilmington, Delaware, 19805.

Publishes FBI Files on 35mm. microfilm. Includes: The FBI Counterintelligence Program; Martin Luther King, Jr. Assassination File; J. Robert Oppenheimer Security File; Malcolm X Surveillance File; Marcus Garvey Investigation File.

Documents Available in FBI Reading Room

The FBI Reading Room at FBI Headquarters, J. Edgar Hoover Building, Washington, D.C., keeps 600,000 pages of FBI documents released under FOIA on topics such as: the assassinations of President Kennedy and Dr. Martin Luther King, Jr., COINTELPRO, the women's liberation movement and others.

We print here the listing of documents compiled as of 10/18/79. On 24-48 hours notice, any of the listed documents can be reviewed at FBI Headquarters. You can have copies made at $.10 a page.

Note: Known within FBI as "FOIPA Preprocessed List." Figures in parentheses following each subject matter indicate the number of pages available for viewing in the FBI reading room.

Abel, Rudolf I. (8,537); ACLU (13,180); Barker-Karpis Gang (Summary) (81); Black Panther Party, Winston-Salem, N.C. (1968-1974) (2,895); Burgess, Guy, SEE: Philby, Kim; Capone, Al (Summary) (3); Chambers, Whittaker, SEE: Hiss, Alger/Chambers, Whittaker; Cointelpro (12 Programs) (52,646) — Cointelpro: Black Extremist Hate Groups (6,116), Cointelpro: Espionage Programs (482), Cointelpro: CPUSA (30,779), Cointelpro: Cuban Matters (Pro Castro) (59), Cointelpro: Disruption of White Hate Groups (5,372), Cointelpro: Hoodwink (to cause dispute between CPUSA and "LCN") (60), Cointelpro: Mexican CP Matters (Border Coverage Program) (122), Cointelpro: New Left (6,244), Cointelpro: Puerto Rican (Groups Seeking Puerto Rican Independence) (1,190), Cointelpro: Socialist Workers Party (688), Cointelpro: Special Operations (Nationalities Intelligence) (1,450), Cointelpro: Yugoslav (Violence-prone Yugoslav Emigrees in United States) (84); Dasch, George (8 Nazi Saboteurs) (Summary) (261); deGalindez, Murphy (715); DeMohrenschildt, Robert (1,209); Detroit Riots, July, 1967 (1,313); Dillinger, John (Summary) (47); Earhart, Amelia (33); Eighteen-and-one-half-minute Gap in the White House Tapes (1,924); Floyd, Charles "Pretty Boy" (Summary) (62); Freedom of Information-Privacy Acts Reference Manual (336); Freedom Riders (1,625); Garvey, Marcus (1,400); Georgia Election, 1946 (3,008); German American Bund (Summary) (910) (13 Photos); Graham, Jackson Gilbert (Summary) (203); Hauptmann, Bruno, SEE: Lindbergh, Charles; Hiss,

Alger/Chambers, Whittaker (54,693); Hohenlohe, SEE: Princess Hohenlohe; Integration of Schools, Little Rock, Arkansas (Summary) (2,701); Interpol, FBI Membership in (1936-1950) (1,787); Irish Northern Aid Committee (382); Kelly, "Machine Gun" (Summary) (22); Kennedy, John F. Assassination (120,748) —JFK: Assassination (38,638), JFK: Ruby, Jack (15,845), JFK: Oswald, Lee Harvey (36,122), JFK: Warren Commission (8,150), JFK: Bulky enclosures (21,933); Kennedy, John F. Assassination, Dallas (8,500); Kennedy, John F. Assassination, New Orleans (3,276); Kennedy, Robert F. (3,775) (39 Photos); Kent State Shooting (8,445); Kent State Shooting, ROTC Fire Bomb (1,109); King, Martin Luther, Jr., Assassination (44,873); Law Enforcement Assistance Administration (10,053); Law Enforcement Intelligence Unit (863); Lindbergh, Charles and Hauptmann, Bruno (35,540); Liuzzo, Viola. Murder (Civil Rights Investigation) (1,520); Lusitania (117); MacLean, Donald, SEE: Philby, Kim; Malcolm X (2,360); Manual of Instructions (970); Marcantonio, Vito (964); May Day Tribe/May Day Collective (1971, WDC) (1,963); Nation of Islam (Monographs Only) (235); National Crime Information Center (26,912); National Organization for Women (110); Nazi Saboteurs, SEE: Dasch, George (Summary); Official and Confidential — Martin Luther King (317), Official and Confidential — Synopsis of Hoover's O & C Files (164); Open America — Information Regarding L. Patrick Gray, III — Watergate (888); Oppenheimer, J. Robert (Security Investigation of) (7,234); Oswald, Lee Harvey, SEE: Kennedy, John F.; Oswald, Lee Harvey, Dallas (19,566); Oswald, Lee Harvey, Little Rock (43); Oswald, Lee Harvey, Newark (84); Oswald, Lee Harvey, New Orleans (1,677); Oswald, Marina, Dallas (639); Oswald, Marina, New Orleans (22); Philby, Kim/MacLean, Donald/Burgess, Guy (3,196); Presley, Elvis Aron (87); Princess Hohenlohe (3,634); Project Search (1,759); Remington, William Walter (8,242); Rosenberg, Ethel/Rosenberg, Julius (155,500 Approx.), Case Summary (171); Ruby, Jack, SEE: Kennedy, John F.; Ruby, Jack Leon, Dallas (13,263); Ruby, Jack Leon, New Orleans (85); Sacco-Vanzetti (781); Schmahl, Horace W. (49); Silkwood, Karen (822); Tokyo Rose (Iva Toquri D'Aquino) (742); Unidentified Flying Objects (investigations by FBI) (1,210); Vanzetti, SEE: Sacco-Vanzetti; Wallace, Governor George (shooting) (65); Warren Commission, Dallas (223); Warren Commission, New Orleans (21); Weatherman Underground (Foreign Involvement) (Summary) (420); Women's Liberation Movement (1,960).